BIBLIOGRAPHY OF IAIN CRICHTON SMITH

CW01066536

A BIBLIOGRAPHY
OF
IAIN CRICHTON
SMITH

compiled by Grant F. Wilson

ABERDEEN UNIVERSITY PRESS

First published 1990
Aberdeen University Press

The Publisher acknowledges subsidy from the Scottish Arts Council
towards the publication of this volume.

British Library Cataloguing in Publication Data

Wilson, Grant F.
    A bibliography of Iain Crichton Smith
    1. Fiction in English. Smith, Iain Crichton, 1928- -
    Bibliographies
    I. Title
    016.823914

    ISBN: 0 08 036599 X

Typeset from author-generated discs
and printed by Antony Rowe Ltd, Chippenham, England

For Kim

Table of Contents

Twenty-one years ago a bibliography of Iain Crichton Smith was published in *Lines Review*, 29, a special issue devoted to his work. Since then there have been several other 'bibliographies' — usually of the check-list variety, appended to interviews and articles about his writing. The appearance of new books and their reception by reviewers have also been recorded in the periodical bibliographies, principally the *Annual Bibliography of Scottish Language and Literature*, and in earlier years in *Scottish Literary News*. It might therefore seem that the record is as up to date as it can be, and that the time for a final round-up has not been reached while the author is still writing — least of all when he is still writing so prolifically (and so well) as Iain Crichton Smith.

This bibliography however sets out to cover ground the periodical bibliographies have had to leave untouched over the years. To pick the most glaring omission, these listings do not include periodical verse. Then, in the effort to do some things well, they inevitably do others badly. With a large field to cover, they must present the fruits of an ordered and thus limited search. They cannot list work found a few odd corners, because their *raison d'aitre* would demand that *all* corners equally odd must be searched; listing a review by Iain Crichton Smith from a student magazine would mean listing all reviews by other writers from similar sources, and the work would collapse into a sprawling chaos. Be assured that this bibliography is not afraid to sprawl; possibly it still does not sprawl far enough.

Readers will be pleased if in another twenty years Iain Crichton Smith has made this bibliography as outdated as its predecessor in *Lines 29* is now. But we hope this will be brought about not only by the appearance of new work but by the discovery of more of the old. Contributions have turned up in periodicals from every country Iain Crichton Smith has visited, and some he has not; and one cannot guarantee that every unlikely 'Special Scottish Issue' of every foreign periodical has been discovered. Closer to home, his work has appeared in legions of may-fly poetry magazines that died after their second issue when funds ran out or their student editors graduated. Some editors with due care for posterity and the laws of copyright sent copies to the National Library; inevitably many did not. So while it is hoped that this bibliography will make more of Iain Crichton Smith's work accessible than before, its publication is also intended to advertise the continuing search for undiscovered work. Readers are invited to send details of material that is not listed here to Dr J. H. Alexander of the English Department at Aberdeen University.

This book advertises not only the Department's quest for unrecorded work, but also a facility it is willing to make available to researchers. Like most recent bibliographies it was compiled using a computer, and it is being maintained on-line. The computer ordered the entries; for those with more specialised needs it will make indexes and re-order the citations to taste. The on-line bibliography will also maintain an up-to-date record of work, including categories of material (such as broadcasts) not published here. The Department can make the files available on request to those interested. They were compiled using FAMULUS, which might be familiar to readers who have used their own universities' computing facilities. Assistance will be available for those who have not.

A brief note on editorial procedures introduces each section of the bibliography. Some general points can be made here however. This is a bibliography for students and readers rather than collectors, even if some of Iain Crichton Smith's early books now attract collectors' prices. Physical descriptions of books are not given; title pages are not transcribed; the size of editions is not given; nor is pagination. Editions have not been collated, but new editions as opposed to re-printings have been few. Substantial variants have been noted.

The details given are those considered to be of most use to readers intersted in the chronology of publication of Iain Crichton Smith's work, and the relation of collected to uncollected work. Revisions have been noted where found, though these are quite few. The poet's dissatisfaction with his own handling of a theme or idea in one poem has generally been the motive for a new poem (as readers will have observed) rather than the reworking of the old. Hence, the spur to create new work; hence, the continuity of themes and relatedness of interests; hence, we hope, the usefulness of this bibliography.

Bibliographers are, more than most writers, the slaves of their subjects, and more than usually dependent on the help of other informants. I have to thank many people for their help in producing this book.

Thanks are due in the first place to Iain Crichton Smith, who provided not only the subject for this bibliography but much of the information. I am grateful to him, and his wife Donalda, both for their help and for their hospitality during my visits to their home in Taynuilt.

Among other informants, I wish particularly to thank John Arnott and Stewart Conn of the BBC, and George Bruce their predecessor there; and many editors and past editors of periodicals and anthologies which have published Iain Cricthon Smith's work. These included George Bruce again, Robin Fulton, Robert Nye and Alexander Scott.

Staff at Aberdeen, Glasgow, Strathclyde, Edinburgh and Newcastle University Libraries provided assisance; though perhaps the National Library of Scotland bore the brunt. Tom Hubbard and Tessa Ransford of the Scottish Poetry Library uncovered many recherché items.

The research was carried out during my year as a research assistant at Aberdeen University, under the guidance of a committee drawn from the English and Celtic Departments. I would like to thank J. H. Alexander, D. H. Hewitt, Donald MacAulay and I. M. Murray for their constant help — though staff of both departments gave generous assistance.

The bibliography was compiled on Aberdeen University's Honeywell mainframe, and I am grateful to David Lindsay of the University Computing Centre. Sagesoft Ltd of Newcastle provided setting facilities.

Last and certainly not least, thanks are due to the Aberdeen University Development Trust, whose financial assistance made this research possible.

Introduction

At the time this bibliography was completed Iain Crichton Smith's collected poems numbered just over nine hundred. He had published sixteen English collections and nine Gaelic, excluding selections and anthologies. It is not surprising therefore that they occupy the bulk of these pages. The poems are listed chronologically, according to the publication date of the book where they were first collected; details and cross-references are given to previous and subsequent publication in periodicals, anthologies and later collections.

English and Gaelic writings have been listed together partly because otherwise we would have ended up with too many sections, and partly because some poems appear and re-appear so often in both languages that the two sections would have been hard to separate.

Distinguishing collections from anthologies was also difficult in a few instances. *The White Moon* appears in this section because although Iain Crichton Smith shares the book *New Poets 1959* with two other writers his poems within it were his own selection and have their own collective title. *Penguin Modern Poets 21* has the same format — work by three poets in a single volume — but it is clearly a 'selection' rather than a 'collection'. *Three Regional Voices* was slightly harder to place, but it too was finally grouped with the anthologies.

Iain Crichton Smith's three different *Selected Poems* are treated as collections in their own right; only poems which had not been collected previously are cited individually however.

This chapter of the bibliography is in two parts. The first lists the publication details of each volume, including its contents, and as many reviews as could be found; the second lists full details of each poem.

The Long River (Loanhead: M. Macdonald, 1955)

Reviewed by Laurence Graham, *Lines*, 10 (Dec. 1955), 35; George Bruce, *Saltire Rev.*, 3, no. 8 (Aut. 1956), 71-75 (p. 73).

Contents: 'The Dedicated Spirits'; 'Some Days Were Running Legs'; 'It Was a Country'; 'Prometheus'; 'Calling the Roll'; 'Poem of Lewis'; 'On Such a Night as This'; 'The Train and the Swan'; 'Fog'; 'On Helensburgh Sea-Front'; 'Meditation Addressed to Hugh MacDiarmid'; 'Tiredly the Town Yawned'; 'As Boys Playing Together'; 'Let Go!'; 'I Never Knew what Volume He Was Reading'; 'Silences'; 'Anchored Yachts on a Stormy Day'; 'So Tied to This'; 'Bricks'.

The White Moon, in *New Poets 1959*, edited by Edwin Muir (London: Eyre and Spottiswoode, 1959)

Reviewed by M.L., *Scottish Field*, Feb. 1960, p. 50.

Contents: 'Beautiful Shadow'; 'Encounter'; 'End of the Season on a Stormy Day ...'; 'False Summer Leans'; 'For Sometimes in My Head'; 'For the Unknown Seamen ...'; 'Grace Notes'; 'Highland Sunday'; 'In Luss Churchyard'; 'Inscriptions'; 'Night Walk' (1) and (2); 'Room for Living'; 'School Teacher'; 'Seagulls'; 'Statement by a Responsible Spinster'; 'The Hoarding'; 'The Ladder of Experience'; 'The Widow'; 'The Window'.

Burn is Aran [Bread and Water], Clò-Bhualaidhean Gairm, Leabhar 2 (Glasgow: Gairm, 1960) Second edition, excluding verse, 1974.

Reviewed by *An Gaidheal*, 55 (1960), 130. Poems and short stories. Stories are listed in Section B. 901771-86-4 (2nd edn)

Contents: 'Am Buachaille 's a Leannan'; 'Tha thu air Aigeann m'Inntinn'; 'An Nochd Chaidh Soluis m'Òige Sìos'; 'A' Dol Dachaidh'; 'An Deidh an Dealbh "Dunkirk" Fhaicinn'; 'Tha Iad an Nochd a' Caitheamh Shraidhean'; 'A' Chailleach' ['Tha i an nochd ... ']; 'Aig Clachan Chalanais'; 'Aig a' Chladh'; 'Sùilean'; 'Do Sheonag NicCoinnich a' Seinn "Milleadh nam Bràithrean"'; 'Do Shùilean'; 'Am Breitheamh'; 'De Tha Ceàrr'; 'Do Bhoireannach Aosd'; 'An Litir Araid'; 'Ionndrain Mara'; 'A Nighean Òg'; 'Iomadh Gaol'; 'Làithean Mharlowe'.

Thistles and Roses (London: Eyre and Spottiswoode, 1961)

Reviewed by Donald Hall, *New Stn*, 61 (Jan-June 1961), 484; M.L., *Scottish Field*, May 1961, p. 65; *Spec.*, 206 (1961), 575-76; *TLS*, 9 June 1961, p. 358.

Contents: 'A Blind Negro Singer'; 'A Note on Puritans'; 'A Young Highland Girl Studying Poetry'; 'About That Mile'; 'After the War'; 'At a Ceilidh'; 'By Ferry to the Island'; 'Culloden and After'; 'Dying is not Setting Out'; 'First World War Generals'; 'For Angus MacLeod ...'; 'For My Mother'; 'Girl with Orange Sunshade'; 'Highland Portrait'; 'Home'; 'John Knox'; 'Kierkegaard'; 'Lilac, Snow and Shadow'; 'Love Songs of a Puritan' (A)and (B); 'Luss Village'; 'Of a Rare Courage'; 'Old Woman' ['And she, being old ...']; 'Schoolgirl on Speech-day in the Open Air'; 'Sea-song'; 'Studies in Power'; 'Sunday Morning Walk: Stornoway'; 'The Bore'; 'The Temptation'; 'Three Sonnets'.

Deer on the High Hills (Edinburgh: Giles Gordon; 1962)

Reviewed by W. A. S. Keir, *New Saltire*, 4 (Smr 1962), 82-85 (pp. 83-84); Edwin Brock, *Outposts*, 54 (Aut. 1962), 19-20; W.P.T., *Scottish Field*, June 1962, pp. 22-23. An edition of three hundred and fifty copies for sale; fifty of them signed and numbered.

At Helensburgh : Written when the British Fleet was being reviewed there in 1965. (Queen's University of Belfast: Festival Publications, [1965])

Twelve-page pamphlet. Contents: A sequence of twelve numbered, untitled poems.

Bìobuill is Sanasan-reice [Bibles and Advertisements], Clò-bhualaidhean Gairm 3 (Glasgow: Gairm, 1965)

Reviewed by *An Gaidheal*, 60 (1965), 15-16; George Campbell Hay, *Sctn*, 5 Feb. 1966; Donald MacAulay, 'On Some Aspects of the Appreciation of Modern Gaelic Poetry: being a review of "Bìobuill is Sanasan-reice"', *SGS*, 11, no. 1 (1966), 136-45. Gaelic poems. Most were published in translation as Part One of *The Permanent Island*. Several are taken from *Burn is Aran*.

Contents: 'Am Buachaille 's a Leannan'; 'A Nighean Òg' /'Young Girl'; 'Do Sheana-bhoireannaich' /'To an Old Woman'; 'Tha Thu air Aigeann m'Inntinn' /'You Are at the Bottom of My Mind'; 'A' Dol Dachaidh' / 'Going Home'; 'A' Chailleach' /'The Old Woman' ['Thig am post ...']; 'Aig a' Chladh' /'At the Cemetery'; 'Aig Clachan Chalanais' /'At the Stones of Callanish'; 'De Tha Ceàrr' /'What is Wrong?'; 'Ochd Orain Airson Ceilidh Uir' /'Eight

Songs for a New Ceilidh'; 'An t-Oban' / 'Oban'; 'Nochdadh ri Beanntan na Hearadh' / 'Sighting the Mountains of Harris'; 'Am Muir 's na Creagan' /'The Sea and the Rocks'; 'Oran Ionndrain' / 'Song of Remembrance'; '1941-42'; 'Am Ministear' /'The Minister'; 'An t-Uisge' /'The Rain'; 'Amhran' /Song'; 'Oran Gaoil' / 'Love Song'; 'A' Gaidhealtachd' /'The Highlands'; 'Luss'; 'Lomnochd' / 'Bareness'; 'Air an t-Sraid' /'On the Street'; 'Neochiontas' / 'Innocence'; 'Rubha Chinn Aird'; 'An t-Eilean' /'The Island'; 'Nuair a bha sinn Òg' /'When We Were Young'; 'Air Oidhche Fhoghair' /'On an Autumn Night'; 'Oran' /'Song'; 'Mo Bhardachd' /'My Poetry'; 'Aon Nighean' /'One Girl'; 'Freud'; 'An Eala Bhàn' /'The White Swan'; 'A' Chailleach Bheag' / 'The Little Old Lady'; 'An Tigh a bh'anns a' Ghleann' /'The House in the Glen'; 'Còmhradh' /'Conversation'; 'Meilodian an Spioraid' /'The Melodeon of the Spirit'; 'Dan' / 'Predestination'; 'An Solus' /'The Light'; 'Do Ruaraidh MacThomais' / 'For Derick Thomson'; 'Am Mac Strodhail' / 'Prodigal Son'; 'An Crom-lus' /'Poppy'; 'Di-Sathuirn' /'Saturday'; 'Deirdre'; 'Na Laoich' /'The Heroes'; 'Oran Foghair' /'Autumn Song'; 'Do Mo Mathair' / 'To My Mother'; 'An t-Amadan' /'The Fool'; 'Oran' /'Song'; 'A' Chlach' /'The Stone'; 'A' Chailleach' /'The Old Woman'; 'Air Latha Breagha' /'On a Beautiful Day'; 'Fitheach' /'Raven'.

The Law and the Grace (London: Eyre and Spottiswoode, 1965)

Reviewed by J. L. Bloom, *Library Rev.*, 20 (Winter 1965), 281; Francis Hope, *New Stn*, 70 (June-Dec 1965), 158; Martin Seymour-Smith, *Sctn*, 3 July 1965; Barbara Gibbs, *Stand*, 8, no. 3 (1966/7), 71-75 (pp. 72-73); *TLS*, 14 Oct. 1965, p. 920. Awarded a Scottish Arts Council Literature Prize in 1968, as most notable book of poetry by a younger Scottish poet.

Contents: 'At the Reservoir'; 'This Blue Cauldron'; 'At Tiumpan Head, Lewis'; 'Meeting'; 'Old Woman' ['Your thorned back ...'];

'Living Together'; 'The Witches'; 'Two Girls Singing'; 'Minister'; 'Old Highland Lady Reading Newspaper'; 'Schoolroom Incident'; 'Lenin'; 'The Argument'; 'Cuan Ferry'; 'Schoolroom'; '1964'; 'To a Theologian'; 'Schoolteacher'; 'The Two Clouds'; 'Johnson in the Highlands'; 'Face of an Old Highland Woman'; 'The Clearances'; 'It is the Old'; 'At the Firth of Lorne'; 'The Law and the Grace'; '"Nothing Human"'; 'The Squirrel'; 'Spring Wedding'; 'The Cemetry Near Burns' Cottage'; 'Hume'; 'Rythm'; 'So Many Names'; 'Preparation for a Death'; 'Encounter in a School Corridor'; 'To Forget the Dead'; 'Highlanders'; 'Poem in March'; 'The Song'; 'The Chess-Player'; 'The Wreath'; 'The Lone Rider'; 'The Anglo-Saxon Lecturer Goes to the Cinema every Thursday'; '"Whether Beyond the Stormy Hebrides"'; 'Proposal'; 'Envoi'.

From Bourgeois Land (London: Victor Gollancz Ltd, 1969)

Reviewed by *Blst*, 15 May 1971, p. 770; Ruaraidh MacThomais, *Gairm*, 17 (1968/69), 375-77; J. McQueen, *Lines*, 29 (June 1969), 46-48; *Lsnr*, 28 Aug. 1969, p. 285; A. Brownjohn, *New Stn*, 2 Jan. 1970, pp. 18-20; *Obs.*, 13 July 1969, p. 25; *Poet*, 119 (Dec. 1971), 159; James Aitchison, *Sctn*, 12 July 1969; Edwin Morgan, *Sc. Int.*, 8 (Nov. 1969), 61; *SLN*, 1, no. 1 (Oct. 1970), 26; Alexander Scott, *SSL*, 7 (1969), 211-28 (pp. 213-14); *TLS*, 14 August 1969, p. 898; one of Robert Nye's year's best books, *Sctn*, 24 December 1969. ISBN 0-575-00271-9

Contents: Twenty-six of the poems are identified only by numbers. The others are: (3) 'Speaker' (5) 'Dido and Aeneas' (6) 'Hamlet' (7) 'Epitaph' (8) 'Burns' (9) 'Lenin' (15) 'Farewell Party' (16) 'Church' (19) 'Young Girl Singing Psalm' (20) 'National Service' (21) 'At the Sale' (32) 'Retiral' (33) 'Little Boy'.

Selected Poems (London: Victor Gollancz Ltd, 1970; and Chester-Spring, Pa.: Dufour Editions, [1970])

> Reviewed by Douglas Dunn, *Enc.*, 36 (Mar. 1971), 65-71 (p. 70); Robert Garioch, *Lines*, 36 (March 1971), 41-42; P. Mills, *NER*, 11 (Feb./March 1971), 36-38; Hugh Creighton Hill, *Outposts*, 88 (Spr. 1971), 23-25 (p. 24); Robert Nye, *Sctn*, 24 Oct. 1970; Terry Eagleton, *Stand*, 12, no. 2 (1971), 59-62 (pp. 59-61). Selected from volumes published up to *From Bourgeois Land*, and including previously uncollected verse, particularly from *Lines*, 29 (June 1969). ISBN 0-575-00545-9; U.S. edition ISBN 0-8023-1160-1

> Contents: 'Statement by a Responsible Spinster'; 'For the Unknown Seamen ...'; 'Old Woman' ['And she, being old, ...']; 'Schoolgirl on Speech-day in the Open Air'; 'Sunday Morning Walk'; 'Kierkegaard'; 'By Ferry to the Island'; 'Studies in Power (2)'; 'Home'; 'For My Mother'; 'Deer on the High Hills'; 'World War One'; 'Old Woman' ['Your thorned back ...']; 'Witches'; 'Two Girls Singing'; 'Lenin'; 'Johnson in the Highlands'; 'At the Firth of Lorne'; 'The Law and the Grace'; 'Envoi'; 'She Teaches Lear'; 'Entering Your House'; 'At the Sale'; 'What's Your Success'; 'At the Highland Games'; 'By the Sea'; 'Old Woman with Flowers'; 'Hear Us O Lord'; 'In Old Age'; 'To Settle Down'; 'Jean Brodie's Children'; 'I Build an Orange Church'; 'If You Are About to Die Now'; 'Shall Gaelic Die?'.

Hamlet in Autumn, Lines Editions, 2 (Loanhead: M. Macdonald, 1972)

> Reviewed by Isobel Murray, *AUR*, 45, no. 2 (Aut. 1973), 209-11; Douglas Dunn, *Enc.*, Mar. 1973, 66-71 (pp. 69-70); *GH*, 23 Dec. 1972; James Aitchison, *Glasgow Rev.*, 3, no. 2 (Autumn 1972), 41-42; *Sc. Int.*, 5, no. 7 (Sept. 1972), 33; Thomas Crawford, *SLN*, 3, no. 2 (July 1973), 36; Terry Eagleton, *Stand*, 14, no. 1 (1973), 65-69 (pp. 66-67); *TLS*, 20 Oct. 1972, p. 1249. Winner of a Scottish Arts

Council Book Award (see *Sctn*, 8 January 1973). ISBN
0-9502106-4-1

Contents: 'By the Sea in Autumn'; 'Carol and Hamlet'; 'Chaplin';
'Children in Winter'; 'Christmas, 1971'; 'Dead for a Rat'; 'Dear
Hamlet'; 'Dipping Your Spoon ...'; 'End of Schooldays';
'Everything is Silent'; 'Fairy Story'; 'Films'; 'Finis not Tragedy';
'For Ann in America in the Autumn'; 'For John MacLean ...'; 'For
Keats'; 'Gaelic Songs'; 'Give Me Your Hand'; 'Going Home';
'Good and Evil'; 'Hotel Dining Room'; 'How Often I Feel Like
You'; 'In the Chinese Restaurant'; 'In the Country'; 'In the Time of
the Useless Pity'; 'Lear and Carroll'; 'Lying Ill'; 'Napoleon'; 'Not to
Islands'; 'Oedipus and Others'; 'On a Beautiful Day'; 'On a
Summer's Day'; 'Our Mess Tins ...'; 'Over and Over'; 'Party';
'Return'; 'Russian Poem'; 'Shane'; 'The Fool'; 'The Letter'; 'The
Moon'; 'The Return'; 'The Small Snags'; 'The Stones of Callanish';
'The Tape Runs'; 'This Goodbye'; 'This is the Time of the Body';
'You are at the bottom of my mind'.

Love Poems and Elegies (London: Victor Gollancz Ltd, 1972)

Reviewed by Douglas Dunn, *Enc.*, Mar. 1973, 66-71 (pp. 69-70);
Stewart Conn, *GH*, 19 Aug. 1972; James Aitchison, *Glasgow Rev.*, 3,
no. 2 (Aut. 1972), 41-42; D. Black, *Lines*, 45 (June 1973), 48-53 (pp.
53-53); A MacLean, *Lsnr*, 22 March 1973, p. 389; Alan Brownjohn,
New Stn, 29 Sept. 1972, p. 440; *Obs.*, 3 September 1972; Hugh
Martin Booth, *Outposts*, 96 (Spr. 1973), 27-28; Clive Wilmer, *Spec.*,
24 Feb. 1973, p. 237; Terry Eagleton, *Stand*, 14, no. 1 (1973), 65-67
(pp. 65-66); *The Times*, 14 Dec. 1972; *TLS*, 29 September 1972, p.
1146; Frederick Grubb, *Tribune*, 9 February 1973. Iain Crichton
Smith supplied a brief note for publication by the *Poetry Book
Society Bulletin*, 74 (Autumn 1972) when *Love Poems and Elegies*
was chosen as their Recommendation for Spring 1975. ISBN
0-575-01434-2

Contents: Part One: Elegies 'You Lived in Glasgow'; 'In Your Long Skirts'; 'You Told Me Once'; 'My Sailor Father'; 'That Island Formed You'; 'The Space-ship'; 'All Our Ancestors'; 'Your Brother Clanked His Sword'; 'Those Who are Needed'; 'On Looking at the Dead'; 'Of the Uncomplicated Dairy Girl'; 'The Burial'; 'Tinily a Star Goes Down'; 'The Lilies and the Daffodils'; 'Death and the Politicians'; 'Contrasts'; 'This Clutch of Grapes'; 'Moonlight Over the Island'; 'The Black Jar'; 'The Chair in Which You've Sat'; 'Argument'; 'The Earth Eats Everything' Part Two: Poems for S. 'No One at Home'; 'I Thought I Saw You'; 'Resurrection'; 'The World's a Minefield'; 'Do Not Put on that Wig'; 'What Tragedy Is'; 'The Trees and You'; 'Sleepless'; 'Youth and Age'; 'Love; If You Are Love'; 'I Think We are Both Sick'; 'lace Without Music'; 'The Fever'; 'In the Cinema'; 'The Bouquet'; 'Inside the Poem'; 'On the Train'; 'Guilts'; 'In the Hotel'; 'The Dream'; 'Night'; 'Where Are You Tonight?'; 'At the Scott Exhibition, Edinburgh Festival'.

Rabhdan is Rudan [Ditties and Things], illustrated by Calum Fearghastan. Clò-bhualaidhean Gairm, aireamh 36 (Glasgow: Gairm, 1973)

ISBN 0-902706-16-0

Contents: 'Mo Sheanmhair'; 'An Cuala tu an Tàirneanaich?'; 'Anns an Teine'; 'Dà Bhròig'; 'Anns an Tigh-Dhealbh'; 'Mo Sheanair'; 'Nuair a dh'fhàsas mise mor'; 'Tha mo Mathair 's i 'na h-aparan'; 'A' Ghaoth'; 'Stocainnean daoimein'; 'Taibhs"; 'Am Post'; 'An Deigh'; 'Air an Trìne'; 'Geansaidh donn'; 'Mo Bhàta Beag'; 'Ceise-ball'; 'A' Phoit'; 'Soluis'; 'Solus uaine, solus dearg'; 'Rionnagan'; 'An Ceàrd'; 'T.V.'; 'Am Bìobull'; 'Anns an Sgàthan'; 'M'athair'; 'An Luch'; 'A' Bhùth'; 'Bu Chaomh Leam'; 'Nuair a dh'eireich mi sa' Mhadainn'; 'Bodach Sneachd'; 'Rabhd'; 'An Coileach'; 'Rabhd'; 'Tinn'; 'Tigh'; 'Saighdear'; 'A' Chuthag'; 'An Sgarbh'; 'An Deireadh'.

Eadar Fealla-dha is Glaschu: orain stolda is orain eibhinn [Between Jest and Glasgow: serious poems and light poems] (University of Glasgow: Department of Celtic, 1974)

> Reviewed by Donnchadh MacLabhruinn, *Gairm*, 1974/75, 279-80; Douglas Sealy, *Lines*, 51 (Dec. 1974), 47-49; George Campbell Hay, *Sctn*, 16 Nov. 1974.

> Contents: 'Orain ghoirid' ('"Coinnichidh Sinn"'; 'A' Cheist'; 'An Luchd-turais 's a' Ghaidhlig'; 'Anns a' Mhuseum'; 'Anns na Làithean Ciùin'; 'Breugel'; 'Còmhradh'; 'Cuimhne'; 'Ma Thig thu Tuilleadh'; 'Na Seanfhacail'; 'Thig a-steach'; 'Thusa'); 'Mas e Ghaidhlig an cànan'; 'Haiku'; 'Am na Nollaig'; 'Feasgar agus ceò ann'; 'Innsidh mi dhut mar a thachair'; 'Bothan beag'; 'Eilean Fhraoich'; 'Anns a' chuirt'; 'Sgialachdan Gaidhlig'; 'Latha na Bliadhn' Uir'; '1973'; 'Planaidean is thusa'; 'A' ghealach'; 'Glaschu'; 'Fad a làithan'; 'Nuair a dh'fhagas tu mi'; 'Tha na làithean a' dol seachad'; 'Thàinig sinn a-mach'; "A' ghaoth'; 'Aibidil'; 'Aig an Dorus'; 'Na làithean fad' ud'; 'Madainn earraich'; 'Dealbh le Picasso'; 'An TV'; 'Sgialachd'.

Orpheus and Other Poems (Preston: Akros, 1974)

> Reviewed by Walter Perrie, *Chmn*, 3, no. 5 (1975), 24; Cuthbert Graham, *P&J*, 19 Oct. 1974; George Campbell Hay, *Sctn*, 16 Nov. 1974. Winner of a Scottish Arts Council Book Award, 1973/74. ISBN 0-900036-65-6

> Contents: 'The Island'; 'Skye'; 'Island Poems'; 'The Voice'; 'rocession'; 'In the Dark'; 'Orpheus'; 'The Scholar's Love Story'; 'To Vergil'; 'Poem' ['With all due tenderness ...']; 'Love Poem'; 'Saturday Afternoon'; 'Breughel'; 'Poem for Auden'; 'Painting'; 'Lecturer'; 'The Visitors'; 'Chess'; 'Tonight'; 'In the Bar'; 'The Glass of Water'; 'Something Somewhere'; 'The Wind'; 'Autumn'; 'My Old Typewriter'.

Poems for Donalda (Belfast: Ulsterman Publications, 1974)

Contents: 'Helplessly'; 'Love, do not leave me'; 'By the River, in the Woods'; 'The Present'; '"The Things I Do."'; 'In the Kitchen'; 'Meeting'; 'The Lie'; 'The Shadows'; 'The Blue Carpet'; 'ainting'; 'On Sunday'; 'Who You Are'; 'Books and You'; 'The Wolves'; 'Tonight'; 'Sunday Walk'; 'On the Shore'.

The Notebooks of Robinson Crusoe, and other poems. (London: Victor Gollancz, 1975)

The sequence 'The Notebooks of Robinson Crusoe' was originally published in *Lines Review*, 47 (December 1973), 12-28. Reviewed by *Blst*, 15 Dec. 1977, p. 659; M. Relich, *Calgacus*, 3 (1976), pp. 54-55; Walter Perrie, *Chmn*, 3, no. 5 (1975), 24; Douglas Dunn, *Enc.*, 44 (May 1975), 73-76 (pp. 73-74); C. Small, *GH*, 17 Apr. 1975; P. J. Kavanagh, *Gdn*, 27 Mar. 1975; *Gdn Weekly*, 5 April 1975, p. 21; D. Black, *Lines*, 57 (March 1976), 44-46; C. Falcke, *New Rev.*, 15 (June 1975), 70; Peter Porter, *Obs.*, 27 April 1975; James Aitchison, *P&J*, 5 April 1975; James Aitchison, *Sctn*, 29 March 1975; Terry Eagleton, *Stand*, 16, no. 4 (1974), 72-74 (pp. 72-73); Anthony Thwaite, *TLS*, 23 May 1975, p. 552; *Tribune*, 21 March 1975. Winner of a Scottish Arts Council Book Award; see *Sctn*, 26 January 1976. 0-575-01889-5

Contents: 'Autumn Song'; 'Ceilidh'; 'Chinese Poem'; 'Faustus Speaks'; 'He and She'; 'Help Me'; 'Him'; 'Housman'; 'In the Glen'; 'In the Gods in a Glasgow Theatre'; 'Incident'; 'Insecurity'; 'Jealousy'; 'Journey'; 'Letter' ['You say, "I am alone."']; 'Letter' ['You write from London ...']; 'My Uncle'; 'Old Woman' ['"The Old Age Pensioners ..."']; 'On the Fact that Karl Marx Wrote Love Poems ...'; 'Party'; 'Sketch'; 'The Cat'; 'The Event'; 'The Ex-Skipper'; 'The Fall'; 'The Hero'; 'The Interview'; 'The Lesson'; 'The Lie'; 'The Old Woman' [' ... sat under an autumn tree.']; 'The Prodigal Son'; 'The Sound of Music'; 'The Three'; 'The Workmen';

'Tonight'; 'The Notebooks of Robinson Crusoe' (a numbered sequence of forty-one poems and prose-poems).

The Permanent Island: Gaelic poems translated by the author, Lines Editions, 5 (Loanhead: M. Macdonald, 1975).

ISBN 0-904265-09-9 (Macdonald)

Contents: From *Bìobuill is Sanasan-reice*: 'Young Girl'; 'You are at the Bottom of my Mind'; 'Going Home'; 'To an Old Woman'; 'The Old Woman'; 'At the Cemetry'; 'At the Stones of Callanish'; 'What is Wrong?'; 'Eight Songs for a New Ceilidh'; 'Oban'; 'Sighting the Mountains of Harris'; 'The Sea and the Rocks'; 'Song of Remembrance'; '1941-42'; 'The Minister'; 'The Rain'; 'Song'; 'Love Song'; 'The Highlands'; 'Luss'; 'Bareness'; 'On the Street'; 'Innocence'; 'The Island'; 'When We Were Young'; 'Poem'; 'My Poetry'; 'One Girl'; 'Freud'; 'The White Swan'; 'The Little Old Lady'; 'Conversation'; 'The Melodeon of the Spirit'; 'Predestination'; 'For Derick Thomson'; 'The Prodigal Son'; 'Poppy'; 'Saturday'; 'Deirdre'; 'The Heroes'; Autumn Song'; 'The Fool'; 'To My Mother'; 'The Old Woman'; 'On a Beautiful Day'; 'The Stone'; 'Raven'.

From *Eadar Fealla-dha is Glaschu*: 'Memory'; 'The Question'; 'Conversation'; 'In the Museum'; 'The Visitors and Gaelic'; 'Proverbs'; 'If You Come Again'; 'In the Calm Days'; '"We Will Meet"; 'Come In'; 'You'; 'Six Haiku'; 'Christmastime'; 'On a Misty Evening'; 'I Will Tell You What Happened'; 'A Small Bothy'; 'Island of Heather'; 'In Court'; 'Gaelic Stories'; 'New Year's Day 1973'; 'The Moon'; 'All His Days'; 'When You Leave Me'; 'The Days Are Passing'; 'Those Long Days'; 'The TV'.

In the Middle Gollancz Poets (London: Victor Gollancz, 1977)

> Reviewed by *Blst*, 1 July 1978, p. 1659; C. Small, *GH*, 22 Dec. 1977; Peter Porter, *Obs.*, 18 December 1977, p. 24; Blake Morrison, *PN Rev.*, 8 (5, no. 4: 1978), 46-48 (p. 47); George Mackay Brown, *Sctn*, 24 Sept. 1977; Norman Nicholson, *Sc. Rev.*, 8 (Winter 1977), 45-47 (p. 47); Desmond Graham, *Stand*, 20, no. 1 (1978/79), 65-71 (p. 70); James Shaw Grant, *St. Gaz.*, 4 Mar. 1978; Alexander Scott, *SSL*, 15 (1980), 221-40 (p. 234); J. Symons, *ST*, 11 September 1977; *The Times*, 1 September 1977; Gavin Ewart, *TLS*, 25 Nov. 1977, p. 1381. ISBN 0-575-02227-2

> Contents: 'In the Surgery'; 'In Sleep'; 'Hail Mary'; 'The Elite'; 'The Cool Weather'; 'To Another Country'; 'Waiting for a Letter'; 'The Critic and the Poem'; 'In Yellow'; 'Sometimes'; 'Morning'; 'When Day is Done'; 'In Ireland'; 'Pupil's Holiday Job'; 'In Other Places'; 'The Purple Bucket'; 'The Dog'; 'The Theatre'; 'The Water Skiers'; 'The Lady of Shalott'; 'In Our Safe House'; 'If Ever You Loved Me'; 'The Ducks'; 'Home Coming'; 'You'; 'The Torches'; 'The Horror'; 'When the House is Quiet'; 'After the Sandals of Summer'; 'My Child'; 'Prepare Ye the Way of the Lord'; 'Those Who Move Others'; 'This Bubble'; 'Back to School'; 'The Chair'; 'The Scream'; 'The Nose' (after Gogol); 'Women'; 'Tears Are Salt'; 'The Queen'; 'In the Middle'; 'Evening'; 'The Scholar'; 'The Whirligigs of Time'; 'The Old School Books'; 'The Cows from the Slaughter House'; 'The Winds'; 'Painting the Walls'; 'Duty'; 'Clouds'; 'We Poets'; 'The Scholars'; 'Evening'; 'The Cry'; 'Rainy Day'; 'None is the Same as Another'.

River, River: poems for children (Loanhead: M. Macdonald, 1978)

> Reviewed by R. P. Wells, *Akros*, 39 (Dec. 1978), 111-12; Trevor Royle, *BiS*, 2 (Aut. 1978), 31-32; J. MacInnes, *Lines*, 67 (December

1978), 45-46; George Mackay Brown, *Sctn*, 7 Oct. 1978. ISBN 0-904265-19-6

Contents: 'For Christabel'; 'Life'; 'In the Ark'; 'The Wind'; 'The Lion and the Alligator'; 'The Wildcat'; 'The Dinosaur'; 'The Old Sailing Ships'; 'The Sea'; 'Leaving Home'; 'What's In the Paper?'; 'Coward or Hero'; 'The End of the Western'; 'At Christmas'; 'In the Liquorice House'; 'The Little Shop'; 'In the Garden'; 'The Hosepipe'; 'The Prodigal Son'; 'Reflection'; 'In Chagall's Paintings'; 'The Tramp'; 'The Soldier'; 'Joseph'; 'Halloween'; 'Stormy Night'; 'The Queen'; 'The Ghost'; 'The Clown'; 'Night Falls'; 'Shadow'; 'Sandcastles'; 'River, River'.

Na h-Ainmhidhean [The Animals], illustrated by Domhnall R. MacThomais (Aberfeldy: Clò Chailleann, 1979)

Reviewed by Frank Thompson, *BiS*, 7 (Spr./Smr 1980), 36; Ronald Black, *Sctn*, 29 Nov. 1980. ISBN 0-906623-00-6

Contents: 'A' Bho'; 'A' Chearc'; 'Am Bru-dhearg'; 'Am Muncaidh'; 'An Cat'; 'An Clamhan'; 'An Coileach'; 'An Duine 's na Madaidhean-Allaidh'; 'An Fhaoileag'; 'An Iolaire'; 'An Laogh'; 'An Leomhan 's an Crocodile'; 'An Leomhan 's an am Fiadh'; 'An Luch 's an Cat'; 'An Rabaid 's an Sionnach'; 'An Siorc'; 'An t-Each'; 'An Tiger 's an Zebra'; 'An t-Seil cheag'; 'Na h-Ainmhidhean'; 'Uiseag'.

Writers in Brief, no. 8: Iain Crichton Smith (Glasgow: National Book League, 1979)

ISBN 0-85353-322-9

Contents: 'Anchored Yachts on a Stormy Day'; 'August Poem'; 'By Ferry to the Island'; 'Culloden and After'; 'For the Unknown Seamen'; 'Old Woman' ['Overwhelmed with kindnesses ...'];

'Poem of Lewis'; 'Some Days were Running Legs'; 'The Departing Island'.

Selected Poems, 1955-1980, compiled by Robin Fulton (Loanhead: Macdonald, 1981)

Reviewed by G. Thomson, *Akros*, 17, no. 51 (Oct. 1983), 111-16; I. Campbell, *BiS*, 11 (1982), 20; *BBN*, Dec. 1982, p. 763; Cairns Craig, *Cenc.*, 11 (New Year 1983), 44-45; Ruaraidh MacThomais, *Gairm*, 1981/82, pp. 379-81; Tom Buchan, *GH*, 10 July 1982; Alexander Scott, *Lines*, 82 (Sept. 1982), 39-41; Iain Stephen, *NER*, 61 (Spr. 1983), 32-33; Stephen Regan, *P. Rev.*, 73, no. 1 (Mar. 1983), 64-65; Cuthbert Graham, *P&J*, 19 June 1982; A. Bold, *Sctn*, 26 June 1982; George Bruce, *Sc. Rev.*, 27 (Aug. 1982), 55-56; David MacDuff, *Stand*, 24, no. 3 (1982/83), 67-75 (pp. 68-70); Roderick Watson, *SSL*, 19 (1984), 194-215 (pp. 207-15); Douglas Dunn, *TLS*, 13 August 1982, p. 876; *WLT*, 57 (Spring 1983), 335. Contains poems from published volumes up to *In the Middle*; and verse at that time uncollected that later appeared in *The Exiles*. Received a Scottish Arts Council Book Award in autumn 1982. ISBN 0-904265-55-2

Contents:

I   'Poem of Lewis'; 'The Good Place'; 'For My Mother'; 'lace'; 'Aberdeen'; 'Schoolteacher'; 'The Widow'; 'Statement by a Responsible Spinster'; 'In Luss Churchyard'; 'Luss Village'; 'For the Unknown Seamen ...'; 'Room for Living'; 'Old Woman' ['And she, being old, ...']; 'A Note on Puritans'; 'Schoolgirl on Speech-day in the Open Air'; 'Dying is not Setting Out'; 'About that Mile'; 'Sunday Morning Walk'; 'Love Songs of a Puritan (A)' (extract); 'Love Songs of a Puritan (B)' (extract); 'By Ferry to the Island'; 'Highland Portrait' (extract); 'A Young Highland Girl Studying Poetry'; 'Home'; 'Studies in Power'; 'Lilac, Snow and Shadow' (extract).

II 'Old Woman' ['Your thorned back']; 'Old Highland Lady Reading Newspaper'; 'Face of an Old Highland Woman'; 'It Is the Old'; 'Two Girls Singing'; 'Lenin'; 'Johnson in the Highlands'; 'The Clearances'; 'At the Firth of Lorne'; 'The Law and the Grace'; 'The Cemetry Near Burns' Cottage'; 'Hume'; 'Preparation for a Death'; 'Encounter in a School Corridor'; 'To Forget the Dead'; 'The Chess Player'; 'The Song'; 'Envoi' ['Remember me when you come into your kingdom']; 'World War One' (extract); 'Deer on the High Hills'.

III 'Young Girl'; 'You are at the Bottom of My Mind'; 'Going Home'; 'To an Old Woman'; 'The Old Woman' ['Tonight she is sitting ...']; 'At the Cemetry'; 'At the Stones of Callanish'; 'What is Wrong?'; 'Eight Songs for a New Ceilidh'; 'Oban'; 'Sighting the Mountains of Harris'; 'The Sea and the Rocks'; 'Song of Remembrance'; '1941-42'; 'The Minister'; 'The Rain'; 'Song' ['I got up on a morning of May,']; 'Love Song'; 'The Highlands'; 'Luss'; 'Bareness'; 'On the Street'; 'Innocence'; 'The Island'; 'When We Were Young'; 'Poem' ['Liberal, Labour or Conservative']; 'My Poetry'; 'One Girl'; 'Freud'; 'The White Swan'; 'The Little Old Lady'; 'Conversation'; 'The Melodeon of the Spirit'; 'Predestination'; 'For Derick Thomson'; 'The Prodigal Son'; 'oppy'; 'Saturday'; 'Deirdre'; 'The Heroes'; 'Autumn Song'; 'The Fool'; 'To My Mother'; 'The Old Woman' ['The postman will come tonight']; 'On a Beautiful Day'; 'The Stone'; 'The Raven'.

IV 'Three Poems for Christmas'; 'Why Are You?'; 'I Build an Orange Church'; 'What's Your Success?'; 'Those Who Act'; 'And This Is Hell'; 'Poem' ['Some move others ...']; 'Hamlet'; 'Hear Us O Lord'; 'Glasgow'; 'The House We Lived In'; 'Return to the Council House'; 'At the Highland Games'; 'School Sports, at the Turnstile'; 'Mr M.'; 'In the Classics Room'; 'For L.'; 'The Departing Island'; 'To Have Found One's Country'; 'The Hall'; 'Duncan Ban MacIntyre'; 'Homage to George Orwell'; 'Jean Brodie's Children'; 'She Teaches Lear'; 'Entering Your House'; 'At the Sale'; 'Old Woman With Flowers'; 'Old Woman' ['Now

you sleep away the day ']; 'In Old Age'; 'If You Are About to
Die Now'.

V   'Light to Light' (extract); 'Transparencies' (extract); 'By the Sea'
(extract); 'The White Air of March' (extract); 'Memory'; 'The
Question'; 'Conversation'; 'In the Museum'; 'The Visitors and
Gaelic'; 'Proverbs'; 'If You Come Again'; 'In the Calm Days';
'"We Will Meet"'; 'Six Haiku'; 'On a Misty Evening'; 'I Will Tell
You What Happened'; 'Gaelic Stories'; 'When You Leave Me';
'The Days are Passing'; 'Those Long Days'; 'The TV'

VI   'Return to Lewis'; 'Shall Gaelic Die?'; 'For John MacLean ...';

VII 'On a Summer's Day'; 'The Moon'; 'Oedipus and Others'; 'Good
and Evil'; 'Over and Over'; 'Dead for a Rat'; 'Carol and Hamlet'
(extract); 'Dear Hamlet'; 'How Often I Feel Like You'; 'Russian
Poem' (extract); 'Party'; 'Dipping Your Spoon ...'; 'Shane'; 'End
of Schooldays'; 'For Keats'; 'Gaelic Songs'; 'In the Chinese
Restaurant'; 'The Small Snags'; 'Children in Winter';
'Christmas, 1971'; 'In the Time of the Useless Pity'; 'Finis not
Tragedy'; 'Everything is Silent'; 'This Goodbye'

VIII 'You Lived in Glasgow'; 'In Your Long Skirts'; 'You Told Me
Once'; 'My Sailor Father'; 'That Island Formed You'; 'All Our
Ancestor s'; 'Your Brother Clanked His Sword'; 'Those Who Are
Needed'; 'On Looking at the Dead'; 'Of the Uncomplicated
Dairy Girl'; 'The Burial'; 'Tinily a Star Goes Down'; 'The Lilies
and the Daffodils'; 'Contrasts'; 'The Chair in Which You've Sat';
'The Earth Eats Everything'; 'No One at Home'; 'I Thought I
Saw You'; 'The World's a Minefield'; 'The Bouquet'; 'On the
Train'; 'Where Are You Tonight'; 'At the Scott Exhibition ...';
'Helplessly'; 'Love, Do Not Leave Me'; 'resent'; '"The Things I
Do"'; 'The Shadows'

IX   'The Island'; 'Skye'; 'Island Poems' (extract); 'The Voice';
'rocession'; 'In the Dark'; 'The Glass of Water'; 'Poem for
Auden'; 'Orpheus'; 'Letter'; 'In the Glen'; 'Ceilidh'; 'The Sound
of Music'; 'Incident'; 'Autumn Song'; 'The Old Woman'; 'Old
Woman' ['"The Old Age Pensioners,"']; 'Sketch'; 'The Prodigal

Son'; 'Chinese Poem'; 'The Notebooks of Robinson Crusoe' (extract).

X   'In Sleep'; 'When Day is Done'; 'The Cool Weather'; 'In Yellow'; 'Morning'; 'In Other Places'; 'Pupil's Holiday Job'; 'The Theatre'; 'If Ever You Loved Me'; 'The Torches'; 'This Bubble'; 'The Chair'; 'My Child'; 'Women'; 'Tears Are Salt'; 'In the Middle'; 'None is the Same as Another'; 'Iolaire'; 'On an Icy Day'; 'Speech for Prospero'; 'Chinese Poem'; 'The Red Horse'; 'Autumn'; 'Running Repairs'; 'Speech for a Woman'; 'My Brother'; 'I Remember, I Remember'; 'Remembering'; 'Old Woman'.

Na h-Eilthirich [The Exiles], (University of Glasgow: Department of Celtic, 1983)

Reviewed by Fearghas MacFhionnlaigh, *Gairm*, 1983-84, pp. 375-77; Raghnall Mac Ille Dhuibh, *Sctn*, 9 June 1984.

Contents: 'Na h-eilthirich'; 'Ann an Astràilia'; 'Am fear a chaidh a dh'Astràilia'; 'Na h-Aborigines'; 'Mo thaipwriter'; 'Togamaid'; 'Oran'; 'Leodhas'; 'A' Cheist'; 'Thusa'; 'Nuair a bha mi fàs suas'; 'Clann nighean an sgadain'; 'A' dìreadh 's a' dìreadh'; 'Coisichidh sinn'; 'Aig an abhainn'; 'Ann Coinneachadh'; 'An t-altachadh'; 'Na balaich'; 'Dearcagan'; 'A' bheart-ola'; 'Cianalas eile'; 'Tilleadh'; 'Air madainn samhraidh'; 'An fheadhainn gun thalant'; 'Thusa'; 'Desperate Dan'; 'An òige'; 'Each dochasach'; 'Sinne 's a' chailleach'; 'Footballer'; 'Anns an Uinneig'; 'A' cuimhneachadh'; 'An tilleadh'; 'Air oidhche gheamhraidh'; 'Esan'; 'Nuair a bhios mi leughadh'; 'Air latha foghair'; 'Dealachadh'; 'We Twa Hae Paiddlt'; 'Aig an taigh'; 'A' dol air ais'; 'Anns an taigh dhubh'; 'Ann an Glaschu'; 'Vancouver'; 'Eachunn Macdhomhnaill'.

The Exiles (Manchester: Carcanet, and Dublin: Raven Arts Press, 1984)

Reviewed by Douglas Dunn, *BiS*, 16 (Aut. 1984), 16-17; Ian A. Bell, *BBN*, Sept. 1984, p. 566; David Constantine, *Enc.*, Sept/Oct 1984, pp. 40-44 (pp. 42-43); Edwin Morgan, *Glasgow Mag.*, 5 (Wtr 1984/85), 20-22; *Lsnr*, 19 July 1984, p. 25; George Szirtes, *Lit. Rev.*, 73 (July 1984), 43-44; *Obs.*, 29 July 1984, p. 20; Gerald Mangan, *Sctn*, 16 June 1984; David MacDuff, *Stand*, 26, no. 3 (1984/85), 79; Roderick Watson, *SSL*, 21 (1986), 226-61 (pp. 252-54); *TLS*, 5 Oct. 1984, p. 20; G. Ross Roy, *WLT*, Winter 1985; Cuthbert Graham, *P&J*, 4 June 1984. Iain Crichton Smith supplied a note for the *Poetry Book Society Bulletin*, 121 (Summer 1984) when *The Exiles* was made the month's Choice. ISBN 0-856354-95-3 (Carcanet), 0-906897-73-4 (Raven)

Contents: 'Always'; 'At the Funeral of Robert Garioch'; 'Australia'; 'Autumn'; 'Breughel'; 'Cinderella'; 'Early Australian'; 'Envoi'; 'For Poets Writing in English over in Ireland'; 'Halloween'; 'Home'; 'In the Spring'; 'Iolaire'; 'Lost'; 'Next Time'; 'No Return'; 'Owl and Mouse'; 'Poem' ['It is always evening ...']; 'Power Cut'; 'Prince Charles'; 'Reading Shakespeare'; 'Returning Exile' ['Home he came after Canada ...']; 'Returning Exile' ['You who come home ...']; 'Snow Poems'; 'Speech for a Woman'; 'Speech for Prospero'; The "Ordinary" People'; 'The Church'; 'The Exiles'; 'The Legend'; 'The Man Without a Name'; 'The New Houses'; 'The Schoolmaster'; 'The Survivors'; 'There Is No Sorrow'; 'When My Poetry Making has Failed'; 'When They Reached the New Land'; 'Who Daily'; '"You'll Take a Bath"'; 'Youth'.

Selected Poems (Manchester: Carcenet, 1985)

Reviewed by Douglas Dunn, *BiS*, 18 (Smr 1985), 13-14; James Aitchison, *GH*, 18 May 85; Cuthbert Graham, *P&J*, 25 May 1985;

Sctn, 22 June 1985; Kevin McCarra, *SLJ* Supplement, no. 23 (Winter 1985), 64-65; Hugh Buckingham, *Stand*, 27, no. 3 (1985/86), 71-72; Iain Stephen, *St. Gaz.*, 25 Sept. 1982; included by Douglas Dunn in his best books of the year, *GH*, 28 Dec. 1985. Robin Fulton's selection is its base, it also finds room for almost half of *The Exiles*.

Contents: 'Poem of Lewis'; 'Aberdeen' ['Mica glittered ...'];
'Statement by a Resposible Spinster'; 'Luss Village'; 'For the Unknown Seamen ...'; 'Old Woman' ['And she, being old, ...'];
'Sunday Morning Walk'; 'By Ferry to the Island'; 'A Young Highland Girl Studying Poetry'; 'Home'; 'Old Woman' ['Your thorned back, ...']; 'Two Girls Singing'; 'Lenin'; 'At the Firth of Lorne'; 'The Law and the Grace'; 'Hume'; 'Envoi' ['Remember me ...']; 'Deer on the High Hills'; 'Young Girl'; 'You are at the Bottom of my Mind'; 'Going Home'; 'To an Old Woman'; 'The Old Woman' ['Tonight she is sitting ...']; 'At the Cemetry'; 'Eight Songs for a New Ceilidh'; 'When We Were Young'; 'Freud'; 'odigal Song'; 'The Poppy'; 'To My Mother'; 'I Build an Orange Church'; 'What's Your Success'; 'Hear Us O Lord'; 'At the Highland Games'; 'In the Classics Room'; 'The Departing Island'; 'To Have Found One's Country'; 'Jean Brodie's Children'; 'She Teaches Lear'; 'At the Sale'; 'Old Woman with Flowers'; 'Old Woman' ['Overwhelmed with kindnesses ...']; 'If You Are About to Die Now'; 'The White Air of March' (extract); 'The TV'; 'Shall Gaelic Die'; 'For John MacLean ...'; 'On a Summer's Day'; 'Dead for a Rat'; 'How Often I Feel Like You'; 'End of Schooldays'; 'For Keats'; 'Gaelic Songs'; 'In the Chinese Restaurant'; 'Christmas 1971'; 'In the Time of the Useless Pity'; 'Finis Not Tragedy'; 'Everything is Silent'; 'You Lived In Glasgow'; 'All Our Ancestors'; 'Of the Uncomplicated Dairy Girl'; 'At the Scott Exhibition'; 'In the Dark'; 'The Glass of Water'; 'Orpheus'; 'Chinese Poem'; 'The Notebooks of Robinson Crusoe' (extract); 'When Day is Done'; 'The Chair'; 'My Child'; 'Women'; 'Tears Are Salt'; 'None is the Dame as Another'; 'The

Iolaire'; 'Autumn'; 'My Brother'; 'Remembering'; 'Next Time';
'Returning Exile' ['Home he came ...']; 'The Exiles'; 'Australia';
'No Return'; 'Reading Shakespeare'; 'Speech for Prospero'; '"You'll
Take a Bath'"; 'Breughel'; 'Owl and Mouse'; 'For Poets Writing in
English over in Ireland'; 'Halloween'; 'The "Ordinary" People';
'At the Funeral of Robert Garioch'; 'Who Daily'; 'Envoi' ['There
are'].

A Life (Manchester: Carcanet, 1986)

Reviewed by *BBN*, Aug. 1986; Carol Gow, *Lines*, 99 (Dec. 1986),
46-48; Cuthbert Graham, *P&J*, 24 Jan. 1987; George MacKay
Brown, *Sctn*, 9 August 1986; J. H. Alexander, *SLJ*, Supplement no.
26 (Spr. 1987), 25-27; Frank Thompson, *WHFP*, 11 July 1986;
Writer's Monthly, Oct. 1986, p. 35; picked by both James Aitchison
and Douglas Dunn as 'Critics' Choice, 1986', *GH*, 29 Nov. 1986;
and included in Alan Taylor's selection of the year's best books,
GH, 27 December 1986. ISBN 0-85635-644-1

An t-Eilean agus An Cànan [The Island and The Language] (Glasgow
University: Department of Celtic, 1987)

Reviewed by Christopher Whyte, *Chmn*, 49 (9, no. 6: Smr 1987), 83;
Crisdean Whyte, *Gairm*, 1987/88, pp. 87-89.

Contents: two sequences of poems and prose-poems; 'An Cànan'
has twenty parts, and 'An t-Eilean' eighty-seven.

The Long River (1955)

1   'Anchored Yachts on a Stormy Day' Fourteen rhymed lines. First line: 'Nine yachts are rocking in the sullen water,'

2   'As Boys playing Together' Three rhymed eight-line stanzas. First line: 'As boys playing together'

3   'Bricks' Eleven lines, mainly in pairs. First line: 'blockishly squat in rising pools'

4   'Calling the Roll' Previously published in *Stand*, 7 (Spr. 1954), 23. Three half-rhymed stanzas of fourteen, thirteen and sixteen lines. First line: 'Those elemental ones who have'

5   'Fogs' Previously published in *Poet*, 11 [1955]. Six three-line stanzas, closing with a couplet. First line: 'drags matter close: red lights of venomous cars'

6   'I never Knew what Volume He was Reading' Three rhymed six-line stanzas. First line: 'I never knew what volume he was reading'

7   'It was a Country' Previously published in *Outposts*, 25 (1954), 9. Five half-rhymed six-line stanzas. First line: 'It was a country white and clear as diamond:'

8   'Let Go!' Twenty-six lines in four irregular rhymed stanzas. First line: 'Let go! as on a swing'

9   'Meditation Addressed to Hugh MacDiarmid' Fourteen rhymed eight-line stanzas. First line: 'To you a tenant of the most perilous places'

10   'On Helensburgh Sea-front' Three stanzas of sixteen, seven and eight lines, rhymed. First line: 'Let me abolish from my verse'

11   'On Such a Night as This' Previously published in *Zebra*, 2, no. 1 (Smr 1955), 2, ed Derek Maggs (Bristol). Also published in *Lines*, 9 (Aug. 1955), 26. Four rhymed eight-line stanzas. First line: 'On such a night as this'

12   'Poem of Lewis' Previously published in *Lines*, 6 (Sept. 1954), 21. Reprinted in *Scotland's Magazine*, 59, no. 3 (Mar. 1963), 38. Translated in *Moznaim*, Oct.-Nov. 1984, p. 29 by Yair Hurvitz (Israel). Twenty-two lines. First line: 'Here they have no time for the fine graces'

13   'Prometheus' Previously published in *Poet*, 7 [1954]. Seven seven-line stanzas. First line: 'Ash where the earth burned'

14   'Silences' Four quatrains. First line: 'First, there's the silence when the heart, full-fed,'

15   'So Tied to This' Sonnet. First line: 'So tied to this and wishing so to leave,'

16   'Some Days were Running Legs' Previously published in *Lines*, 3 (Smr 1953), 23. Four four-line stanzas. First line: 'Some days were running legs and joy'

17   'The Dedicated Spirits' Previously published in *Poet*, 6 [1953]. Six six-line rhymed stanzas. First line: 'The dedicated spirits grow'

18   'The Trains and the Swan' Thirty-four lines. First line: 'Marble masks faces readying for work.'

19   'Tiredly the Town Yawned' Four eight-line stanzas. First line: 'Tiredly the town yawned.'

The White Moon (1959)

20 ' Beautiful Shadow' Three rhymed stanzas of nine, four and six stanzas. First line: 'Beautiful shadow, cool, fastidious, '

21   'Encounter' Twelve rhymed lines. First line: 'Cool and bitter as a lemon'

22   'End of the Season on a Stormy Day — Oban' Seventeen lines in five part-rhymed three and four line stanzas. First line: 'In the dead park a bench sprawls drunkenly.'

23   'False Summer Leans' Previously published in *Saltire Rev.*, 3, no. 8 (Aut. 1956), 13. Also published in *Best Poems of 1956: Borestone Mountain Poetry Awards 1956. A Compilation of Original Poetry pubished in Magazines of the English-speaking World in 1956: Ninth Annual Issue* (Stanford, Ca.: Stanford

University Press, 1957). Four rhymed six-line stanzas. First line: 'False summer leans across the dwindling veins:'

24 'For Sometimes in my Head' Four rhymed eight line stanzas. First line: 'For sometimes in my head there's a sweet planet'

25 'For the Unknown Seamen of the 1939-45 War Buried in Iona Churchyard' Five rhymed five-line stanzas. First line: 'One would like to be able to write something for them'

26 'Grace Notes' Sequence of five sonnets numbered 1, 2A, 2B, 2C, and 3 First lines: (1) 'Nod nod go churchbells with their hollow helms.' (2A) 'Grace is what speaks behind the words you speak.' (2B) 'I also speak of the slim cormorant's grace' (2C) 'And lastly I speak of the grace that musicks us' (3) 'Today this poster wears a calm green light.'

27 'Highland Sunday' Two rhymed stanzas of five and nine lines. First line: 'Striped-trousered, hard-black-hatted, sunday-sunned,'

28 'In Luss Churchyard' Previously published in *Saltire Rev.*, 4, no. 10 (Spr. 1957), 32-33. Originally entitled 'In the Churchyard at Luss'. Nine rhymed six-line stanzas. First line: 'Light strikes the stone bible like a gong:'

29 'Inscriptions' Five quatrains. First line: '"There is no going backward now"'

30 'Night Walk — 1' Previously published in *Saltire Rev.*, 4, no. 11 (Smr 1957), 47. Two half-rhymed stanzas of eleven and six lines. First line: 'Someone had painted a moon on the sky.'

31 'Night Walk — 2' Two rhymed stanzas of thirteen and nine lines. First line: 'The tall lamps burn their sockets late'

32 'Room for Living' Five rhymed six-line stanzas. First line: 'You should stop here and not step'

33 'School Teacher' Four rhymed stanzas of seventeen, two, seventeen and nine lines. First line: 'She was always earlier than the bell at nine.'

34 'Seagulls' Three half-rhymed stanzas of seventeen lines. First line: 'These have the true cold avarice beyond'

35 'Statement by a Responsible Spinster' Six half-rhymed four-line stanzas. First line: 'It was my own kindness brought me here'

36 'The Hoarding' Previously published in *Lines*, 11/12 (Smr 1956), 38. Two rhymed six-line stanzas. First line: 'From the red hoarding at the waterside'

37 'The Ladder of Experience' Three seven-line stanzas. First line: 'From the calm step above he gazes down'

38 'The Widow' Three rhymed verse paragraphs of fourteen, forty-eight and twenty-four lines. First line: 'That's his harem on the shelves. I don't know'

39 'The Window' Ten quatrains. First line: 'We walked that night between the piled houses.'

Bùrn is Aran (1960)

40 'A Nighean Og' Reprinted in *Bìobuill is Sanasan-reice* with a translation, included in *The Permanent Island* and Donald MacAulay's bilingual anthology, *Nua-bàrdachd Ghàidhlig/Modern Scottish Gaelic Poems* (1976) Four quatrains. First line: 'A nighean òg a dh'fhalbhas'

41 'A' Chailleach' Reprinted in *Bìobuill is Sanasan-reice* Five part-rhymed four-line stanzas. First line: 'Tha i an nochd 'na suidhe ri uinneig'

42 'A' Dol Dhachaidh' Previously published in *Gairm*, 7 (1958/59), 125. Reprinted in *Bìobuill is Sanasan-reice*, with a translation which also appears in *Hamlet in Autumn* and *The Permanent Island*. Printed with a translation in *Scot. Int.*, 4 (Oct/Nov 1968), 48; and translated into modern Irish by Louis de Paor, *Innti* 10 (Christmas 1986), 8. Three stanzas of five lines and one of ten. First line: 'Am màireach theid mi dhachaidh do m'eilean'

43 'Aig a' Chladh' Reprinted in *Bìobuill is Sanasan-reice*. Five part-rhymed four-line stanzas. First line: 'Chunna mi aig a' chladh an de iad,'

44 'Aig Clachan Chalanais' Reprinted in *Bìobuill is Sanasan-reice*. Eight rhymed lines. First line: 'Aig clachan Chalanais an de'

45 'Am Breitheamh' Three four-line stanzas. First line: 'Ars esan: "Tha dithis no triùir a' moladh"'

46 'Am Buachaille 's a Leannan (Bho'n Bheurla aig Marlowe)' Reprinted in *Bìobuill is Sanasan-reice*. An earlier version of this poem was published anonymously in the *Nicolson Institute Annual*, 1946. Four quatrains. First line: 'O thugainn leam 's thoir dhomh do ghràdh'

47 'An Deidh an Dealbh "Dunkirk" Fhaicinn' Previously published in *Gairm*, 7 (1958/59), 209. Two part-rhymed fourteen-line stanzas. First line: 'An e so ceart mar a thachair?'

48   'An Litir Araid' Reprinted in *Bìobuill is Sanasan-reice*. Two four-line stanzas. First line: 'Chuir mi litir gu mo ghaol,'

49   'An Nochd Chaidh Soluis m'Oige Sìos' Previously published in *Gairm*, 6 (1957/58), 125. Four rhymed six-line stanzas. First line: 'An nochd chaidh soluis m'oige sìos'

50   'De Tha Ceàrr' Reprinted in *Bìobuill is Sanasan-reice*. Three rhymed five-line stanzas. First line: 'Co 's urrainn innse de tha ceàrr?'

51   'Do Bhoireannach Aosd' Fifty-one lines in nine stanzas of three to twelve lines. First line: 'Tha thu san eaglais ag eisdeachd,'

52   'Do Sheonag NicCoinnich a' Seinn "Milleadh nam Bràithrean"' Four quatrains. First line: 'Tha thu a' seinn an amhrain-s' mar gum biodh màthair'

53   'Do Shùilean' Two quatrains. First line: ''S ghlais thu do shùilean ri mo shùilean:'

54   'Iomadh Gaol' Three quatrains. First line: '"Tha iomadh gaol ann," arsa esan, ars esan'

55   'Ionndrain Mara' Three quatrains. First line: 'Innsidh mi dhut de bha dhìth orm'

56   'Làithean Mharlowe' Four quatrains. First line: ''S a nis tha làithean Mharlowe seachad.'

57   'Sùilean' Two four-line stanzas. First line: 'Tha saoghal anns gach sùil agad'

58   'Tha Iad an Nochd a' Caitheamh Shràidean' Seven part-rhymed four-line stanzas. First line: 'Tha iad an nochd a' caitheamh shràidean,'

59   'Tha thu air Aigeann m'Inntinn' Previously published in *Gairm*, 1, no. 2 (An Geamradh 1952), 87 Included in *Criochan Ura*, edited by Iain A. MacDhomhnaill (1958). Reprinted in *Bìobuill is Sanasan-reice*, with a translation which also appears in *Hamlet in Autumn* and *The Permanent Island*. Included in Donald MacAulay 's bilingual anthology, *Nua-bhàrdachd Ghàidhlig/Modern Scottish Gaelic Poems* (1976). Translated into modern Irish by Louis de Paor, *Innti*, 10 (Christmas 1986), 9. Three rhymed six-line stanzas. First line: 'Gun fhìos dhomh tha thu air aigeann m'inntinn'

Thistles and Roses (1961)

60   'A Blind Negro Singer' Four rhymed six-line stanzas. First line: 'A blind man stamps and sings. The great guitar'

61   'A Note on Puritans' Previously published in *Honour'd Shade* (see Section E). Six rhymed five-line stanzas. First line: 'There was no curtain between them and fire.'

62   'A Young Highland Girl studying Poetry' Five quatrains. First line: 'Poetry drives its lines into her forehead'

63   'About that Mile' Seven rhymed six-line stanzas. First line: 'It all grew in a garden, all that sin,'

64   'After the War' Two lyrics; one of five rhymed six-line stanzas, the other a sonnet. First line: 'After the War had said its last' 'Their sheets are waters of the porpoise blue.'

65   'At a Ceilidh' Four three-line stanzas. First line: 'The pianist hollows out repetitive teeth.'

66   'By Ferry to the Island' Published in *Observer Mag.*, 14 Aug. 1966, 17; accompanied by photograph and introductory caption, as part of an article called 'Poets and Their Worlds' by Colin Cross and Jane Bown. Six five-line rhymed stanzas. First line: 'We crossed by ferry to the bare island'

67   'Culloden and After' Previously published in *New Stn*, 58 (June–Dec 1959), 167. Three rhymed six-line stanzas, concluding with a three-line stanza linked in terza rima to the foregoing. First line: 'You understand it? How they returned from Culloden'

68   'Dying is not Setting Out' Four half-rhymed quatrains. First line: 'Dying is not setting out'

69   'First World War Generals' Five quatrains. First line: 'These are of a different sort,'

70   'For Angus MacLeod: Headmaster, and Editor of Gaelic Poems' Previously published in *Sidewalk*, 1, no. 1 [1960], 41. Five quatrains. First line: 'Today they laid him in the earth's cold colour,'

71   'For my Mother' Four five line stanzas. First line: 'She is tougher than me, harder.'

72   'Girl with orange Sunshade' Previously published in *New Stn*, 59 (Jan-June 1960), 420. Sonnet. First line: 'An orange sunshade wheels about her head.'

73   'Highland Portrait' Four rhymed six-line stanzas. First line: 'Castles draw in their horns. The stones are streaming'

74   'Home' Previously published in CQ, 2 (1960), 232. Three rhymed nine-line stanzas. First line: 'To have to stay'

75   'John Knox' Sonnet. First line: 'That scything wind has cut the rich corn down —'

76   'Kierkegaard' Four half-rhymed six-line stanzas. First line: 'Forced theologian of the minimum place,'

77   'Lilac, Snow and Shadow' Four lyrics, in rhymed and unrhymed two and three-line stanzas. First line: 'A lilac dress casting a long shadow' 'I think of my friends, of sixteen years' silence' 'Or think how it was, four hundred years ago,' 'The lilac veins pulse with a cruel blood.'

78   'Love Songs of a Puritan (A)' Previously published in *London Magazine*, o.s. 6, no. 10 (Oct. 1959), 15-16. Four sections, the first three in quatrains, the last in rhymed six-line stanzas. First lines: 'You've put salt on my bread' 'My eyes are heresies to the clear' 'The day's in love with you as suns with gardens.' 'I know a young girl of great wit'

79   'Love Songs of a Puritan (B)' Sequence of ten poems, nine of which are sonnets. The second has two eight-line rhymed stanzas. Only the seventh, 'The Sick Gull', is titled. First lines: (1) 'Only in winter can I see you best.' (2) 'White paper boils before the moving boat' (3) 'The piper, marching in his peacock style' (4) 'There was a mountain veiled in level black' (5) 'There is a mountain stony, bleak and tall,' (6) 'The weighted mountain broods in changing water' (7) 'What is that dumb posterity to me?' (8) 'Searching yourself to find a saving God' (9) 'Bald insect heads are gossiping on a leaf' (10) 'To stand so steady that the world is still'

80   'Luss Village' Previously published in *Sctn*, 12 Sept. 1959. Sonnet. First line: 'Such walls, like honey, and the old are happy'

81   'Of a Rare Courage' Five quatrains. First line: 'A man of a rare courage, not oppressive.'

82   'Old Woman' Previously published in *Honour'd Shade* (1959). Six half-rhymed four-line stanzas. First line: 'And she, being old, fed from a mashed plate'

83 'Schoolgirl on Speech-day in the Open Air' Six quatrains. First line: 'Here in their health and youth they're sitting down'

84 'Sea-Song' Six rhymed five-line stanzas. First line: 'I walked one day by the composed water'

85 'Studies in Power' Previously published in *New Stn*, 60 (July-Dec 1960), 93. Two sonnets First line: 'Today at a meeting while I sat confused' 'I thought of power and its sources while'

86 'Sunday Morning Walk: Stornoway' Previously published in *Saltire Rev.*, 6, no. 23 (Wtr 1961), 66. Ten quatrains. First line: 'Sunday of wrangling bells — and salt in the air —'

87 'The Bore' Four quatrains. First line: 'The whirring bullets drone through his conversation'

88 'The Temptation' Four seven-line part-rhymed stanzas. First line: 'Imagine, say, a medieval window'

89 'Three Sonnets' First lines: (1) 'Leaves, crisped by heat, droop in tormenting air.' (2) 'One precious Sunday we sat in the calm park.' (3) 'Nor did the trees adore you, that's quite silly.'

Deer on the High Hills (1962)

90 'Deer on the High Hills: A Meditation' Previously published in *New Saltire*, 2 (1961), 27-38. Sequence of fourteen lyrics; all, except the first which is a single couplet, in rhymed three-line stanzas. First lines: (1) 'A deer looks through you to the other side,' (2) 'Yesterday three deer stood at the roadside.' (3) 'One would be finished with these practical things' (4) 'Forget these purple evenings and these poems' (5) 'You must build from the rain and stones,' (6) 'Duncan Ban MacIntyre, the poet,' (7) 'What is the knowledge of the deer?' (8) 'Supposing God had a branched head like this' (9) 'Deer on the high peaks, calling, calling,' (10) 'Deer on the high peaks, the wandering senses' (11) 'Deer on the high peaks, let me turn' (12) 'Deer on the high hills, in your halfway kingdom,' (13) 'Do colours cry? Does "black" weep for the dead?' (14) 'There is no metaphor. The stone is stony.'

At Helensburgh (1965)

91 'At Helensburgh (1)' Six lines. First line: 'Ship in the misty bay. Now it is autumn.'

92 'At Helensburgh (2)' Four three-line stanzas. First line: '"Different from the world of the happy"'

93 'At Helensburgh (3)' Six half-rhymed pairs. First line: 'The gale corrects a dumb reality.'

94 'At Helensburgh (4)' Two poems. The first has three stanzas of three lines and one of six. The second has three pairs and one single line. First lines: (a) 'The idiot sea trying to speak' (b) 'There is a being here trying to reach us'

95 'At Helensburgh (5) Five three-line stanzas. First line: 'Out in the bay the grey destroyers wait.'

96 'At Helensburgh (6)' Six lines. First line: 'The yachts slide, are different colours —'

97 'At Helensburgh (7)' Six three-line stanzas. First line: 'This that's here cannot be spoken of'

98 'At Helensburgh (8)' Ten lines, half-rhymed. First line: '"How much can neither kings nor laws cure."'

99 'At Helensburgh (9)' Three stanzas of four, eight and four lines. First line: 'Huge mirror of the sea. I look in you.'

100 'At Helensburgh (10)' Seventeen lines. First line: 'The free wind dies on us.'

101 'At Helensburgh (11)' Thirteen lines. First line: 'The day is cooling now.'

102 'At Helensburgh (12)' Sequence of three poems, one of nine and two of eight lines. First lines: (a) 'Summer is leaving us and the white sun' (b) 'Now the benches empty and the blue' (c) 'Where shall I find you, you who are more than idea?'

Bìobuill is Sanasan-reice (1965)

103 '1941-42' Translated in *The Permanent Island*. Six lines. First line: 'Na làithean ud air an reidio —' / 'Those days, on the radio'

104 'A Nighean Og'/'Young Girl' Previously published in *Bùrn is Aran*. See A00. Translated in *The Permanent Island*. First line: 'A nighean òg a dh'fhalbhas'/'A young girl goes with a straight back'

105 'A' Chailleach Bheag'/'The Little Old Lady' Translated in *The Permanent Island*. Eight lines. First line: 'A' chailleach bheag leis a' bheannaig dhuibh'/'The little old lady with the black hood'

106 'A' Chailleach'/'The Old Woman' Translated in *The Permanent Island*. Eight lines. First line: 'Thig am post an nochd'/'The postman will come to-night'

107 'A' Chailleach'/'The Old Woman' Previously published in *Bùrn is Aran*. First line: 'Tha i an nochd 'na suidhe ri uinneig'/'To-night she is sitting by a window'

108 'A' Chlach'/'The Stone' Translated in *The Permanent Island*. Nineteen lines. First line: 'Innsidh mi dhut, a rùin, na facail a thubhairt a' chlach rium.'/'I will tell you my dear the words that the stone told me.'

109 'A' Dol Dhachaidh'/'Going Home' Previously published in *Bùrn is Aran*. First line: 'Am màireach theid mi dhachaidh do m'eilean'/'Tomorrow I will go home to my island'

110 'A' Ghaidhealtachd'/'The Highlands' Translated in *The Permanent Island*. Five lines. First line: 'Uibhir de thalàmh, uibhir de fhairge,'/'So much land, so much sea,'

111 'Aig a' Chladh'/'At the Cemetry' Previously published in *Bùrn is Aran*. First line: 'Chunna mi aig a' chladh an de iad,'/'I saw them yesterday at the cemetr y,'

112 'Aig Clachan Chalanais'/'At the Stones of Callanish' Previously published in *Bùrn is Aran*. First line: 'Aig clachan Chalanais an de'/'At the stones of Callanish yesterday'

113 'Air an t-Sràid'/'On the Street' Translated in *The Permanent Island*. Six lines. First line: 'Seana bhoireannach a' gal air sràid.'/'An old woman crying in the street.'

114 'Air Latha Breagha'/'On a Beautiful Day' Translated in *The Permanent Island* and *Hamlet in Autumn*. Published in translation in the *Lit. Rev.*, 18, no. 3 (Spring 1975), 336. Nineteen lines. First line: 'Bho'n chreig'/'From the stone'

115 'Air Òidhche Fhoghair'/'On an Autumn Night' Seventeen lines. First line: 'Air òidhche fhoghair'/'On an autumn night'

116 'Am Buachaille 's a Leannan (Bho'n Bheurla aig Marlowe)' Previously published in *Bùrn is Aran*.

117 'Am Mac Strodhail' / 'The Prodigal Son' Translated in *The Permanent Island*. Six eight-line stanzas. First line: 'Fo rionnagan na dorainn' / 'Under the stars of grief'

118 'Am Ministear' / 'The Minister' Translated in *The Permanent Island*. Seven three-line stanzas. First line: 'Ann an coilltean Chinn-tire' / 'In the woods of Kintyre'

119 'Am Muir 's na Creagan' / 'The Sea and the Rocks' Translated in *The Permanent Island*. Eight lines. First line: 'Ballet a' choip ris a' chreig' / 'Ballet of foam against the rocks'

120 'Amhran' / 'Song' Translated in *The Permanent Island*. Two four-line stanzas. First line: 'Dh'eirigh mi moch madainn Cheitein'

121 'An Crom-lus' / 'The Poppy' Ten lines in pairs. First line: 'Tha flùran Flanders dearg san adhar ghorm.' / 'The flower of Flanders is red in the blue sky.'

122 'An Eala Bhàn' / 'The White Swan' Translated in *The Permanent Island*. Printed with a translation in *Scot. Int.*, 4 (Oct/Nov 1968), 49. Four four-line stanzas. First line: 'Tha an eala bhàn an còmhnaidh' / 'The white swan is always there'

123 'An Litir Aràid' Previously published in *Bùrn is Aran*.

124 'An Solus' / 'The Light' Twenty-one lines. First line: 'Ann an uinneag tigh a' ghlinne' / 'In the window of the house of the glen'

125 'An t-Amadan' / 'The Fool' Translated in *The Permanent Island*. Ten lines. First line: 'Ann an aodach an amadain,' / 'In the dress of the fool,'

126 'An t-Eilean' / 'The Island' Translated in *The Permanent Island*. Six pairs. First line: 'Tha eilean an còmhnaidh anns an spiorad' / 'There is an island always in the spirit.'

127 'An Tigh a bh'anns a' Ghleann' / 'The House in the Glen' Four four-line stanzas. First line: 'Tha an cruinne-ce nas aingidh' / 'The universe is more hostile'

128 'An t-Oban' / 'Oban' Translated in *The Permanent Island*. Five poems of eight to ten lines, in single stanzas or quatrains. First line: 'Tha an t-uisg a' drùdhadh air an Oban,' / 'The rain is penetrating Oban,' 'An tog mi baile de phàipear?' / 'Shall I raise a town of paper?' 'Tha am muir an nochd mar

shanas-reice.'/'Tonight the sea is like an advertisement.' 'Dh'fhalbh an sarcas dhachaidh.'/'The circus has gone home.' 'Thoisich an cl ag mor a' bualadh.'/'The big bell began to peal.'

129 'An t-Uisge'/'The Rain' Translated in *The Permanent Island*. Six rhymed lines. First line: 'An t-uisge dortadh air an t-sràid.'/'The rain pouring on the street.'

130 'Aon Nighean'/'One Girl' Translated in *The Permanent Island*. Three four-line stanzas. First line: 'Aon nighean a chunna mi'/'One girl I saw'

131 'Còmhradh'/'Conversation' Translated in *The Permanent Island*. Four four-line stanzas. First line: '"Tha thusa aosd, is mise òg,"'/'"You are old, and I am young,"'

132 'Dan'/'Predestination' Translated in *The Permanent Island*. This poem has also been translated in *Poetry Australia*, 63 (May 1977), 91 — a special issue selected and introduced by Derick Thomson. Five four-line stanzas. First line: 'Nam bithinn air sud a dheanamh,'/'If I had done that, if I had done this,'

133 'De tha Ceàrr'/'What is Wrong?' Previously published in *Bùrn is Aran*. First line: 'Co 's urrainn innse de tha ceàrr?'/'Who can tell me what is wrong?'

134 'Deirdre' Translated in *The Permanent Island*. Three four-line stanzas. First line: 'O gleann Eite, O gleann Eite, '/'O Glen Etive, O Glen Etive,'

135 'Di-Sathuirn'/'Saturday' Translated in *The Permanent Island*. Twenty-five lines. First line: 'An so air feasgar Di-Sathuirn'/'Here on Saturday evening'

136 'Do mo Mhàthair'/'To my Mother' Translated in *The Permanent Island*. Published in translation in *Poetry Australia* 63 (May 1977), 92. It has also been translated into modern Irish by Louis de Paor, *Innti*, 10 (Christmas 1986), 8. Four eight-line stanzas. First line: 'Bha thus' a' sgoltadh sgadain'/'You were gutting herring'

137 'Do Ruaraidh MacThomais'/'For Derick Thomson' Translated in *The Permanent Island*. Five lyrics; four in four-line, one in three-line stanzas. First lines: (1) 'Thogadh sinn am Pabail còmhla.'/'We were brought up in Bayble together.' (2) 'Tha beinn mhor ann, beinn na bàrdachd.'/'There is a tall mountain, the mountain of poetry.' (3) 'Pabail 's Athens, nach e chompaist'/'Bayble and Athens, isn't the compass' (4) '"Na gob thog i Leodhas is Pabail.'/'In his beak he lifted Lewis and Bayble.' (5) 'Tha chuthag ann am beul na seabhaig.'/'The cuckoo is in the hawk's mouth.'

138 'Do Sheana-bhoireannach' / 'To an Old Woman' Translated in *The Permanent Island*. Fifty-one lines in nine stanzas of three to twelve lines. First line: 'Tha thu san eaglais ag eisdeachd' / 'You are in the church listening'

139 'Fitheach' / 'The Raven' Translated in *The Permanent Island*. Five four-line stanzas. First line: 'A' sgrìobhadh nam facal mu dheireadh' / 'Writing the last words'

140 'Freud' Translated in *The Permanent Island*. Six eight-line stanzas. First line: 'Duine mor a Vienna' / 'Great man from Vienna'

141 'Lomnochd' / 'Bareness' Translated in *The Permanent Island*. Seven lines. First line: "Se lomnochd a tha mi 'g iarraidh, ' / 'It is bareness I want,'

142 'Luss' Translated in *The Permanent Island*. Two four-line stanzas. First line: 'Ròsan a' slugadh na cloich', ' / 'Roses swallowing the stone,'

143 'Meileoidian an Spioraid' / 'The Melodeon of the Spirit' Translated in *The Permanent Island*. Five four-line stanzas. First line: 'E hi o ro, e hi o ri,'

144 'Mo Bhàrdachd' / 'My Poetry' Two four-line stanzas. First line: 'Uill, cha do dh'ionnsaich mi gaol bhuat.' / 'Well, I did not learn love from you.'

145 'Na Laoich' / 'The Heroes' Translated in *The Permanent Island*. Two four-line stanzas. First line: 'Tha feadhainn ann nach bris am bas' / 'There are whom some death will not break'

146 'Neochiontas' / 'Innocence' Translated in *The Permanent Island*. The Gaelic original is included in Donald MacAulay's bilingual anthology, *Nua-bhàrdachd Ghàidhlig/Modern Scottish Gaelic Poetry* (Edinburgh, 1976). Five lines. First line: 'Tha am muir gorm 'na dhaoimeanan.' / 'The blue sea is like diamonds.'

147 'Nochdadh ri Beanntan na Hearadh' / 'Sighting the Mountains of Harris' Translated in *The Permanent Island*. Two rhymed eight-line stanzas. First line: 'Nochdadh ri beanntan na Hearadh' / 'Sighting the mountains of Harris'

148 'Nuair a Bha Sinn Og' / 'When We Were Young' Translated in *The Permanent Island*. Six three-line stanzas. First line: 'Nuair a bha sinn òg bhiodh uisge ann,' / 'When we were young it would be raining'

149 'Ochd Orain airson Ceilidh Uir' / 'Eight Songs for a new Ceilidh' Previously published in *Gairm*, 11 (1962/63), 378-82. Eight poems of two to six four-line stanzas. First lines: (1) 'Dh'iarr thu òran orm dhut fhein' / 'You asked me for a poem for yourself' (2) 'Nuair a thug i 'n cuan mor

oirr'' / 'When she took the great sea on her' (3) 'Chunna mi ann an càmpa mi' / 'I saw myself in a camp' (4) "Nar seasamh aig bun na màthair-uisge' / 'Standing at the edge of the reservoir' (5) 'Cha dirich mi na beanntan ud,' / 'I will not climb these mountains,' (6) 'Cha teid mi chaoidh do'n Fhraing,' / 'I will never go to France,' (7) '"Thoir Lunnainn ort," thubhairt iad rium.' / '"Go to London," they said to me.' (8) 'Am falbh thu leam, a rìbhinn òg,' / 'Will you go with me, young maiden,'

150   'Oran Foghair' / 'Autumn Song' Translated in *The Permanent Island*. Six lines. First line: 'Chuir iad an t-arbhar a steach, phaisg iad na beanntan.' / 'They have taken the corn in, they have folded up the mountains,'

151   'Oran Gaoil' / 'Love Song' Printed with a translation in *Scot. Int.*, 4 (Oct/Nov 1968), 49. Translated in *The Permanent Island*. Five lines. First line: '"Dh'fhàg thu mi is m'inntinn trom,"' / '"You left me and my mind was heavy,"'

152   'Oran Ionndrain' / 'Song of Remembrance' Translated in *The Permanent Island*. Seven lines. First line: 'Soraidh slàn le Stèornabhagh' / 'Good-bye to Stornoway'

153   'Oran' / 'Song' Translated in *The Permanent Island*. Seven lines. First line: 'Liberal, Labour no Conservative,' / 'Liberal, Labour or Conservative,'

154   'Oran' / 'Song' Two four-line stanzas. First line: 'Dh'fhalbh na feidh, a Dhonnchaidh Bhàin.' / 'The deer have gone, O Duncan B an.'

155   'Rubha Chinn Aird (air eadar-theangachadh bho Sheòras Bruce)' Three stanzas of two, ten and four lines. First line: 'Tha mi a' dol tuath, gu fuachd, gu dachaidh, gu Ceann Ard,'

156   'Tha thu air aigeann m'inntinn' / 'You are at the bottom of my mind' Previously published in *Bùrn is Aran*. This translation was also published in *Poetry Australia*, 63 (May 1977). Printed with a translation in *Scot. Int.*, 4 (Oct/Nov 68), 47. Translated in *The Permanent Island*. Three six-line stanzas. First line: 'Gun fhìos dhomh tha thu air aigeann m'inntinn' / 'Without my knowing it you are at the bottom of my mind,'

The Law and the Grace (1965)

157   '1964' Five quatrains. First line: '1964 is come around'

158   'At the Firth of Lorne' Four quatrains. First line: 'In the cold orange light we stared across'

159 'At the Reservoir' Five rhymed five-line stanzas. First line: 'I sat beside you on the stone stair.'

160 'At Tiumpan Head, Lewis' Previously published in *Scotland's Magazine*, 59, no. 3 (Mar. 1963), 40. Three quatrains. First line: 'I looked out across the water,'

161 'Cuan Ferry' Two half-rhymed quatrains. First line: 'We looked out across the water'

162 'Encounter in a School Corridor' Five quatrains. First line: 'Supposing today walking along this passage'

163 'Envoi' Translated into Polish by Andrzej Szuba in *Litteratura na Swiecie*, 10 (135: 1982). Four three-line stanzas. First line: 'Remember me when you come into your kingdom.'

164 'Face of an Old Highland Woman' Three half-rhymed quatrains. First line: 'This face is not the Mona Lisa's'

165 'Highlanders' Three half-rhymed quatrains. First line: 'They sailed away into the coloured prints'

166 'Hume' Four part-rhymed quatrains. First line: 'More than this I do not love you,'

167 'It is the Old' Three six-line stanzas. First line: 'It is the old'

168 'Johnson in the Highlands' Broadcast on the Third Programme before publication. Six three-line stanzas. First line: 'A reasoning mind travels through this country.'

169 'Lenin' Six quatrains. First line: 'In a chair of iron'

170 'Living Together' Four quatrains. First line: 'So sensitive my fingers hardly'

171 'Meeting' Seven quatrains. First line: '"They threw stones at me," the old man said.'

172 'Minister' Three quatrains. First line: 'In a moral cage all his days,'

173 '"Nothing Human"' Six half-rhymed quatrains. First line: '"Nothing human is alien to me."'

174 'Old Highland Lady Reading Newspapers' Three quatrains. First line: 'Grasping the newspapers in kneaded hands'

175 'Old Woman' Broadcast on the Third Programme before publication. Also published in *P. Rev.*, 3, no. 2 (1984), ed. Eugene van Itterbeek(Leuven). Nine rhymed three-line stanzas. First line: 'Your thorned back'

176 'Poem in March' Three part-rhymed quatrains. First line: 'Old cans sparkle. Tie slaps at the chin.'

177 'Preparation for a Death' Previously published in *Glasgow Rev.*, 1, no. 1 (Spr. 1964), 11. Four half-rhymed quatrains. First line: 'Have I seen death conquered at last in you'

178 'Rythm' Many times anthologised. Nineteen rhymed lines. First line: 'They dunno how it is. I smack a ball'

179 'Schoolroom' Five part-rhymed three-line stanzas. First line: 'My room is bare and has no pictures in it,'

180 'Schoolroom Incident' Five rhymed five-line stanzas. First line: 'Whose fault was this?'

181 'Schoolteacher' Four quatrains. First line: 'Roman lady, in your distant gown'

182 'So Many Names' Three triplets. First line: 'So many names cut into the grey stone —'

183 'Spring Wedding' Three quatrains. First line: 'Step out, my dear, down the aesthetic aisles'

184 'The Anglo-Saxon Lecturer goes to the Cinema every Tuesday' Eight quatrains. First line: 'Monogrammed lady with her loaded tray'

185 'The Argument' Seven rhymed five-line stanzas. First line: '"Our world is not predestined." So he chose'

186 'The Cemetry near Burns' Cottage' Three rhymed five-line stanzas. First line: 'Tombs of the Covenanters nod together'

187 'The Chess Player' Six rhymed five-line stanzas. First line: 'When the badness came he was playing chess again.'

188 'The Clearances' Four three-line stanzas. First line: 'The thistles climb the thatch. Forever'

189 'The Law and the Grace' Five quatrains. First line: 'It's law they ask of me and not grace.'

190 'The Lone Rider' Five rhymed five-line stanzas. First line: 'It's not the worst ones that things happen to.'

191 'The Proposal' Seven three-line stanzas. First line: 'This is my hairy hand. I am a killer.'

192 'The Song' Two quatrains. First line: '"Never again will we part." So says the song.'

193 'The Squirrel' Six quatrains. First line: 'The squirrel lay on the cold stone'

194 'The Two Clouds' Three triplets. First line: 'What has this to do with "the good"?'

195 'The Witches' Four quatrains. First line: 'Coveys of black witches gather'

196 'The Wreath' Five rhymed five-line stanzas. First line: 'She broke the stalks clean off; stuck wire instead'

197 'This Blue Cauldron' Four quatrains. First line: 'This blue cauldron of a stunned cold'

198 'To a Theologian' Fifteen lines in terza rima. First line: 'In the world of Kierkegaard and Bonhoeffer'

199 'To Forget the Dead' Three quatrains. First line: 'To forget the dead. How to forget the dead'

200 'Two Girls Singing' Previously published in GH, 11 Nov. 1961. Broadcast on 'Time for Verse', 26 Aug. 1987 (Radio 4). Translated into Polish by Andrzej Szuba in Litteratura na Swiecie, 10 (135: 1982) Four three-line stanzas. First line: 'It was neither the words nor yet the tune.'

201 '"Whether beyond the stormy Hebrides"' Four rhymed five-line stanzas. First line: 'Too simple an ending that,'

202 'World War One' Previously published in New Saltire, 4 (Smr 1962), 21-27. The seventh poem of the original sequence is omitted. Its first line is, 'I cannot find a place', and it is of twenty-seven lines in mainly five-line stanzas. Sequence of seven poems. The first, 'Haig', has seventeen lines in stanzas of five and six lines. The second has six three-line, and the third three nine-line stanzas. The fourth, 'The Soldier's Wish', has twenty-four lines in half-rhymed couplets, and 'November 1961' is of four quatrains. The sixth has five rhymed seven-line stanzas closed by two quatrains; the last poem is of nine rhymed lines. First lines: (1) 'These stumbling men (later to be translated)' (2) 'They droop out of the twilight, slack-rifled,' (3) 'Lucky for them that they died perhaps' (4) 'I want fat cigars to explode' (5) 'I can't cry for these men.' (6) 'Here at the droning sermon' (7) 'Poppies defencelessly bared like hearts'

From Bourgeois Land (1969)

203 'From Bourgeois Land 1' Ten rhymed five-line stanzas. First line: 'One might still argue that it's possible'

204 'From Bourgeois Land 2' Nine rhymed five-line stanzas. First line: 'Entering your house I sniff again'

205 'From Bourgeois Land 3: Speaker' Seven half-rhymed quatrains. First line: 'Ah, well, let the sun shine on you'

206 'From Bourgeois Land 4' Six quatrains. First line: 'Poets aren't dangerous, you think.'

207 'From Bourgeois Land 5: Dido and Aeneas' Seven quatrains. First line: 'What did the papers say of that romance'

208 'From Bourgeois Land 6: Hamlet' Five quatrains, the last split three and one. First line: 'Sick of the place, he turned him towards night.'

209 'From Bourgeois Land 7: Epitaph' Sonnet. First line: 'This is the Law. What you love best you get.'

210 'From Bourgeois Land 8: Burns' Five rhymed six-line stanzas. First line: '"Ah such a genius," the church intones.'

211 'From Bourgeois Land 9: Lenin' Seven quatrains. First line: 'You heard his voice, that terrible blunt voice.'

212 'From Bourgeois Land 10' Seven quatrains. First line: 'All night the poet drinks and all the day.'

213 'From Bourgeois Land 11' Eight pairs. First line: 'It was the heavy jokes, the dreadful jokes,'

214 'From Bourgeois Land 12' Published in *Radical Scotland*, 22 (Aug/Sept 1986), 38 with notes by Frederic Lindsay. Seven quatrains. First line: 'My Scottish towns with Town Halls and with courts,'

215 'From Bourgeois Land 13' Six quatrains. First line: 'When you were young, my dear, you could be found'

216 'From Bourgeois Land 14' Five rhymed five-line stanzas. First line: 'In youth to have mocked the pompous and shot down'

217 'From Bourgeois Land 15: Farewell Party' Six quatrains. First line: 'Oh, it was such a party. Miss MacMillan'

218 'From Bourgeois Land 16: Church' Ten quatrains. First line: 'Once more you speak, once more I hear your words.'

219 'From Bourgeois Land 17' Eight lines in three stanzas of two and three. First line: 'The wind roars. Thousands of miles it came'

220 'From Bourgeois Land 18' Three quatrains. First line: 'The zebra's running free. Then the wild dogs,'

221 'From Bourgeois Land 19: Young Girl Singing Psalm' Nine rhymed pairs. First line: 'Just for a moment then as you raised your book —'

222 'From Bourgeois Land 20: National Service' Eight rhymed five-line stanzas. First line: 'A small neat man, bright as a silver buckle,'

223 'From Bourgeois Land 21: At the Sale' Previously published in *TLS*, 31 Aug. 1967, p. 780. Eight rhymed six-line stanzas. First line: 'Old beds, old chairs, old mattresses, old books,'

224 'From Bourgeois Land 22' Three quatrains. First line: 'Could I but love you then your hands are green,'

225 'From Bourgeois Land 23' Four quatrains. First line: 'Take, O take that book away.'

226 'From Bourgeois Land 24' Fifteen rhymed pairs. First line: 'More than twenty years ago you heard it'

227 'From Bourgeois Land 25' Two rhymed pairs. First line: 'I take it from you — a small token of esteem —'

228 'From Bourgeois Land 26' Six rhymed pairs. First line: 'I don't love you. You have surrendered too much.'

229 'From Bourgeois Land 27' Five rhymed five-line stanzas. First line: 'Shyly she said: "I so admire your work."'

230 'From Bourgeois Land 28' Two rhymed pairs. First line: 'To hell with this poetry reading, he cried —'

231 'From Bourgeois Land 29' Seven rhymed pairs. First line: 'The hall is large and echoing. Your are small.'

232 'From Bourgeois Land 30' Thirteen rhymed pairs. First line: 'I know you, Hawthorne, I know all your ways,'

233 'From Bourgeois Land 31' Seven rhymed pairs. First line: 'The lawyer stands beside the sea'

234 'From Bourgeois Land 32: Retiral' Seven numbered sections, each of two rhymed pairs. First line: 'You say goodbye and hand the banknotes over'

235 'From Bourgeois Land 33' Seven rhymed pairs. First line: 'What were you in search of, RLS,'

236 'From Bourgeois Land 34' Four rhymed pairs. First line: 'What's your Success to me who read the great dead,'

237 'From Bourgeois Land 35' Ten lines in triplets and single last line. First line: 'It is the night, night of the yellow moon,'

238 'From Bourgeois Land 36' Five three-line stanzas. First line: 'Love, if you had been love you would have spoken.'

239 'From Bourgeois Land 37' Previously published in *Transatlantic Review*. Fifteen lines. First line: 'Your face is a white moon rising over Islay,'

240 'From Bourgeois Land 38: Little Boy' Ten half-rhymed pairs and one triplet. First line: 'Little boy, carefully stringing your bow'

241 'From Bourgeois Land 39' Eight rhymed pairs. First line: 'Children, follow the dwarfs and the giants and the wolves,'

Selected Poems (1970)

242 'Am Faigh a' Ghàidhlig Bas?' / 'Shall Gaelic Die?' Previously published in *Lines*, 29 (June 1969), 33-41; with an English translation in the following pages (41-45). Only the English text is printed in *Selected Poems* (1970). Sequence of twenty-five poems, of two to twenty lines. First lines: (1) 'Chàn eil gramar ann an dealbh.' / 'A picture has no grammar.' (2) 'Sanasan-reice ann an neon' / 'Advertisements in neon' (3) 'Tha facail ag eirigh as an duthaich.' / 'Words rise out of the country.' (4) 'Thogh iad tigh' / 'They built a house' (5) 'Am fear a chailleas a chanain,' / 'He who loses his language,' (6) 'Thàinig mise le "sobhrach" nam bheul.' / 'I came with a "sobhrach" in my mouth.' (7) '"An ni air nach urrainn dhut bruidhinn"' / '"That thing about which you cannot speak"' (8) '"Am faigh a' Ghàidhlig bas?"' / '"Shall Gaelic die?"' (9) 'Ma chanas mi eaglais òrange' / 'If I say "an orange church"' (10) 'Ars' an Domhnallach: "'S e Ghàidhlig a bh'aig Adhamh,"' / 'Said Alexander MacDonald, "It was Gaelic that Adam"' (11) 'Am faigh a' Ghàidhlig bas?' / 'Shall Gaelic die?' (12) 'Eaglais òrange' / 'An orange church' (13) 'An robh thu riamh ann am maze?' / 'Were you ever in a maze?' (14) 'Nuair a thàinig an apa a nios as na craobhan' / 'When the ape descended from the trees' (15) 'Thàinig an

calman air ais gu Noah' / 'The dove returned to Noah' (16) 'Tha an sgoilear na shuidhe' / 'The scholar is sitting' (17) 'Co th'agad anns an lion?' / 'Whom have you got in the net?' (18) '"Nuair a chuireas tu cul ris an dorus,"' / '"When you turn your back on the door,"' (19) 'Tha muillion dath nas fheàrr na aon dath,' / 'A million colours are better than one colour,' (20) 'Mar bhoga-froise, mar chrayons,' / 'Like a rainbow, like crayons, ' (21) 'Tha Dia air tu-muigh a' chanain' / 'God is outside language,' (22) 'Tha am Bas air tu-muigh a chanain.' / 'Death is outside the language.' (23) 'Nuair a dh'eigheadh "Adhamh"' / 'When the name "Adam" was spoken' (24) 'Chan urrainn dhut "Neo-Adhamh" eigheachd.' / 'You cannot say "Not-Adam."' (25) 'Tha an or ur. Cha mheirg e.' / 'The gold is new. It will not rust.'

243 'At the Highland Games' Previously published in *Lines*, 28 (Mar. 1969), 12-13. Included in *Poems of the Sixties*, ed. F. E. S. Finn (London, 1970). Nine rhymed pairs, opened by a single line. First line: 'Like re-reading a book which has lost its pith.'

244 'By the Sea' Previously published in *Scottish Poetry Three* (Edinburgh, 1968). A fourteen-poem sequence, totalling two hundred and thirty lines. The poems are predominantly in short, rhymed stanzas; two are in couplets. Some of the poems are titled; the fourth 'In the Cafe', the sixth 'Dumbarton', the eighth 'After the Gale', the ninth 'Young Girl', the tenth 'Dunoon and the Holy Loch', the eleventh 'Tourist Driver', the twelfth 'In the Park', and the last 'At the Silent Films'. First lines: (1) 'Sitting here by the foreshore day after day' (2) 'At Helensburgh the tide is out again —' (3) 'These hundred-year-olds preserved in glazed' (4) 'The leaf-fringed fountain' (5) 'Milk jugs, cups,' (6) 'They're pulling down the Bingo hall today.' (7) 'Out of the grey the white waves mouth at the shore.' (8) 'The stunned world stops on its axis.' (9) 'Nothing more impermanent, it appears,' (10) 'The huge sea widens from us, mile on mile.' (11) 'He tells us there's a cow and there's a cow.' (12) 'Over the shoes in pebbles I sit here. ' (13) 'Days when the world seems like an old French film' (14) 'O Chaplin with your little black moustache,'

245 'Hear Us O Lord' Previously published in *Lines*, 29 (June 1969), 13-14. The punctuation of the title and first line are changed. The last stanza is split into a pair and two single lines. Twenty lines in four-line stanzas. First line: 'Hear us, O Lord, aggression is part of us.'

246 'I Build an orange Church' Previously published in *Sctn*, 25 Jan. 1969. Four three-line stanzas. First line: 'I build an orange church and put inside it'

247 'If You are About to Die Now' Previously published in *Scot. Int.*, 6 (Apr. 1969), 31-32. Translated into Polish by Andrzej Szuba in *Litteratura na Swiecie*, 10 (135: 1982). Thirty-nine lines in seven and eight-line stanzas. First line: 'If you are about to die now'

248 'In Old Age' Previously published in *Sctn*, 17 May 1969. Eleven lines. First line: 'Now you sleep away the day which has nothing to offer.'

249 'Jean Brodie's Children' Previously published in *Sctn*, 25 Jan. 1969. Seventeen lines in six stanzas of two and three lines. First line: 'Jean Brodie's children in your small green caps,'

250 'Old Woman with Flowers' Previously published in *Lines*, 29 (June 1969), 3. Eight rhymed lines. First line: 'These are your flowers. They were given to you'

251 'She Teaches Lear' Previously published in *TLS*, 17 June 1965, p. 520. Also appeared in *Three Regional Voices* (See Section E). Thirteen rhymed six-line stanzas. First line: 'Much to have given up? Martyr, one says?'

252 'To Settle Down' Previously published in *Sctn*, 17 May 1969. Sixteen lines. First line: 'To settle down into religion with'

Hamlet in Autumn (1972)

253 'By the Sea in Autumn' Four stanzas: the first and last of two lines, the two others four. First line: 'The mussels clamp their miniature helmets to'

254 'Carol and Hamlet' (Excerpts from a sonnet sequence) Previously published in CQ, 9 (1967), 230-33. *Critical Quarterly* prints two other sonnets from the sequence; see section C. First lines: [1] 'Small and small-breasted you scribble in your jotter.' [2] 'The light of order (false and yet not false)' [3] 'That leaf you see touching the window now —' [4] 'That's why Hamlet always talks of death.' [5] 'I too was terrified of words once.' [6] 'I've seen you often standing at the wall' [7] 'As now I see you individual'

255 'Chaplin' Previously published in *Sctn*, 6 Dec. 1969. Twelve lines. First line: 'Everything seems pasted on,'

256 'Children in Winter' Ten lines in four and three-line stanzas. First line: 'In the dark mornings'

257 'Christmas, 1971' Previously published in *Sctn*, 25 Mar. 1972. Fourteen lines. First line: 'There's no snow this Christmas ... there was snow'

258 'Dead for a Rat' Previously published in *Agenda*, 5, no. 4: 6, no. 1 (Aut./Wtr 1967/68), 84. Thirty-three lines in stanzas of four, five, six and nine lines. First line: 'What snarls'

259 'Dear Hamlet' Previously published in *Sctn*, 18 May 1968. One stanza of three lines, seven of four. First line: 'Dear Hamlet, you were pushed beyond your strength'

260 'Dipping your Spoon ...' Included in *New Poems 1972-1973*, edited by Douglas Dunn (London: Hutchinson, 1973). Fifteen lines, in stanzas of two, five and six. First line: 'Dipping your spoon in the mash of TV'

261 'End of Schooldays' Previously published in *Sctn*, 30 Aug. 1969. Four stanzas; three of six and one of five lines. First line: 'Captains, this is your last day in school.'

262 'Everything is Silent' Previously published in *Aquarius*, 3 (1970), 43. Originally entitled simply 'Poem'. Published as 'Everything is Silent' in *Sctn*, 20 June 1970; and included in *Scottish Poetry Six* (Edinburgh, 1972). Four five-line stanzas. First line: 'Everything is silent now'

263 'Fairy Story' Five four-line stanzas. First line: 'Snow. Much snow. Ice. A cottage.'

264 'Films' Ten lines in stanzas of one, two and four lines. First line: 'These serious tedious Scandinavian films'

265 'Finis not Tragedy' Previously published in *Sctn*, 5 Oct. 1968. Also appeared in *Scottish Poetry Four* (Edinburgh, 1969). Six three-line stanzas. First line: 'All is just. The mouth you feed turns on you'

266 'For Ann in America in the Autumn' Previously published in *Akros*, 2, no. 4 (Jan. 1967), [n.p.]. Three six-line stanzas. First line: 'When the wind dies in New Jersey'

267 'For John MacLean, Headmaster, and Classical and Gaelic Scholar' Sequence of seven poems, each of three rhymed six-line stanzas; except the first, which has a five-line second stanza. First lines: (1) 'The coloured roses fade along the wall.' (2) 'For you it was the case that Homer lived' (3) 'I know that it is waning, that clear light' (4) 'You were a teacher also: what we've learned' (5) 'The October leaves are falling. None condemns' (6) 'Though it is finished now, that scholarship,' (7) 'So with your battered helmet let you be'

268 'For Keats' Thirty-three lines in eight stanzas of three to five lines. First line: 'Genius is so strange,'

269 'Gaelic Songs' Previously published in *Sctn*, 20 June 1970. Broadcast on 'MacGregor's Gathering', Radio Scotland (16 Apr. 1984 and repeated 27 Aug. 1986). Two stanzas, of five and twenty lines. First line: 'I listen to these songs'

270 'Give me your Hand' A revised Gaelic text with a translation appears in *Nua-bhàrdachd Ghàidhlig*; a Welsh text translated from the Gaelic appears in *Cerddi Gaeleg Cyfoes*. See Section E. Six five-line stanzas. First line: 'Give me your hand.'

271 'Going Home' Prose translation from Gaelic. This translation first appeared in *Bìobuill is Sanasan-reice*.

272 'Good and Evil' Previously published in *Sctn*, 5 June 1971. Fifteen lines. First line: '"Good" is not like "yellow" or like "green".'

273 'Hotel Dining Room' Previously published in *Sctn*, 15 May 1971. Fourteen lines. First line: 'Our mouths work in the hotel dining room,'

274 'How Often I Feel Like You' Previously published in *Sctn*, 26 Sept. 1970. Original title, 'Russian Poem'. Twenty-three lines. First line: 'Ah, you Russians, how often I feel like you'

275 'In the Chinese Restaurant' Two stanzas, of twelve and six lines. First line: 'Because we'd never go there, it was good, '

276 'In the Country' Previously published in *Sctn*, 18 May 1968. Seven four-line stanzas. First line: 'Everyone is so nice.'

277 'In the Time of the Useless Pity' Previously published in *Sctn*, 5 Oct. 1968. Included in *Scottish Poetry Four* (Edinburgh, 1969), and *Contemporary Scottish Verse* (London, 1970). Thirteen lines. First line: 'In the time of the useless pity I turned away'

278 'Lear and Carroll' Four lines. First line: 'Those child-loving nonsense-writing Victorian uncles,'

279 'Lying Ill' Previously published in *English*, 16 (1966/67), 240-41. Twenty-five lines in nine stanzas of one to five lines. First line: 'Lying here for three days I might ask,'

280 'Napoleon' Previously published in *Scot. Int.*, Sept. 1971, p. 25. Twenty-four lines. First line: 'So you came back and then stretched wide your arms'

281 'Not to Islands' Previously published in *Sctn*, 18 May 1968. Originally printed as two six-line stanzas. Twelve lines. First line: 'Not to islands ever returning now'

282 'Oedipus and Others' Seventeen lines. First line: 'The god Apollo scratched out both his eyes.'

283 'On a Beautiful Day' Prose translation from Gaelic: six lines. This translation first appeared in *Biobuill is Sanasan-reice*.

284 'On a Summer's Day' Previously published in *Sctn*, 30 Aug. 1969. Six three-line stanzas. First line: 'Thus it is.'

285 'Our Mess Tins ...' Six six-line stanzas. First line: 'Our mess tins soggy with stew'

286 'Over and Over' Previously published in *Akros*, 6, no. 16 (Apr. 1971), 59. Five unrhymed pairs. First line: 'They came for him at night in the light of Homer.'

287 'Party' Thirteen lines, in stanzas of five, two and six. First line: 'Cigarette ends mounting slowly in the ashtray,'

288 'Return' Previously published in *Sctn*, 30 Aug. 1969. Four five-line stanzas. First line: 'I lived in that room fifteen years ago'

289 'Russian Poem' Sequence of ten poems. The first has thirty lines; the second fifteen in three stanzas. The third has ten lines in pairs and single lines, the fourth six lines in three-line stanzas. The fifth has seven lines in two stanzas; the sixth four three-line stanzas, and the seventh eighteen lines in a repeated pattern of three, two, and four-line stanzas. The eighth has thirteen lines, the ninth nine in two and three-line stanzas, and the last eighteen lines in stanzas of one to five lines. First lines: (I) 'I am too old for you. ' (II) 'Ennui covers the land.' (III) 'Hear us, philosophy will not save us.' (IV) 'Gogol, how your troika sparkled down our leaf-fringed lanes.' (V) 'In the siding the red light veins his beard.' (VI) '"We shall soon go to Moscow," say the sisters' (VII) 'Sometimes I think of the Cossacks wolfing their hunks of flesh' (VIII) 'The idiot stands on the pavement' (IX) 'I hear that he came in a sealed train.' (X) 'Sonia, my fine ghost,'

290 'Shane' Previously published in *Sctn*, 6 Dec. 1969. Ten lines. First line: 'He comes out of some place where he has invented justice.'

291 'The Fool' Prose translation from Gaelic; six lines. This translation first appeared in *Biobuill is Sanasan-reice*. It also appeared in *The Permanent Island*, and *Literary Rev.*, 18, no. 3 (Spring 1975), 336. First line: 'In the dress of the fool, the two colours'

292 'The Letter' Previously published in *Ariel*, 2, no. 3 (July 1971), 61. Twenty-seven lines, in stanzas of two to four lines. First line: 'Here is my letter out of the mirror'

293 'The Moon' Previously published in *Sctn*, 15 May 1971. Twelve lines. First line: 'The bronze curtains hang at the window.'

294 'The Return' Thirty-five lines in five rhymed stanzas of one to sixteen lines. First line: 'Continuous music in the restaurant'

295 'The Small Snags' Previously published in *Sctn*, 1 Feb. 1969. Two stanzas, of nine and six lines. First line: 'The small snags tug at us. The flag will not unfold'

296 'The Stones of Callanish' A prose translation from Gaelic, which first appeared in *Bìobuill is Sanasan-reice*. The poem also appears in translation in *The Permanent Island*, and was published in the *Literary Rev.*, 18, no. 3 (Spring 1975), 335. First line: 'At the stones of Callanish yesterday'

297 'The Tape Runs' Previously published in *Spirit*, 38, no. 2 (Smr 1971), 35-37. Twenty-five lines, in four-line stanzas, except second which is five. First line: 'The tape runs'

298 'This Goodbye' Previously published in *Akros*, 6, no. 16 (Apr. 1971), 59. Four three-line stanzas. First line: 'This goodbye'

299 'This is the Time of the Body ...' Four five-line stanzas. First line: 'This is the time of the body not the mind'

300 'You are at the Bottom of my Mind' Previously published in *Bìobuill is Sanasan-reice*. Prose translation of Gaelic poem; fourteen lines. First line: 'Without my knowing it, you are at the bottom of my mind,'

301 'All our Ancestors' Previously published in *Stand*, 12, no. 2 (1971), 6. Original is untitled. Eleven lines in rhymed two and three-line stanzas. First line: 'All our ancestors have gone abroad.'

Love Poems and Elegies

Part One

302 'Argument' Previously published in *Stand*, 12, no. 3 (1971), 43-4. Originally untitled. Thirteen rhymed seven-line stanzas. First line: 'He said: 'We argue and we come to this, ''

303 'Contrasts' Previously published in *Stand*, 12, no. 3 (1971), 41. Originally untitled. Five triplets. First line: 'Against your black I set the dainty deer'

304 'Death and the Politicians' Previously published in *Stand*, 12, no. 3 (1971), 40. Originally untitled. Four three-line stanzas. First line: 'The politicians gesture in this bland'

305 'In Your Long Skirts' Previously published in *Stand*, 12, no. 2 (1971), 5. Originally untitled. Three three-line stanzas. First line: 'In your long skirts among the other girls'

306 'Moonlight over the Island' Previously published in *Stand*, 12, no. 3 (1971), 42. Originally untitled. Four three-line stanzas. First line: 'Moonlight over the island, our people gathered'

307 'My Sailor Father' Previously published in *Stand*, 12, no. 2 (1971), 5. Originally untitled. Two quatrains. First line: 'My sailor father died in hospital'

308 'Of the Uncomplicated Dairy Girl' Previously published in *Sctn*, 9 Jan. 1971. Four seven-line stanzas. First line: 'Of the uncomplicated dairy girl'

309 'On Looking at the Dead' Previously published in *Sctn*, 9 Jan. 1971. Thirty-nine lines, in unrhymed pairs and single lines. First line: 'This is a coming to reality.'

310 'That Island formed You' Previously published in *Stand*, 12, no. 2 (1971), 5. Originally untitled. Slightly revised. Thirteen rhymed lines. First line: 'That island formed you, its black hatted men'

311 'The Black Jar' Previously published in *Stand*, 12, no. 3 (1971), 42. Originally untitled. Eight lines in pairs. First line: 'Exemplar of the exotic with that jar'

312 'The Burial' Previously published in *Sctn*, 9 Jan. 1971. Four half-rhymed quatrains. First line: 'The coffin is let down into the grave,'

313 'The Chair in which you've Sat' Previously published in *Stand*, 12, no. 3 (1971), 40. Originally untitled. Five half-rhymed six-line stanzas. First line: 'The chair in which you've sat's not just a chair'

314 'The Earth eats Everything' Translated for Israel's evening paper, *Yedioth Ahronoth*, 2 Nov. 1984 by Yair Hurvitz. This translation also appeared in *Moznaim*, Oct.-November 1984, p. 29. Nine lines. First line: 'The earth eats everything there is.'

315   'The Lilies and the Daffodils' Two three-line stanzas. First line: 'The lilies and the daffodils shade your face.'

316   'The Space-ship' Previously published in *Stand*, 12, no. 2 (1971), 6. Originally untitled. Four three-line stanzas. First line: 'I think of you and then I think of this'

317   'This Clutch of Grapes' Previously published in *Stand*, 12, no. 3 (1971), 41. Originally untitled. Four three-line stanzas. First line: 'This clutch of grapes is a clutch of black stars.'

318   'Those Who are Needed' Previously published in *Stand*, 12, no. 2 (1971), 6. Originally untitled. Fourteen rhymed lines. First line: 'Those who are needed do not easily die'

319   'Tinily a Star goes Down' Six lines in pairs. First line: 'Tinily a star goes down'

320   'You Lived in Glasgow' Previously published in *Stand*, 12, no. 2 (1971), 4. Originally untitled. Two eleven and three ten-line stanzas. First line: 'You lived in Glasgow many years ago.'

321   'You Told Me Once' Previously published in *Stand*, 12, no. 2 (1971), 5. Originally untitled. Two rhymed six-line stanzas. First line: 'You told me once how your younger brother died.'

322   'Your Brother Clanked his Sword' Previously published in *Stand*, 12, no. 2 (1971), 6. Originally untitled. Four three-line stanzas. First line: 'Your brother clanked his sword for the Boer War.'

Part Two

323   'At the Scott Exhibition, Edinburgh Festival' Two lyrics, of twelve and eleven lines. First line: 'He will out last us, churning out his books,' 'It was all in his life, not in his books'

324   'Do not Put on that Wig' Eight lines in couplets. First line: 'Do not put on that wig. Be what you are.'

325   'Guilts' Ten lines. First line: 'Your father played a piano made of bone.'

326   'I Think We are both Sick' Two stanzas of three lines. First line: 'I think we are both sick.'

327 'I Thought I Saw You' Two rhymed six-line stanzas. First line: 'I thought I saw you on the street just now'

328 'In the Cinema' Two three-line stanzas. First line: 'You rest your head on my shoulder. Wellington says:'

329 'In the Hotel' Later published in *Antaeus*, 12 (Wtr 1973), 115. Two stanzas of two lines. First line: 'In the hotel a wash basin and a mirror.'

330 'Inside the Poem' Twelve lines in four stanzas of two, three and four lines. First line: 'All night I have been writing.'

331 'Love, if You are Love' Eight lines. First line: 'Love, if you are love why do you fail?'

332 'Night' Six four-line stanzas. First line: 'Night and we are drinking yet again,'

333 'No one at Home' Twenty-two lines. First line: 'There is never anyone at home when I call.'

334 'On the Train' Previously published in *Sctn*, 6 May 1972. Eight lines. First line: 'Nothing is cool and green any more. '

335 'Resurrection' Two quatrains. First line: 'You rise from the dead ghosts of last night's party'

336 'Sleepless' Four lines in pairs. First line: 'Sleepless in one room thinking of another room,'

337 'The Bouquet' Two stanzas of two lines. First line: 'You brought me a bouquet, salt with brine.'

338 'The Dream' Twelve lines. First line: 'I tremble like a needle on a compass.'

339 'The Fever' Two three-line stanzas. First line: 'Our heads burn together but our hands are cold.'

340 'The Place without Music' Previously published in *Sctn*, 6 May 1972. Nine lines. First line: 'Look steadily at the place without music'

341 'The Trees and You' Six lines in pairs. First line: 'If it were that the trees would ripen with fruit'

342 'The World's a Minefield' Two quatrains. First line: 'The world's a minefield when I think of you.'

343 'What Tragedy is' Two three-line stanzas. First line: 'What tragedy is is to hope for the one thing forever.'

344 'Where Are You Tonight?' Translated in Israel's evening paper, *Yedioth Ahronoth*, 2 Nov. 1984 by Yair Hurvitz. Twenty lines. First line: 'Where are you tonight as the rain falls?'

345 'Youth and Age' Five lines in stanzas of two and three. First line: 'In youth engagements are not perilous'

Rabhdan is Rudan (1973)

346 'A' Bhùth' Two four-line stanzas. First line: 'Tha buth bheag sa' bhail' againn'

347 'A' Chuthag' Two four-line stanzas. First line: 'Tha chuthag a' seinn'

348 'A' Ghaoth' Three four-line stanzas. First line: 'Cia as a thàinig a' ghaoth?'

349 'A' Phoit' Two four-line stanzas. First line: 'Tha poit air an làr,'

350 'Air an Trìne' Ten lines. First line: 'Tha mi fhìn is Sìne'

351 'Am Bìobuill' Two four-line stanzas. First line: 'Tha Bìobuill aig mo sheanmhair'

352 'Am Post' Four two-line stanzas. First line: 'Thig am post an diugh 's an ath-latha'

353 'An Ceàrd' Four four-line stanzas. First line: 'Thàinig an ceàrd chun an doruis'

354 'An Coileach' Two four-line stanzas. First line: 'Than an coileach anns a' mhadainn'

355 'An Cuala tu an Tàirneanaich?' Two four-line stanzas. First line: 'An cuala tu an tàirneanaich'

356 'An Deigh' Eight lines. First line: 'Tha an deigh air an lòn'

357 'An Deireadh' Two four-line stanzas. First line: 'Theid an toiseach chun an deireadh'

358 'An Luch' Three four-line stanzas. First line: "Se luch bheag a th'annam-sa'

359 'An Sgarbh' Two four-line stanzas. First line: 'Ha ha ha'

360 'Anns an Sgàthan' Two four-line stanzas. First line: 'A' sealltainn anns an sgàthan'

361 'Anns an Teine' Two four-line stanzas. First line: 'Chi mi anns an teine'

362 'Anns an Tigh-Dhealbh' Eight lines. First line: 'Chunna mise san tigh-dhealbh'

363 'Bodach Sneachd' Two four-line stanzas. First line: 'Rinn sinn bodach sneachda'

364 'Bu Chaomh Leam' Two four-line stanzas. First line: 'Bu chaomh leam bhith air drifter'

365 'Ceise-Ball' Four lines. First line: 'Ceise-ball, ceise-ball,'

366 'Dà Bhròig' Two four-line stanzas. First line: 'Dà bhròig air an làr'

367 'Geansaidh Donn' Eight lines. First line: 'Geansaidh donn,'

368 'M'Àthair' Two four-line stanzas. First line: "Se iasgair tha 'nam àthair'

369 'Mo Bhàta Beag' Four lines. First line: 'Tha mo bhàta beag a' seòladh'

370 'Mo Sheanair' Eight lines. First line: 'Tha feusag fhada'

371 'Mo Sheanhmair' Four lines. First line: 'Bidh mo sheanmhair a' toirt dhomh'

372 'Nuair a dh'Eirigh mi sa' Mhadainn' Two four-line stanzas. First line: 'Nuair a dh'eirigh mi sa' mhadainn'

373 'Nuair a dh'Fhàsas Mise Mor' Two four-line stanzas. First line: 'Nuair a dh'fhàsas mise mor'

374 'Rabhd' Two four-line stanzas. First line: 'Uaine airson talàmh,'

375 'Rabhd' Six lines. First line: 'Rabaid agus geàrr,'

376 'Rionnagan' Two four-line stanzas. First line: 'Tha muillion rionnag anns an adhar'

377 'Saighdear' Two four-line stanzas. First line: 'Bu chaomh leam bhith 'nam shaighdear'

378 'Soluis' Eight lines. First line: 'Chì thu air na sràidean'

379 'Solus Uaine, Solus Dearg' Two four line stanzas. First line: 'Solus uaine, solus dearg,'

380 'Stocainnean Daoimein' Two four-line stanzas. First line: 'Stocainnean daoimein'

381 'T.V.' Two four-line stanzas. First line: 'An caomh leat SOFTLY SOFTLY'

382 'Taibhs'' Two four-line stanzas. First line: 'Tha taibhs' aig ceann a' ghàrraidh'

383 'Tha mo Mhàthair 's i 'na h-Aparan' Two four-line stanzas. First line: 'Tha mo mhàthair 's i 'na h-aparan'

384 'Tigh' Two four-line stanzas. First line: 'Thog mi tigh de phlastasan'

385 'Tinn' Two four-line stanzas. First line: 'Aon latha bha mi tinn'

386 'A' Ghaoth' Twelve lines. First line: 'Tha a' ghaoth a' seideadh anns an t-simileir.'

387 'A' Ghealach' Translated as 'The Moon' in *The Permanent Island*. Sequence of thirteen three-line poems. First lines: (1) 'A' ghealach' (2) 'Air lòn' (3) 'Air aodann' (4) 'Air faochagan' (5) 'Air a' chuan' (6) 'Air an rathad' (7) 'Air an leabaidh' (8) 'Air canastairean' (9) 'Air a' ghùn' (10) 'Air na sgàthain,' (11) 'Air an tigh' (12) 'Air an tigh' (13) 'Air balach'

388 'Abidil' 'Alphabet poem' in eighteen three-line and one five-line stanzas. First line: 'airson abhall,'

389 'Aig an Dorus' Nine lines in stanzas of six and three. First line: 'Ai ai'

390 'Am na Nollaig' Translated as 'Christmastime' in *The Permanent Island*. Sequence of fifteen three-line poems. First lines: (1) 'Am na Nollaig.' (2) '"A bheil rùm anns an tigh-òsda?"' (3) 'Chan eil fhìos aig an aiseal' (4) 'Sgrìobh Hèrod òrdugh' (5) 'Bha sùilean an leinibh ' (6) 'Na ciobairean air a' bheinn,' (7) 'Chuire Moire an saoghal' (8) 'Dh'fhosgail an Diabhal' (9) 'Dannsairean, dannsairean,' (10) 'Anns an dealbh' (11) '"'S e an leanabh mo nàmhaid,"' (12) '"Nuair nach còrd sgialachd ri leanabh,"' (13) '"nuair a dh'fhàsas E suas,"' (14) '"Nuair a dh'fhàsas E suas,"' (15) 'Sheas na h-ainglean aig an dorus.'

391 'An TV' Translated as 'The TV' in *The Permanent Island* Sequence of fourteen three-line poems. First lines: (1) 'Tha a' ghrian ag eirigh gach latha' (2) 'Cha do chreid sinn gu robh Eirinn ann' (3) 'Tha e nas fhaisge air Humphrey Bogart' (4) 'Arsa Plato —' (5) ' Thàinig nighean a-steach do rùm' (6) 'Mu dheireadh chaill e an saoghal' (7) 'Cheannaich e "War and Peace",' (8) 'Nuair a chuir as an TV.' (9) 'Cha dàinig a lamhan air ais thuisge' (10) 'Ròs ann am bola air an TV,' (11) 'Fhuair e e fhein ann an

sgialachd ' (12) 'Bha e anns an sgialachd:' (13) "'S tu a ghràidh is fheàrr leam' (14) 'An seòmraichean glaiste le geatachan iarain'

392 'Anns a' Chuirt' Translated as 'In Court' in *The Permanent Island*. Four stanzas of seven lines. First line: 'Thubhairt an siorraidh'

393 'Bothan Beag' Translated as 'A Small Bothy' in *The Permanent Island*. Five lines. First line: '"Bothan beag"'

394 'Dealbh le Picasso' Nine lines. First line: 'Shìos ris a' chladach tha amadam le aodach daoimeanach'

395 'Eilean Fraoich' Translated as 'Island of Heather' in *The Permanent Island*. Four lines. First line: '"Eilean fraoich, eilean fraoich,"'

396 'Fad a Làithean' Translated as 'All his Days' in *The Permanent Island*. Two seven-line stanzas. First line: 'Fad a làithean'

397 'Feasgar Agus Ceò Ann' Translated as 'On a Misty Evening' One five-line and three six-line stanzas. First line: 'Feasgar agus ceò ann'

398 'Glaschu' Eighteen poems of three to sixteen lines. First lines: (1) 'An raoir ann an Glaschu' (2) 'Soluis gun sgur' (3) 'Anns an tigh-òsda' (4) 'Sràidean glasa,' (5) 'Nas bòidhche' (6) 'Thoir dhomh do làmh' (7) 'Gach taobh dhinn' (8) 'Sgian uaine' (9) 'Os cionn Ghlaschu' (10) 'Duine' (11) 'Coire' (12) 'YA BAS' (13) 'He mandu' (14) 'Leagh am ministear' (15) 'Thoir dhomh do làmh.' (16) 'Tha a' ghaoth' (17) 'Rangers' (18) 'Glaschu'

399 'Haiku' Translated in *Poetry Australia*, 63 (May 1977), 92-93. Eight three-line poems; the first six translated in *The Permanent Island*. First lines: (1) 'Tha sneachd air na beantann' (2) 'Piano san fhàsach' (3) 'Cuibhle a' cur char dhìth.' (4) 'Aingeal aig dorus.' (5) 'Cailleach a' nighe' (6) 'Nighean le naidhlons' (7) 'Ròs anns a' mhadainn' (8) 'Mo nàire mo nàire'

400 'Innsidh mi Dhut Mar a Thachair' Translated as 'I will Tell You what Happened' in *The Permanent Island*. Forty-two lines in five stanzas of six to thirteen lines. First line: 'Innsidh me dhut mar a thachair.'

401 'Latha na Bliadhn' Uir', 1973' Translated as 'New Year's Eve, 1973' in *The Permanent Island*. Five lines. First line: 'An diugh tha mi da fhichead bliadhna 's a coig'

402 'Madainn Earraich' Five lines. First line: 'Tha am bùrn a' ruith anns na pìoban'

403 'Mas e Ghàidhlig an Cànan' Sequence of six poems, eight to twenty-four lines in length. First lines: (1) 'Mas e Ghàidhlig an cànan' (2) 'Mas e Ghàidhlig an cànan' (3) 'Mas e Ghàidhlig an cànan' (4) 'Mas e Ghàidhlig an cànan' (5) 'Arsa Eubha ri Adhamh,' (6) 'Nuair a ràinig i buth'

404 'Na Làithean Fad' Ud' Translated as 'These Long Days' in *The Permanent Island*. Ten lines. First line: 'Na làithean fad' ud'

405 'Nuair a dh'Fhàgas Tu Mi' Translated as 'When You Leave Me' in *The Permanent Island*. Two four-line stanzas. First line: 'Nuair a dh'fhàgas tu mi'

406 'Orain ghoirid — "Coinnichidh Sinn"' Translated as 'We will Meet' in *The Permanent Island*. Two five-line stanzas. First line: '"Coinnichidh sinn uaireigin,"'

407 'Orain ghoirid — A' Cheist' Translated as 'The Question' in *The Permanent Island*. Five lines. First line: "S tu 'nad sheasamh ri craoibh, crùn 'na do làimh'

408 'Orain ghoirid — An Luchd-turais 's A' Ghàidhlig' Translated as 'The Visitors and Gaelic' in *The Permanent Island*. Six lines. First line: 'Tha an luchd-turais an còmhnaidh a-mach air bàtaichean'

409 'Orain ghoirid — Anns a' Mhuseum' Translated as 'In the Museum' in *The Permanent Island*. Four lines. First line: 'Sinn le cheile anns a' mhuseum'

410 'Orain ghoirid — Anns na Làithean Ciùin' Translated as 'In the Calm Days' in *The Permanent Island*. Four lines. First line: 'Anns na làithean ciùin'

411 'Orain ghoirid — Breugel' Eight lines. First line: "Se so an aon pheantair'

412 'Orain ghoirid — Còmhradh' Translated as 'Conversation' in *The Permanent Island*. Six lines. First line: '"Tha thu airson m'fhàgail, tha mi 'g aithneachadh.'

413 'Orain ghoirid — Cuimhne' Translated as 'Memory' in *The Permanent Island*. Five lines. First line: 'Ged nach till sinn dhachaidh tuilleadh'

414 'Orain ghoirid — Ma Thig thu Tuilleadh' Translated as 'If You Come Again' in *The Permanent Island*. Four lines. First line: 'Ma thig thu tuilleadh cuimhnich gun toir thu leat'

415 'Orain ghoirid — Na Seanfhacail' Translated as 'The Proverb' in *The Permanent Island*. Six lines. First line: 'Shèol na seanfhacail'

416 'Òrain ghoirid — Thig a-steach' Translated as 'Come In' in *The Permanent Island*. Nine lines. First line: 'Thig a-steach,'

417 'Òrain ghoirid — Thusa' Translated as 'You' in *The Permanent Island*. Five lines. First line: 'Nuair a dh'eireas a'ghrian dhubh'

418 'Planaidean is Thusa' Eighteen lines in three stanzas. First line: 'A rùin'

419 'Sgialachd' Eighteen three-line poems. First line: (1) 'Bhiodh i a' leughadh' (2) 'Aon latha choinnich i e.' (3) 'Thubhairt iad rithe:' (4) 'Cheannaich e na h-aibhnichean,' (5) 'Ach bha car aige' (6) 'Thubhairt iad rithe:' (7) 'Phòs i e.' (8) 'Thòisich i leughadh' (9) '"A, mo rùn," ars esan,' (10) 'Tha do shùilean mar dhearcagan' (11) 'Thug e dhi dealbhàn' (12) 'Thubhairt e rithe aon latha.' (13) '"O," ars ise' (14) 'Aon oidhche dh'fhàg i.' (15) '"Tha e 'g ràdh anns a' Bhioball'" (16) 'Dh'fhàg i am Bioball' (17) '"S phòs i a rithist' (18) '"Oir," ars ise,'

420 'Sgialachdan Gaidhlig' Translated as 'Gaelic Songs' in *The Permanent Island*. Sequence of eighteen three-line poems. First line: (1) 'Iasgair ann am bòtannan mora,' (2) 'Sgialachd' (3) 'Te' (4) 'Melòdeon.' (5) 'Croit.' (6) 'Te a Glaschu' (7) 'An cuan' (8) 'Fear a bha 'n Astràilia' (9) '"Romance"' (10) 'Glaschu' (11) 'Dà bhoireannach' (12) 'Uilebhiasd' (13) 'Comadaidh' (14) 'Comhràdh' (15) 'Comhràdh' (16) 'Comhràdh' (17) 'Comhràdh' (18) 'Gealach'

421 'Tha na Làithean a' Dol Seachad' Translated as 'The Days are Passing' in *The Permanent Island*. Thirteen lines in stanzas of eight and five. First line: 'Tha na làithean a' dol seachad,'

422 'Thàinig Sinn a-Mach' Eighteen lines. First line: 'Thàinig sinn a-mach gu sràidean Ghlaschu'

Orpheus and Other Poems (1974)

423 'Autumn' Eight lines. First line: 'Accept now what you are. The leaves are brown,'

424 'Breughel' Previously published in *Stand*, 14, no. 3 (1973), 50. Reprinted in *The Exiles*. Seven half-rhymed pairs. First line: 'A bony horse with a bird on it droops its head.'

425 'Chess' Previously published in *Tablet*, 227 (1973), 777. Ten lines. First line: 'Night after night we play chess in the old house,'

426 'In the Bar' Previously published in *Tablet*, 227 (1973), 850. *Tablet* has 'leases' in the first line, but 'eases' is correct. Eight lines. First line: 'Ice-cold, perched on a stool, she eases her thighs out.'

427 'In the Dark' Previously published in *Stand*, 14, no. 3 (1973), 51. Original title was 'Crossing a Field in the Dark' Four half-rhymed quatrains. First line: 'Feeling across a field in the dark'

428 'Island Poems' Previously published in *Akros*, 8, no. 24 (Apr. 1974), 14-15. Five poems. The first, 'Kilnave Churchyard, Islay', is of nineteen lines. The second, 'On the Beach, Islay', is of eight unrhymed three-line stanzas. The third, 'An Islander Speaks', is of two four-line stanzas. The fourth is untitled, and has four three-line stanzas. The last, also untitled, is of ten lines. First line: (1) 'In this calm place the graves are very old,' (2) 'This shore is strewn with bones, bottles of Parozone' (3) 'I was born in this village seventy years ago.' (4) 'Let us lie here and sleep' (5) 'You say, "I am leaving the island."'

429 'Lecturer' Twenty-four lines. First line: 'Listen to him speaking. It is Sunday.'

430 'Love Poem' Six six-line stanzas. First line: 'The ways will never part'

431 'My Old Typewriter' Eight five-line stanzas. First line: 'Goodbye, black-toothed one,'

432 'Orpheus' The first four sonnets were published in *Sctn*, 13 Jan. 1973. Sequence of seven poems. The first four are sonnets; the other three could be considered as being made up of three 'sonnets' each, comprising alternating eight and six line stanzas, or pairs of seven line stanzas. First line: (1) 'And he said, I am come in search of her' (2) 'And he said, that is great condemnation,' (3) 'And he to the god, If you should let her go' (4) 'And the god to him, Now I must tell you clear' (5) 'And he to the god, Tell me about the shades.' (6) 'And he to the god, I have descended from' (7) 'And Orpheus walked among the broken slums'

433 'Painting' Ten lines. First line: 'Clear cold Vermeer'

434 'Poem' Eight lines. First line: 'With all due tenderness I gaze into your eyes'

435 'Poem for Auden' Thirty-seven lines in eight stanzas of three to six lines. First line: 'When you died'

436 'Saturday Afternoon' Thirteen lines. First line: 'The dog says Come in, and licks your face.'

437 'Skye' Eleven half-rhymed lines. First line: 'Stone and rain and mist on the mountains.'

438 'Something Somewhere' Previously published in *Sctn*, 17 Nov. 1973. Six stanzas of three lines and one of two. First line: 'Something somewhere is destroying us.'

439 'The Glass of Water' Previously published in *Sctn*, 17 Nov. 1973. Two seven-line stanzas. First line: 'My hand is blazing on the cold tumbler.'

440 'The Island' Previously published in *Aquarius*, 6 (Scottish issue: 1973), 24. Five lines. First line: '"And as for that island," so he said,'

441 'The Procession' Twelve lines. First line: 'Clad all in black, they bear the coffin over'

442 'The Scholar's Love Story' Fourteen lines. First line: 'She said, "There is someone else," and it was like'

443 'The Visitors' Thirty-two lines. First line: 'The bell rings.'

444 'The Voice' Fourteen lines. First line: 'I hear in this valley which is loud with streams'

445 'The Wind' Two four-line stanzas. First line: 'The wind is strong again. It has upset our ludo board.'

446 'To Vergil' Ten lines. First line: 'Why should you write about Rome? It wasn't your metier.'

447 'Tonight' Sixteen lines. First line: 'Tonight is wet and dull, Edgar Allan Poe weather.'

Poems for Donalda ([1974])

448 'Books and You' Two four-line stanzas. First line: 'As I leafed through some of my books'

449 'By the River, in the Woods' Three quatrains. First line: 'We walked in the woods, looking at the trees.'

450 'Helplessly' Previously published in *Stand*, 14, no. 3 (1973), 51. Originally entitled 'Poem'. Six lines. First line: 'Helplessly I wait for you.'

451 'In the Kitchen' Eleven rhymed lines. First line: 'You wash the dishes like someone I once knew.'

452 'Love, do not Leave Me' Five half-rhymed quatrains. First line: 'Love, do not leave me.'

453 'Meeting' Sonnet. First line: 'We meet again in April, after all that —'

454 'On Sunday' Eight rhymed lines. First line: 'Go to church on Sunday'

455 'On the Shore' Ten rhymed five-line stanzas. First line: 'We walked together on the shore'

456 'Sunday Walk' Seven five-line stanzas. First line: 'The horses crop beside the gorse,'

457 '"The Things I Do"' Fourteen lines. First line: '"The things I do," you said, "injecting sheep,"'

458 'The Blue Carpet' Two three-line stanzas. First line: 'When I came home one day'

459 'The Lie' Later published in *Orpheus*. Three half-rhymed quatrains. First line: 'The lie that nearly killed them was a slight'

460 'The Painting' Four four-line stanzas. First line: 'She's in the act of pouring'

461 'The Present' Three quatrains. First line: 'I brought you a green belt'

462 'The Shadows' Five rhymed five-line stanzas. First line: '"I think," she said, "we shall not see again"'

463 'The Wolves' Two five-line stanzas. First line: 'The wolves follow the sledge'

464 'Tonight' Re-published in *The Notebooks of Robinson Crusoe*. Eight rhymed six-line stanzas. First line: 'Tonight you are a hundred miles away'

465 'Who You Are' Sonnet First line: 'I'm trying to remember who you are.'

The Notebooks of Robinson Crusoe (1975)

466 'Autumn Song' Two four-line stanzas. First line: '"I'll be seeing you"'

467 'Ceilidh' Re-published in *Radical Scotland*, 22 (Aug/Sept 1986), 38 with notes by Frederic Lindsay. Six rhymed six-line stanzas. First line: 'Some ragged tartans hang above the stage.'

468 'Chinese Poem' Five poems, of thirteen, sixteen, sixteen, eleven and eleven lines. First line: (1) 'To Seamus MacDonald, now resident in Edinburgh —'

(2) 'The dog brought your letter today' (3) 'There is a man here who has been building a house' (4) 'Today I read five books.' (5) 'A woman arrived today'

469   'Faustus Speaks' Twenty-one lines. First line: 'You on your light tiptoe at the ballet,'

470   'He and She' Twenty-four lines. First line: '"I shall not visit them again," he said,'

471   'Help Me' Two stanzas of six and five lines. First line: 'Help me, mother, they are kicking me.'

472   'Him' Previously published in *Antaeus Review*, 12 (Wtr 1973), 116. Original title 'Ambitious Man'. Fifteen lines. First line: 'Talking till 2 a.m. "What makes him tick?"'

473   'Housman' Previously published in *Antaeus Review*, 12 (Wtr 1973), 118. Twelve lines. First line: 'Queen of the air and darkness, I know you.'

474   'In the Glen' Twenty-nine lines. First line: 'The stags come down from the hills and he comes over.'

475   'In the Gods in a Glasgow Theatre' Eight rhymed six-line stanzas. First line: 'We climb the stairway to the very top'

476   'Incident' Forty-two lines. First line: 'She watched him with her children and she thought'

477   'Insecurity' Five quatrains. First line: 'He feared that he might leave her and she feared'

478   'Jealousy' Previously published in *Tablet*, 227 (1973), 922. Eleven lines. First line: 'Firstly I dreamed of a cat that ate a snake'

479   'Journey' Twenty-two lines. First line: 'At nighttime we drive home under the trees.'

480   'Letter' Fourteen lines. First line: 'You say, "I am alone. Are you alone?"'

481   'Letter' Two eight-line stanzas. First line: 'You write from London to me. "I hate Art."'

482   'My Uncle' Ten rhymed five-line stanzas. First line: 'In '18 the M.O. said:'

483   'Old Woman' Two rhymed eleven-line stanzas. First line: '"The Old Age Pensioners," she said,'

484 'On the Fact that Karl Marx Wrote Love Poems when he was Young' Seven half-rhymed couplets. First line: 'Ah, Herr Marx, to write about roses'

485 'Party' Twenty-four lines. First line: 'I put my hand under your bum. You're drunk.'

486 'Sketch' Four half-rhymed pairs. First line: 'The squashed church leans out of the thumnderstorm.'

487 'The Cat' Eight lines. First line: 'The cat pads home with a mouse in its mouth.'

488 'The Event' Three stanzas of twenty, four and three lines. First line: 'It is true I didn't do anything about it because I was frightened'

489 'The Ex-Skipper' Sixteen half-rhymed lines. First line: 'Squat-bodied ex-skipper from the China Seas,'

490 'The Fall' Six rhymed eight-line stanzas. First line: 'The Art or life? Which is the way to go?'

491 'The Hero' Forty-four lines. First line: 'He stayed in the black tent, alone, withdrawn.'

492 'The Interview' Seven rhymed six-line stanzas. First line: 'The place had stairs and washrooms. Would they ask,'

493 'The Lesson' Stanzas of twenty-seven, four and four lines. First line: 'The cold wind of his mind passed over them.'

494 'The Lie' Included in *Poems for Donalda*.

495 'The Old Woman' Fifteen lines. First line: 'The old woman sat under an autumn tree.'

496 'The Prodigal Son' Five half-rhymed six-line stanzas. First line: '"All day," he said, "I've been trying to write a play"'

497 'The Sound of Music' Four rhymed nine-line stanzas. First line: 'After the Sound of Music we mooned out'

498 'The Three' Thirty lines. First line: '"He asked me to marry him," you wrote.'

499 'The Workmen' Previously published in *Scottish Poetry Seven* (Edinburgh, 1974). Five rhymed seven-line stanzas. First line: 'The workmen sing like birds in the scaffolding'

500 'Tonight' Previously published in *Poems for Donalda*.

501 'The Notebooks of Robinson Crusoe: 1 — Resources' A List of thirty-three items, in thirty-three lines. This sequence of poems (to 541) was first published in *Lines*, 47 (Dec. 1973), 12-28.

502 'The Notebooks of Robinson Crusoe: 2 — Extract from Log' Twelve-line prose poem. First line: 'Labour will sustain me, to permit my soul enter iron,'

503 'The Notebooks of Robinson Crusoe: 3 — Looking at ruined rigging remember' Seven-line prose poem. First line: 'Captain on bridge resplendent in yellow and blue, burdened'

504 'The Notebooks of Robinson Crusoe: 4 — Remember Margaret' Thirteen lines. First line: 'How once uncovering breasts'

505 'The Notebooks of Robinson Crusoe: 5' Eight-line prose poem. First line: 'With knife carved Margaret: arms raised, shaking out'

506 'The Notebooks of Robinson Crusoe: 6' Ten-line prose poem. First line: 'Today I wished to write a story. It would be of a man'

507 'The Notebooks of Robinson Crusoe: 7' Published in *Lines*, 47; but first published Glasgow Rev., 3, no. 1 (Smr 1972), 32. Four lines. First line: 'At my killed goat wild-cats nuzzle, seethe: legs working:'

508 'The Notebooks of Robinson Crusoe: 8' Six lines. First line: 'Evenings: the sea monotonous:'

509 'The Notebooks of Robinson Crusoe: 9' Twenty-three lines. First line: 'One place'

510 'The Notebooks of Robinson Crusoe: 10' Three rhymed six-line stanzas. First line: 'I'

511 'The Notebooks of Robinson Crusoe: 11' First published *Glasgow Rev.*, 3, no. 1 (Smr 1972), 31. Ten-line prose poem. First line: 'The wind blows in my chimney. How mournful it is! I can'

512 'The Notebooks of Robinson Crusoe: 12' Eleven-line prose poem. First line: 'Last night I drank much rum. I dreamed that you were in my'

513 'The Notebooks of Robinson Crusoe: 13' Nine lines. First line: 'Today I stupefied myself with rum. The world became rum-coloured.'

514 'The Notebooks of Robinson Crusoe: 14 — Landscape' First line: 'This landscape is my diary.'

515 'The Notebooks of Robinson Crusoe: 15' Six-line prose poem. First line: 'If I eat the green leaves for a long time, shall I turn green?'

516 'The Notebooks of Robinson Crusoe: 16' Eighteen-line prose poem. First line: 'Today I saw Dan-Dare, silver-winged,'

517 'The Notebooks of Robinson Crusoe: 17' Sixteen lines. First line: 'In my leafed chapel I pray to God.'

518 'The Notebooks of Robinson Crusoe: 18' Six rhymed seven-line stanzas. First line: 'The thunder-roared,'

519 'The Notebooks of Robinson Crusoe: 19' First published *Glasgow Rev.*, 3, no. 1 (Smr 1972), 30. Twelve-line prose poem. First line: 'Last night I saw in the moonlight'

520 'The Notebooks of Robinson Crusoe: 20' Sixteen-line prose poem. First line: 'I dreamed that a girl called Lavender'

521 'The Notebooks of Robinson Crusoe: 21' Nine lines. First line: 'March and the world is white again'

522 'The Notebooks of Robinson Crusoe: 22' Eight-line prose poem. First line: 'There is no other world but this:'

523 'The Notebooks of Robinson Crusoe: 23' Eight lines. First line: 'When the storm came I saw the headlights again.'

524 'The Notebooks of Robinson Crusoe: 24' First published *Glasgow Rev.*, 3, no. 1 (Smr 1972), 31. Five three-line stanzas. First line: 'I shall clamp my teeth.'

525 'The Notebooks of Robinson Crusoe: 25 — Memory' Twelve lines. First line: 'I put my hand in yours, adored phantom.'

526 'The Notebooks of Robinson Crusoe: 26' Nine-line prose poem. First line: 'Today there were washed ashore one powder puff,'

527 'The Notebooks of Robinson Crusoe: 27' Nineteen-line prose poem. First line: 'It is possible that I shall grow used to this'

528 'The Notebooks of Robinson Crusoe: 28 — Names' Three prose poems, of five, eight and six lines. First line: 'Noon: and the gluttonous ocean sparkles.'

529 'The Notebooks of Robinson Crusoe: 29' Seventeen-line prose poem. First line: 'When I was young I was allowed'

530 'The Notebooks of Robinson Crusoe: 30' Previously published in *Glasgow Rev.*, 3, no. 1 (Smr 1972), 32. Sixteen lines. First line: 'Island, what shall I say of you, your peat bogs, your lochs, your moors and berries?'

531 'The Notebooks of Robinson Crusoe: 31' Twenty-three-line prose poem. First line: 'I propped the mirror against a rock.'

532 'The Notebooks of Robinson Crusoe: 32' Twenty-four-line prose poem. First line: 'Today on a headland I devoured a bunch of old comics'

533 'The Notebooks of Robinson Crusoe: 33' Ten-line prose poem. First line: 'When they rescue me I shall return'

534 'The Notebooks of Robinson Crusoe: 34' Fourteen-line prose poem. First line: 'I have read them all, Sartre, Wittgenstein, Ryle.'

535 'The Notebooks of Robinson Crusoe: 35' Six lines. First line: 'The cannibals suck bones around the fire, their clubs laid aside, hair hiding their ridged limited foreheads.'

536 'The Notebooks of Robinson Crusoe: 36' Three four-line stanzas. First line: 'Friday'

537 'The Notebooks of Robinson Crusoe: 37' Sixteen-line prose poem. First line: 'An imperfect me, Friday walks amiably at my back,'

538 'The Notebooks of Robinson Crusoe: 38' Ten lines. First line: '"Wat is dis angels?" he says. "Wat is dis resurrection?"'

539 'The Notebooks of Robinson Crusoe: 39 — Friday's Fragments' Twenty-four lines. First line: 'Our fat'

540 'The Notebooks of Robinson Crusoe: 40' Sixteen-line prose poem. First line: 'I think perhaps this is where I wished to be,'

541 'The Notebooks of Robinson Crusoe: 41' Twelve-line prose poem. First line: 'It is not with sorrow that I stand on deck'

In the Middle (1977)

542 'After the Sandals of Summer' Eight lines. First line: 'After the sandals of summer'

543 'Back to School' Twelve lines. First line: 'Tomorrow they will go back to school'

544 'Clouds' Four lines. First line: 'Black clouds in the sky'

545 'Duty' Fourteen lines in four stanzas of two to five lines. First line: 'Duty tells you what to do.'

546 'Evening' Twelve lines. First line: 'The late sun shines on the chair.'

547 'Evening' Five half-rhymed quatrains. First line: 'Over the moor the late sun is shining,'

548 'Hail Mary' Five four-line stanzas. First line: 'Hail Mary, will you tell me something?'

549 'Home Coming' Two four-line stanzas. First line: 'Well, the evening has brought you home again'

550 'If Ever You Loved Me' Two four-line stanzas. First line: 'If ever you loved me'

551 'In Ireland' Previously published in *Sctn*, 15 Nov. 1975. Included in *Scottish Poetry Nine* (Manchester, 1976) One six- and two four-line stanzas. First line: 'In Ireland the horse and cart go over'

552 'In Other Places' One quatrain, two unrhymed pairs. First line: 'In other places all sorts of things are going on,'

553 'In Our Safe House' Ten lines. First line: 'In our safe house we hear a strange noise.'

554 'In Sleep' Eight lines. First line: 'Sometimes when I sleep I am among the dead.'

555 'In the Middle' Twenty-four lines in eleven one to three-line stanzas. First line: 'In the middle'

556 'In the Surgery' Four poems totalling thirty-five lines. First line: (1) 'What in this place are they waiting to be cured of?' (2) 'The receptionist has said: No dogs permitted.' (3) 'The doctor says: there's nothing wrong with you' (4) 'So I went away and stared into the water.'

557 'In Yellow' Previously published in *Sctn*, 15 Nov. 1975. Originally in three stanzas of three and four lines. Two stanzas, of four and seven lines. First line: 'The Chinamen sing Chinese songs'

558 'Morning' Previously published in *Sctn*, 15 Nov. 1975 Three four-line stanzas. First line: 'The white egg boils in the new saucepan'

559 'My Child' Eight three-line stanzas; a single line between the sixth and seventh. First line: 'My child, where are you?'

560 'None is the Same as Another' Twenty lines, in stanzas of two and four lines. First line: 'None is the same as another, '

561 'Painting the Walls' Five three-line stanzas. First line: 'All day we've been painting the walls of the room.'

562 'Prepare Ye the Way of the Lord' Four four-line stanzas. First line: 'Prepare ye the way of the Lord,'

563 'Pupil's Holiday Job' Nineteen lines. First line: 'The girl who was reading Milton'

564 'Rainy Day' Thirteen lines, in stanzas of two, four and five lines. First line: 'Rain all day.'

565 'Sometimes' Two four-line stanzas. First line: 'Sometimes the world appears unreal —'

566 'Tears are Salt' Six four-line stanzas. First line: 'Tears are salt like the sea.'

567 'The Chair' Three four-line stanzas. First line: 'The tall green-backed chair'

568 'The Cool Weather' Twelve lines. First line: 'After the tropical heat was over'

569 'The Cows from the Slaughter House' Four three-line stanzas. First line: 'Late at night the cows from the slaughterhouse moo.'

570 'The Critic and the Poem' Four four-line stanzas; first and last are two and five lines. First line: 'The critic goes looking for a carcass'

571 'The Cry' Thirteen, in two-line and one three-line stanzas. First line: 'Nothing is louder than this cry,'

572 'The Dog' Seventeen lines in six part-rhymed stanzas. First line: 'The dog that barked all day at passing cars'

573 'The Ducks' Two four-line stanzas. First line: 'The ducks waddle about so stupidly'

574 'The Elite' One stanza of four lines and two of six. First line: 'There's no use worrying about it'

575 'The Horror' Five four-line stanzas. First line: 'The horror, the horror.'

576 'The Lady of Shalott' Two three-line stanzas and two pairs, unrhymed. First line: 'She was killed by reality'

577 'The Nose' (after Gogol) Twenty-nine lines in six stanzas of four to eight lines. First line: 'The nose went away by itself'

578 'The Old School Books' Twenty-eight lines in seven stanzas of two to eight lines. First line: 'Do you remember'

579 'The Purple Bucket' Fifteen lines in stanzas of three, four and eight lines. First line: 'The purple bucket sits in the corner'

580 'The Queen' Ten lines. First line: 'Seated on the throne crying'

581 'The Scholar' Twelve three-line stanzas. First line: 'The scholar says: Why is the world changing?'

582 'The Scholars' Twelve lines in stanzas of two and three lines. First line: 'In the garden where the windows bulge I have seen the scholars walking,'

583 'The Scream' Previously published in *Sctn*, 27 Sept. 1975. One two-, one three-, and four four-line stanzas. First line: 'The scream rips through the forest'

584 'The Theatre' Two four-line stanzas. First line: 'The theatre that we found among the trees'

585 'The Torches' Two four-line stanzas. First line: 'The newspapers create news.'

586 'The Water-skiers' Three three-line stanzas. First line: 'In the evening'

587 'The Whirligigs of Time' Seven five-line stanzas. First line: 'The scholar sits by the fire reading.'

588 'The Winds' Ten lines. First line: 'The winds hold us together'

589 'This Bubble' Ten lines in stanzas of three and four. First line: 'In this stained bubble'

590 'Those Who Move Others' Previously published in *Sctn*, 27 Sept. 1975. Original title 'Who Move Others'. Nineteen lines, in five stanzas of two, three, four and six. First line: 'Those who move others'

591 'To Another Country' Fifteen lines in stanzas of five, four and eight lines. First line: 'When I went to another country for the first time'

592 'Waiting for a Letter' Two three- and one five-line stanzas. First line: 'Every morning she waits for a letter.'

593 'We Poets' Thirty lines, in seven stanzas of three to six lines. First line: 'We are everywhere, we poets,'

594 'When Day is Done' Previously published in *Scottish Poetry Nine* (Manchester, 1976). Eight lines. First line: 'Sorrow remembers us when day is done.'

595 'When the House is Quiet' Four four-line stanzas. First line: 'When the house is quiet'

596 'Women' Six four-line stanzas. First line: 'Bewildered and angry is the sap of women'

597 'You' One three-line and four four-line stanzas. First line: 'You began by listening to pop songs'

River, River (1978)

598 'At Christmas' One two-line and three four-line stanzas. First line: 'At Christmas bring me the gift I need,'

599 'Coward or Hero' Seven quatrains. First line: 'Coward! they shouted at him.'

600 'For Christabel' Two quatrains. First line: 'Your face is framed in the window'

601 'Halloween' Five pairs. First line: 'At night we walked the street'

602 'In Chagall's Paintings' Two three-line and four two-line stanzas. First line: 'In Chagall's paintings'

603 'In the Ark' Eight rhymed pairs. First line: 'The ark is sailing on'

604 'In the Garden' Twelve lines in five stanzas of one to three lines. First line: 'What are you doing, child,'

605 'In the Liquorice House' Four three-line stanzas. First line: 'In the liquorice house'

606 'Joseph' Five three-line stanzas. First line: 'Wearing his coloured coat'

607 'Leaving Home' Thirteen quatrains. First line: 'Tonight I'm leaving the island'

608 'Life' Six triplets and a couplet. First line: 'No matter what happens,'

609 'Night Falls' Five two-line and one three-line stanzas. First line: 'Night falls.'

610 'Reflection' Four pairs. First line: 'In the oval mirror'

611 'River, River' Fifteen lines in five stanzas of two to four lines. First line: 'River, river,'

612 'Sandcastles' Five pairs. First line: 'The tide is flowing in'

613 'Shadow' Four quatrains. First line: 'The boy walks with his shadow'

614 'Stormy Night' Four lines. First line: 'The thunder walks with his big boots about the heavens.'

615 'The Clown' Two four-line stanzas. First line: 'They throw water at the clown'

616 'The Dinosaur' Five three-line stanzas. First line: 'Often I think of the dinosaur'

617 'The End of the Western' Nineteen lines. First line: 'At the end of the Western'

618 'The Ghost' Nine pairs. First line: 'Who is this coming towards you'

619 'The Hosepipe' Two quatrains. First line: 'Like a green snake is the green hosepipe.'

620 'The Lion and the Alligator' Six quatrains. First line: 'The lion went down to the water'

621 'The Little Shop' Four three-line stanzas. First line: 'Do you remember the little shop in the village'

622 'The Old Sailing Ships' Three rhymed six-line stanzas. First line: 'The old sailing ships have gone and with them the pirates,'

623 'The Prodigal Son' Nine quatrains. First line: 'The Prodigal Son left the farm behind him.'

624 'The Queen' Four four-line stanzas. First line: 'The queen sits in the throne room'

625 'The Sea' Eight two line stanzas. First line: 'At night the sea speaks to itself'

626 'The Soldier' Four pairs. First line: 'The soldier came home from the war'

627 'The Tramp' Fourteen pairs. First line: 'The tramp goes from country to country'

628 'The Wildcat' Four four-line stanzas. First line: 'The wildcat sits on the rock.'

629 'The Wind' Thirteen rhymed pairs. First line: 'If I was the wind I'd peer in everywhere.'

630 'What's in the Paper?' Six quatrains. First line: 'What's in the paper this morning?'

Na h-Ainmhidhean (1979)

631 'A' Bhò' Fourteen lines. First line: 'Latha an dèidh latha tha a' bhò ag ithe feur.'

632 'A' Chearc' Fourteen lines. First line: 'Gog gog, their a' chearc'

633 'Am Brù-dhearg' Five lines. First line: 'Aig am sneachda bidh am brù-dhearg a' tighinn do d'dhoras'

634 'Am Muncaidh' Eleven lines. First line: 'Tha am muncaidh a' leum bho chraobh gu chraobh.'

635 'An Cat' Eleven lines. First line: 'Tha an cat 'na laighe ris an teine'

636 'An Clàmhan' Eight lines. First line: 'Bidh an clàmhan dubh a' falbh air feadh na mòintich.'

637 'An Coileach' Eighteen lines. First line: 'Anns a' mhadainn dhealtach'

638 'An Duine 's na Madaidhean-Allaidh' Fourteen lines. First line: 'Tha e fuar is reòite. Tha sneachd air an talàmh.'

639 'An Fhaoileag' Ten lines. First line: 'Tha an fhaoileag 'na seasamh ris a' chladach'

640 'An Iolaire' Thirteen lines. First line: 'Tha an iolair' a' tionndadh anns an adhar'

641 'An Laogh' Sixteen lines. First line: 'A h-uile madainn bhiodh sinn a' dol a thoirt biadh do'n laogh'

642 'An Leòmhan 's am Fiadh' Fourteen lines. First line: 'Tha an leòmhann buidhe a' tighinn a-mach as an fhasach.'

643 'An Leòmhan 's an Crocodile' Seventeen lines. First line: 'Thàinig an leòmhan sios chun na h-aibhne'

644 'An Luch 's an Cat' Seventeen lines. First line: 'Thig an luch a-mach as a toll is seallaidh i mun cuairt oirre.'

645 'An Rabaid 's an Sionnach' Twenty-three lines. First line: 'Tha an rabaid bheag dhonn a' cluich air an faiche.'

646 'An Siorc' Eight lines. First line: 'Tha an siorc gun iochd, gun thruas.'

647 'An t-Each' Twelve lines. First line: 'Tha an t-each 'na sheasamh anns an uisge,'

648 'An Tìgeir 's an Zebra' Fourteen lines. First line: 'Thàinig an tìgeir a-mach 'as a' choille'

649 'An t-Seilcheag' Nine lines. First line: 'Tha an t-seilcheag bheag dhubh'

650 'Na h-Ainmhidean' Thirty-seven lines. First line: 'Tha an saoghal làn de ainmhidhean,'

651 'Uiseag' Eight lines. First line: 'Uiseag, tha mi gad chluintinn a' seinn'

Selected Poems 1955-1980 (1981)

653 'Aberdeen' Previously published in *Lines*, 24 (Smr 1967), 7. Included in *Contemporary Scottish Verse* (1970). Also appeared in *Aberdeen* (Smr 1988), ed. Keith Murray (a tourist magazine). Four four-line stanzas. First line: 'Mica glittered from the white stone.'

654 'And This is Hell' Previously published in *Lines*, 28 (Mar. 1969), 15. Two stanzas of five and one of ten lines. First line: '"And this is hell,"'

655 'Chinese Poem' Previously published in *Sctn*, 3 Mar. 1979. Twenty-six lines in four stanzas of three to ten lines. First line: 'The darkness lightens. The yellow army sets out'

656 'Duncan Ban MacIntyre' Previously published in *Lines*, 28 (Mar. 1969), 13-14. Four rhymed eight-line stanzas. First line: 'This Gaelic bard fell in love with a small corrie.'

657 'For L.' Previously published in *Lines*, 29 (June 1969), 3. Later published in *Lit. Rev.*, 18, no. 3 (Spring 1975), 334. Three half-rhymed five-line stanzas. First line: 'Practical girl, worker of cloth and of silver,'

658 'Glasgow' Previously published in *Lines*, 29 (June 1969), 5. Six half-rhymed pairs. First line: 'City, cauldron of a shapeless fire,'

659 'Homage to George Orwell' Previously published in *Lines*, 29 (June 1969), 15-17. Sequence of five poems, of ten to twenty-four lines. First line: (1) 'You knew well in advance' (2) 'In my little house' (3) 'Lorca falls' (4) 'The pack surround him,' (5) 'Lorca goes marching underground'

660 'I Remember I Remember' Previously published in *Chmn*, 6, no. 1 (Aut. 1979), 23. Four unrhymed pairs. First line: 'I remember I remember the house where I was born,'

661 'In the Classics Room' Previously published in *Lines*, 29 (June 1969), 9. Eighteen lines in seven stanzas of two and three lines. First line: 'In summer how lovely the girls are'

662 'Light to Light' Originally a TV poem, the complete script of which is unpublished. Part of it was published in *Lines*, 26 (Smr 1968), 9-11, and this is the section re-printed in *Selected Poems*. The published extract is one hundred and eleven lines long.

663 'Mr M.' Previously published in *Lines*, 29 (June 1969), 8-9. Thirty lines in nine stanzas of two to four lines. First line: 'O how Mr M's Latin gown'

664 'My Brother' Previously published in *Chmn*, 6, no. 1 (Aut. 1979), 24. Also published in New Poetry, 48 (Spring 1980), 12, ed. Norman Hidden. Sixteen lines. First line: 'My brother, today the rain is falling,'

665 'Old Woman' Previously published in *Chmn*, 6, no. 1 (Aut. 1979), 25. Nine rhymed lines. First line: 'Your face is wrinkled'

666 'Old Woman' Previously published in *TLS*, 14 Jan. 1965, p. 26. Also appeared in Scottish Poetry One (Edinburgh, 1966) and *Three Regional Voices* (London, 1968). The *TLS* version has three stanzas of six, four and five lines. Sixteen lines in four stanzas of three to five lines. First line: 'Overwhelmed with kindnesses — and you have nothing.'

667 'On an Icy Day' Previously published in *Sctn*, 16 Feb. 1980. Eleven lines in four stanzas of two and three lines. First line: 'We walk on mirrors today just like Hamlet.'

668 'Poem' Previously published in *Contemporary Scottish Verse* . Ten lines in couplets. First line: 'Some move others but themselves are stone.'

669 'Remembering' Later published in *The Exiles* as 'Youth': Six lines. First line: 'When the wind blows the curtains wide, do you not remember'

670 'Return to Lewis' Previously published in *Lines*, 51 (Dec. 1974), 15-6. Sequence of seven poems, of sixteen to fifty-two lines, in couplets. First line: (1) 'The hills are stony as they've always been' (2) 'This old black pot is boiling with the soul.' (3) 'Time hangs heavy here. On certain days' (4) 'This is the place I grew in. Barefoot, I' (5) 'All night the wind blows round the house, and rain' (6) 'Down on the sand the visitors turn brown.' (7) '"I'll tell you something, lad" he sits and says.'

671 'Return to the Council House' Previously published in *Lines*, 29 (June 1969), 6. Six four-line stanzas. First line: 'Box on box, on ledge after ledge rising'

672 'Running Repairs' Previously published in *Stand*, 21, no. 3 (1979/80), 66. Sixteen rhymed lines. First line: 'A fight? she asks. A button from your blazer'

673 'School Sports, at the Turnstiles' Previously published in *Lines*, 29 (June 1969), 8. Three five-line stanzas. First line: 'This is impossible. Though I know'

674 'The Departing Island' Previously published in *Saltire Rev.*, 6, no. 22 (Aut. 1960), 51. Translated in *Moznaim*, Oct.-Nov. 1984, p. 29 by Yair Hurvitz (Israel). Included in *Three Regional Voices*. Three rhymed six-line stanzas. First line: 'Strange to see it — how as we lean over'

675 'The Good Place' Previously published in *Lines*, 16 (Wtr 1960), 36. Four quatrains. First line: 'You'd say it was a good place if you knew it,'

676 'The House We Lived In' Previously published in *Lines*, 29 (June 1969), 5. Eight four-line stanzas. First line: 'The house we lived in for five years'

677 'The Place' Previously published in *Lines*, 22 (Wtr 1966), 39. Four four-line stanzas. First line: 'To reach the place where there is no enigma'

678 'The Red Horse' Previously published in *Chmn*, 25 (6, no. 1: Aut. 1979), 23. Two four- and two five-line stanzas. First line: '"Art costs everything," I said.'

679 'Those Who Act' Previously published in *Contemporary Scottish Verse* (1970). Thirteen lines, part-rhymed, in stanzas of one to three. First line: 'Those who act,'

680 'Three Poems for Christmas' Previously published in *Lines*, 28 (Mar. 1969), 10-11. Sequence of three poems, the second four five-line stanzas, the others five four-line stanzas. First line: (I) 'The dark begins to close in.' (II) 'Now the radiator fumes in the lobby.' (III) 'In the terrible white of the light I hear ticking.'

681 'To Have Found One's Country' Previously published in *Contemporary Scottish Verse* (See Section E). Four rhymed eight-line stanzas. First line: 'To have found one's country'

682 'Transparencies' Previously published in *Lines*, 29 (June 1969), 20-32. *Selected Poems 1955-1980* reprints numbers 3, 7, 10, 11, 21, and 31-34. Sequence of thirty-nine poems, of four to twenty-nine lines. First line: (1) 'She eases down into the deck-chair:' (2) 'The five year old rolls the segmented ball.' (3) 'The old lady's head nods endlessly, without speech.' (4) 'The old lady reads the Record.' (5) 'A long road up the brae.' (6) 'Delirious with delight'

(7) 'Does the Renaissance' (8) 'None of us is' (9) 'Girls,' (10) 'Across the water,' (11) 'Roses in every garden —' (12) 'Victorian bench' (13) 'She builds' (14) 'Biro in mouth,' (15) 'Long legs, ' (16) 'The great roses sway in the breeze.' (17) 'The library's' (18) 'The fountain's' (19) 'She smiles' (20) 'Mouths.' (21) 'In the evening' (22) 'At night the cars burn past.' (23) 'Thwackety thwack goes the train' (24) 'Morning begins in gladness.' (25) 'This place is calm with' (26) 'German lady' (27) 'Smoke rises' (28) 'Ninety,' (29) 'Triangles of red bulbs, ' (30) 'One has to be fit' (31) 'I would love' (32) 'They come off the buses' (33) 'The clock ticks' (34) 'Ah, how the yachts' (35) 'On the blue —' (36) 'My name' (37) 'Beautiful' (38) 'I open the bathroom door.' (39) 'The Graham Greene'

683 'Why are You' Previously published in *Lines*, 29 (June 1969), 19. Three three-line stanzas. First line: 'Why are you always going to the library?'

Na h-Eilthirich (1983)

684 'A' Bheart-ola' Seventeen lines in five stanzas of two to five lines. First line: 'Tha thu a' coimhead a' bheart-ola anns a' bhàgh'

685 'A' Cheist' Prose poem in thirteen lines. First line: 'A bheil Carlos Williams cho dlùth dhomh'

686 'A' Cuimhneachadh' Previously published in *Gairm*, 1980/81, p. 159. Three stanzas of four, three and four lines. First line: 'Tha cuideigin a' cluich air melòdeon'

687 'A' Dìreadh 's a' Dìreadh' Two stanzas of seven and four lines. First line: 'A' dìreadh 's a' dìreadh'

688 'A' Dol Air Ais' Eighteen lines in six stanzas of two to four lines. First line: 'A' dol air ais a dh'Obair-dheadhain'

689 'Aig an Abhainn' Prose poem. Fourteen lines. First line: 'O abhainn'

690 'Aig an Taigh' Six three-line stanzas. First line: 'Nuair a thill mi dhachaigh'

691 'Air Latha Foghair' Thirteen lines in three stanzas of four and five lines. First line: 'Air latha foghair tha a' chlann a' dol air ais don sgoil'

692 'Air Madainn Samhraidh' Eight lines in stanzas of three, one and four. First line: 'Air madainn samhraidh'

693 'Air Oidhche Gheamhraidh' Nineteen lines in five stanzas of three and four lines. First line: 'Chuala mi fear a' dol seachad air an t-sràid.'

694 'Am Fear a Chaidh a dh'Astràilia' Previously published in *Gairm*, 1979/80, p. 279. Originally entitled, 'Am Fear a dh'fhàg a Dhùthaich'. Fourteen lines. First line: 'Cha thill thu tuilleadh a Astràilia'

695 'An Coinneachadh' Six three-line stanzas. First line: 'Chan eil cuimhn' am air d'ainm'

696 'An Fheadhainn Gun Thalant' Five four-line stanzas. First line: 'Ciamar as urrainn dhaibh bhith beò'

697 'An Oige' Three stanzas of four, and one of three lines. First line: '"Feasgar agus ceò ann"'

698 'An t-Altachadh' Twelve lines. First line: 'Tha thu nad shuidhe aig a' bhòrd'

699 'An Tilleadh' Sixteen lines. First line: 'Bliadhnachan air ais bha thu nurs' anns na Hearadh.'

700 'Ann an Astràilia' Previously published in *Gairm*, 1979/80, p. 279. Also published in *An Teachdaire Gaidhealach*, 10 (Dec. 1981), 2-3 (Sydney), with a translation. The middle lines of the first poem are revised; it originally had nine lines. Two poems of eight and nine lines. First line: (1) 'Anns a' mhadainn tha thu a' cluinntinn isean' (2) 'Mar gum biodh dràma a' dol a thòiseachadh'

701 'Ann an Glaschu' Ten lines in three stanzas of three and four lines. First line: 'Ann am baile Ghlaschu'

702 'Anns an Taigh Dhubh' Thirteen lines in four stanzas of three and four lines. First line: 'Tha mi ann an taigh dubh'

703 'Anns an Uinneig' Eleven lines. First line: 'Anns an uinneig'

704 'Cianalas Eile' Three four-line stanzas. First line: 'Nuair a thàinig an droch rud,'

705 'Clann Nighean an Sgadain' Two seven-line stanzas. First line: 'Clann nighean an sgadain'

706 'Coisichidh Sinn' Four pairs. First line: 'Coisichidh sinn eadar dà rann'

707 'Dealachadh' Eleven lines in three stanzas of three and four lines. First line: 'Nuair a dh'fhàg am bàt' an cidhe'

708 'Dearcagan' Previously published in *International Poetry Rev.*, 5, no. 1 (Celtic Issue: Spr., 1979), 54-55. Translated into modern Irish by Louis de Paor, *Innti*, 10 (Christmas 1986), 9. Twelve lines. First line: 'Chruinnich sinn dearcagan air feasgar foghair'

709 'Desperate Dan' Ten lines in stanzas of two and six lines. First line: 'Desperate Dan le d'aodann solt,'

710 'Each Dochasach' Previously published in *Gairm*, 1980/81, p. 160. Its original title was 'Nuair a thug iad'. One of the four-line stanzas was printed as two pairs. Two three- and two four-line stanzas. First line: 'Nuair a thug iad a WIZARD 's a HOTSPUR air falbh bhuam'

711 'Eachunn MacDhomhnaill' Previously published in *Gairm*, 1980/81, p. 159. Eighteen lines. First line: 'Bha a' Ghàidhlig air do bhilean'

712 'Esan' Fifteen lines. First line: 'Chan eil mi airson bàrdachd "mhor" a dhèanamh tuilleadh'

713 'Footballer' Five three-line stanzas. First line: 'Bha thu uair'

714 'Leodhas' Previously published in *Sctn*, 7 Oct. 1978. The poem's original title was 'Bho 'n Chuimneachan Cogaidh'. Two stanzas of twenty-one and two lines. First line: 'Bho 'n Chuimhneachan Cogaidh'

715 'Mo Thaipwriter' Nine lines. First line: 'Mo thaipwriter air a' bhòrd,'

716 'Na Balaich' Previously published in *Sctn*, 3 Mar. 1979. Nine lines. First line: 'Na balaich a bha còmhla rium anns na làithean a thrèig'

717 'Na h-Aborigines' Previously published in *Gairm*, 1979/80, p. 278. Twelve lines. First line: 'Tha iad a' cladhach airson ola'

718 'Na h-Eilthirich' Translated into modern Irish by Louis de Paor, *Innti*, 10 (Christmas 1986), 9. Two stanzas of six and eight lines. First line: 'A liuthad soitheach a dh'fhàg ar dùthaich'

719 'Nuair a Bha mi Fas Suas' Twelve lines. First line: 'Nuair a bha mi fàs suas'

720 'Nuair a Bhios mi Leughadh' Five four-line stanzas. First line: 'Nuair a bhios mi leughadh'

721 'Oran' Two stanzas of seven and two lines. First line: 'Thoir dhomh do làmh. Tha an cuan stoirmeil an-diugh.'

722 'Sinne 's a' Chailleach' Two three-line stanzas. First line: 'A' chailleach air am biodh sinn a' fanoid'

723 'Thusa' Thirteen lines in stanzas of three, one, three and six lines. First line: 'Tha thu cluiche reacordan le Elvis Presley'

724 'Thusa' Nine lines. First line: 'Tha d'aodann preasach'

725 'Tilleadh' Two five-line stanzas. First line: 'Aig deireadh an fhoghair'

726 'Togamaid' Eight lines. First line: 'Togamaid togamaid'

727 'Vancouver' Twenty-two lines. First line: 'Ann a Chinatown'

728 'We Twa Hae Paiddlt' Two four-line stanzas. First line: 'Co às a tha am bùrn seo a' tighinn'

The Exiles (1984)

729 'Always' Previously published in *PN Rev.,* 28 (9, no. 2: 1982), 56. Five three-line stanzas. First line: 'Always in the same way the poets die'

730 'At the Funeral of Robert Garioch' Previously published in *Lines,* 77 (June 1981), 5. The original has the same lines, but grouped instead in eight two and four-line stanzas. Seven four-line stanzas. First line: 'Something about the April day'

731 'Australia' Four sections of ten to twenty lines. First line: (1) 'In Australia the trees are deathly white,' (2) 'Naturally there are photographs of Ned Kelly' (3) 'No, you will not return from Australia' (4) 'All day the kookaburra is laughing'

732 'Autumn' Previously published in *Stand,* 21, no. 3 (1979-80), 66. Seventeen rhymed lines in three-line stanzas, closed by a pair. First line: 'Autumn again. A wide-eyed absence in'

733 'Breughel' Previously published in *Orpheus and Other Poems.*

734 'Cinderella' Four three-line stanzas. First line: 'Always in rough cloth she scrubs the floor.'

735 'Early Australian' Six lines. First line: 'If the cards should turn out right, let your butler'

736 'Envoi' Two stanzas of six and twenty-four lines. First line: 'There are'

737 'For Poets writing in English over in Ireland' Previously published in *Stand,* 19, no. 2 (1978), 24-25 under the title, 'On Meeting in Ireland some Young Poets who Write in English'. Nineteen three-line stanzas. First line: '"Feeling," they said,'

738 'Halloween' Previously published in *TLS,* 12 Feb. 1982, p. 165. Fourteen lines. First line: 'Someone was playing the piano when quite suddenly'

739 'Home' Previously published in *Sctn,* 25 Sept. 1982. Twenty lines. First line: 'Home from Zimbabwe you look tired and ill'

740 'In the Spring' Five pairs. First line: 'In the spring, air returns to us,'

741 'Iolaire' Previously published in *Stand*, 12, no. 2 (1971), 45-46. Considerably revised. Forty-six lines; only one more than in the original. First line: 'The green washed over them. I saw them when'

742 'Lost' Fifteen lines in seven stanzas of one to three lines. First line: 'Lost, we go from street to street'

743 'Next Time' Previously published in *PN Rev.*, 24 (8, no. 4: Aut. 1981), 44. Original has a stanza of eleven lines, and one line more in total. Twenty-seven lines in five stanzas of four to ten lines. First line: 'Listen, when you come home'

744 'No Return' Previously published in *Sctn*, 22 June 1974. Ten five-line stanzas. First line: 'No, really you can't go back to'

745 'Owl and Mouse' Previously published in *Chmn*, 4, no. 3 (1976), 29. In *Chapman* this poem was entitled 'Photograph', and was one of seven inspired mainly by paintings. Four pairs. First line: 'The owl wafts home with a mouse in its beak.'

746 'Poem' Five three-line stanzas. First line: 'It is always evening in a German poem,'

747 'Power Cut' Twenty-one lines in six stanzas of three and four lines. First line: 'Suddenly there was darkness'

748 'Prince Charles' Six three-line stanzas. First line: 'To the Highlands he came, boyishly running.'

749 'Reading Shakespeare' Previously published in *PN Rev.*, 28 (9, no. 2: 1982), 56. Four three-line stanzas. First line: 'On a dark day in winter I read Shakepeare'

750 'Returning Exile' Previously published in *Lsnr*, 77 (Jan-June 1967), 135. Also published in *Three Regional Voices* (London, 1968) Twenty-three lines; the original has one line more. First line: 'Home he came after Canada'

751 'Returning Exile' Previously published in *St. Gaz.* shortly before, although the exact issue has not been traced. Three three-line stanzas. First line: 'You who come home do not tell me'

752 'Snow Poems' Previously published in *Sctn*, 23 Jan. 1982. Originally entitled 'Three Winter Poems'. The order of the sequence is reversed, and the irregular stanzas re-arranged into three-line stanzas. Three poems in five to eight three-line stanzas. First line: (1) 'Not through snow the ancient

heroes walk,' (2) 'Much more than ghost or essence, much more palpable,' (3) 'A rat-shaped smoky cloud in the sky'

753 'Speech for a Woman' Previously published in *Sctn*, 3 Mar. 1979. Thirty lines in seven stanzas of two to nine lines. First line: 'One night'

754 'Speech for Prospero' Previously published in *TLS*, 7 Dec. 1979, p. 84. Also appeared in *Sctn*, 16 Feb. 1980. Originally entitled 'Prospero', and set out in five stanzas. Twenty-seven lines. First line: 'When I left that island I thought I was dead. Nothing'

755 'The "Ordinary" People' Previously published in *Enc.*, Sept. 1981, 21. Original title 'Ordinary People'. Six three-line stanzas and one single line. First line: 'The "ordinary" people sing on the edge of the grave.'

756 'The Church' Twenty-three lines in seven stanzas of three and four lines. First line: 'I imagine a gothic church'

757 'The Exiles' (translated from the author's own Gaelic). The Gaelic original with this translation is published in Donald MacAulay's bilingual anthology, *Nua-bhàrdachd Ghàidhlig/Modern Scottish Gaelic Poetry* (Edinburgh, 1976). The English text was re-published in *PN Rev.*, 56 (13, no. 6: 1987), 10; and *Artful Reporter*, May 1984, p. 16, which also has a report on Iain Crichton Smith's visit to Manchester with Norman MacCaig. Fourteen lines. First line: 'The many ships that left our country'

758 'The Legend' Seven three-line stanzas. First line: 'Today, receiving a letter from a friend'

759 'The Man without a Name' Fifty-seven lines in eleven stanzas of two to thirteen lines. First line: 'He exists somewhere, perhaps in America,'

760 'The New Houses' Previously published in *Sctn*, 25 Sept. 1982. Re-printed in *Sctn*, 1 October 1983. The first version has the same number of lines, but divided into five short stanzas. Its title is 'Canadian Exile'. Twenty-three lines. First line: 'Across the road they are building new flats,'

761 'The Schoolmaster' Seven pairs closed by a single line. First line: 'Sometimes I see the schoolmaster on the boat'

762 'The Survivors' Seven three-line stanzas. First line: 'How can they survive the days'

763 'There is no Sorrow' Twenty-four lines in four stanzas of four to eight lines. First line: 'There is no sorrow worse than this sorrow'

764 'When my Poetry Making has Failed' Previously published in *Words*, 7, p. 13. Originally called 'Not Writing'. Ten lines. First line: 'When my poetry making has failed'

765 'When they reached the New Land' Ten pairs. First line: 'When they reached the new land they rebuilt the old one,'

766 'Who Daily' Six lines. First line: 'Who daily at the rickety table'

767 '"You'll take a Bath"' Previously published in *Stand*, 23, no. 1 (1981/82), 23. Twenty-four lines in three rhymed stanzas of six and twelve lines. First line: '"And now you'll take a bath," she'd always say,'

768 'Youth' Two three-line stanzas. First line: 'When the wind blows the curtains wide, do you not remember'

A Life (1986)

769 'Aberdeen University 1945-49 (1)' Included in *Under Another Sky: The Commonwealth Poetry Prize Anthology*, edited by Alastair Niven (Manchester: Carcanet, 1987). Six half-rhymed quatrains. First line: 'The glitter of the water and the wake ...'

770 'Aberdeen University 1945-49 (2)' Four quatrains. First line: 'The prim historian talks of Robespierre.'

771 'Aberdeen University 1945-49 (3)' Five half-rhymed three-line stanzas. First line: '"Youse students with the cash," says Mrs Gray,'

772 'Aberdeen University 1945-49 (4)' Three three-line stanzas and one pair. First line: 'Beowulf dives into mysterious depths ...'

773 'Aberdeen University 1945-49 (5)' Five three-line stanzas. First line: 'Bicycles sparkle past the market place.'

774 'Aberdeen University 1945-49 (6)' Seven pairs and one three-line stanza. First line: 'Aberdeen, I constantly invoke'

775 'Aberdeen University 1945-49 (7)' Seventeen lines in two and three-line stanzas. First line: 'No library that I haven't loved.'

776 'Aberdeen University 1945-49 (8)' Fourteen lines in five two and three-line stanzas. First line: 'In winter, ice and frosty Aberdeen'

777 'Clydebank and Dumbarton 1952-55 (1)' Four half-rhymed triplets. First line: 'The adjective clause, the adverbial and the noun —'

778 'Clydebank and Dumbarton 1952-55 (2)' Two rhymed seven-line stanzas. First line: 'Alliteration, simile. He composed'

779 'Clydebank and Dumbarton 1952-55 (3)' Five pairs and one three-line stanza. First line: 'The flash of trains on rails, the Cenotaph,'

780 'Clydebank and Dumbarton 1952-55 (4)' Six half-rhymed triplets. First line: 'Seen here from green Argyll, the city is'

781 'Lewis 1928-45 (1)' Nineteen half-rhymed lines. First line: '"When did you come home? When are you leaving?"'

782 'Lewis 1928-45 (2)' Seventeen half-rhymed lines. First line: 'All day she sleeps but often in the night'

783 'Lewis 1928-45 (3)' Sixteen half-rhymed lines. First line: 'Our landmark is the island, complex thing.'

784 'Lewis 1928-45 (4)' Four rhymed five-line stanzas. First line: 'You will not find a Rubens, Rembrandt here,'

785 'Lewis 1928-45 (5)' Five rhymed three-line stanzas, and closing pair linked by rhyme. First line: 'Once famous footballer, he's alcoholic now.'

786 'Lewis 1928-45 (6)' Eight half-rhymed pairs. First line: 'O hi ro O hi ree,'

787 'Lewis 1928-45 (7)' Fourteen rhymed lines. First line: 'In school it was, each morning, and her bum'

788 'Lewis 1928-45 (8)' Six rhymed three-line stanzas. First line: 'Beside the library, I smelt the salt'

789 'Lewis 1928-45 (9)' Five rhymed three-line stanzas closed by a single line. First line: 'Remember how the War brought the News home,'

790 'Lewis 1928-45 (10)' Fourteen pairs. First line: 'Roses, I think there is salt on you,'

791 'Lewis 1928-45 (11)' Eight pairs. First line: 'They get off the buses at the ends of roads,'

792 'Lewis 1928-45 (12)' Eight pairs. First line: 'Stubs of pipes in teeth, the old men'

793 'National Service 1950-52 (1)' Sixteen lines. First line: 'The corporal struts briskly up and down,'

794 'National Service 1950-52 (2)' Sixteen lines. First line: '"Listen, you poof, I'm standing on your hair."'

795 'National Service 1950-52 (3)' Twenty lines. First line: 'Education sergeants, lowest of the low ...'

796 'National Service 1950-52 (4)' Fourteen lines. First line: 'Love O careless love. Irene, Good Night.'

797 'National Service 1950-52 (5)' Six half-rhymed triplets, closed by a single line. First line: 'We marched so beautifully, cleanly, then.'

798 'Oban 1955-82 (1)' Nine rhymed pairs. First line: 'Oban in autumn, and reflective Mull'

799 'Oban 1955-82 (2)' Eight rhymed three-line stanzas. First line: 'A Roman rector, measured gravitas,'

800 'Oban 1955-82 (3)' Five rhymed three-line stanzas. First line: 'To find the way!'

801 'Oban 1955-82 (4)' Six rhymed three-line stanzas. First line: 'That sunny Gaelic world! That Roman rule!'

802 'Oban 1955-82 (5)' Nine half-rhymed pairs. First line: 'Around the library'

803 'Oban 1955-82 (6)' Eighteen lines in terza rima. First line: 'Spinsterish teachers, missing the apples, die'

804 'Oban 1955-82 (7)' Five half-rhymed three-line stanzas. First line: 'Come towards me, immense millions.'

805 'Oban 1955-82 (8)' Twelve half-rhymed lines. First line: 'The unpredicted that I prize'

806 'Oban 1955-82 (9)' Eleven three-line stanzas. First line: 'Peasant that you are, realise'

807 'Oban 1955-82 (10)' Six rhymed pairs. First line: '"Please, sir, I don't read books ..." she says to me.'

808 'Oban 1955-82 (11)' Four quatrains. First line: 'Sometimes in supermarkets at the till'

809 'Oban 1955-82 (12)' Previously published in *North Mag.*, 1 (Wtr 1983/84), 15. Four three-line stanzas. First line: 'The teachers are growing old,'

810 'Oban 1955-82 (13)' Twenty-six lines in seven rhymed stanzas of three to five lines. First line: 'There was a time'

811 'Oban 1955-82 (14)' Four quatrains. First line: '"Sir, we are the stupid ones," they say.'

812 'Taynuilt 1982 — (1)' Four quatrains and a closing linked pair. First line: 'Alone with my old typewriter at last'

813 'Taynuilt 1982 — (2)' Previously published in *Argo*, 2, no. 1 (Spr. 1980), 28-29. The original has two lines fewer and a different stanza arrangement. Forty-three half-rhymed lines in five stanzas of two to twenty-one lines. First line: 'What have I done today?'

814 'Taynuilt 1982 — (3): For Donalda' Previously published in *Lines*, 78 (Sept. 1981), 24-25. Five four-line stanzas. First line: 'So I come home to you'

815 'Taynuilt 1982 — (4)' Previously published in *Sctn*, 17 Mar. 1984. Four three-line stanzas. First line: 'If everything is contingent'

816 'Taynuilt 1982 — (5)' Ten three-line stanzas. First line: 'The joy of the author is beyond speech.'

817 'Taynuilt 1982 — (6)' Thirteen lines in four stanzas of one to five lines. First line: 'Never trust the author, trust the tale.'

818 'Taynuilt 1982 — (7)' Twenty lines in eight stanzas of one to three lines. First line: 'I think you will die easily.'

819 'Taynuilt 1982 — (8)' Three four-line stanzas. First line: 'Your brain is a thorn'

820 'Taynuilt 1982 — (9)' Five three-line stanzas. First line: 'Don Quixote, through appearances'

821 'Taynuilt 1982 — (10): For George Campbell Hay (1915-1984)' Previously published in *Sctn*, 18 May 1985. Thirty-three lines in nine stanzas of two to five lines. First line: 'The vulnerable ones die many deaths'

822 'Taynuilt 1982 — (11)' Five pairs. First line: '"We authors," she will say, who has written nothing'

823 'Taynuilt 1982 — (12)' Five rhymed pairs. First line: 'The jet plane leaves a trail in the blue sky.'

824 'Taynuilt 1982 — (13)' Five stanzas of three and one of four lines. First line: 'Poet, you arise from the dead.'

825 'Taynuilt 1982 — (14)' Forty-four lines in fifteen stanzas of two to six lines. First line: 'Such joy that I have come home to'

826 'Taynuilt 1982 — (15)' Four three-line stanzas. First line: 'Latterly the sea would cast them up,'

827 'Taynuilt 1982 — (16)' Forty-seven lines in eleven stanzas of two to six lines. First line: 'There is no island.'

An t-Eilean agus An Canan (1987)

828 'An Canan (1)' Eleven three-line stanzas. First line: 'Ann an Sabhal Mòr Ostaig'

829 'An Canan (2)' Seven three-line stanzas. First line: 'Sheas mi aig beulaibh an taigh-òsda,'

830 'An Canan (3)' Six three-line stanzas. First line: 'Chuir thu do làmhan mu m'amhaich.'

831 'An Canan (4)'One four-line and ten two-line stanzas. First line: 'Tha uisge tuiteam,'

832 'An Canan (5)' Five three-line stanzas. First line: 'Tha an drungair anns an dìg,'

833 'An Canan (6)' Nine two-line stanzas. First line: 'Tha am Frangach seo ag ionnsachadh na Gaidhlig.'

834 'An Canan (7)' Six pairs. First line: 'Thubhairt Rùnaire na Stàit'

835 'An Canan (8)' Two three- and two two-line stanzas. First line: 'Thubhairt m'uncle rium,'

836 'An Canan (9)' Six stanzas of four lines and two of three. First line: 'Anns a' van gheal'

837 'An Canan (10)' Two four- and one three-line stanzas. First line: 'Aon turas'

838 'An Canan (11)' Four stanzas of one, two, three and four lines. First line: 'Tha i beò air crisps is air lemonade,'

839 'An Canan (12)' One four- and three three-line stanzas. First line: 'Tha a' chlann a' gabhail seachad, innealan-ciùil'

840 'An Canan (13)' Nine three-line stanzas. First line: 'Tha thu togail ort dhachaigh,'

841 'An Canan (14)' Three three-line stanzas. First line: 'Ged a tha thu bòidheach,'

842 'An Canan (15)' Two four- and three three-line stanzas. First line: 'Tha sinn a' cladhach,'

843 'An Canan (16)' Four pairs. First line: 'Na guthan àrd ud,'

844 'An Canan (17)' Six stanzas of two lines and one of three. First line: 'Tha gach ainmhidh coimhlionta'

845 'An Canan (18)' Seven three-line stanzas. First line: 'Thachair thu rium,'

846 'An Canan (19)' Two three- and three two-line stanzas. First line: 'Bidh na facail ag èirigh às an talàmh'

847 'An Canan (20)' Two three- and three three-line stanzas. First line: 'Chunna mi planaidean anns an adhar'

848 'An t-Eilean (1)' Prose poem; fifteen lines. First line: 'Anns an eilean ud, tha Dia, coltach ri gobha,'

849 'An t-Eilean (2)' Prose poem; seventeen lines. First line: 'Nuair a bha sinn òg, a bheil cuimhn agaibh?'

850 'An t-Eilean (3)' Prose poem; twenty lines in five paragraphs. First line: 'Bha i ceithir fichead 's a dhà-dheug.'

851 'An t-Eilean (4)' Prose poem; seventeen lines. First line: 'Tha e feitheamh air cidhe Steòrnabhaigh,'

852 'An t-Eilean (5)' Prose poem; nine lines. First line: 'Aig am na Nollaig tha solais Airnis a' deàlradh troimh 'n dorchadas.'

853 'An t-Eilean (6)' Prose poem; eleven lines. First line: 'Aon latha chunna mi e sealltainn a-mach'

854 'An t-Eilean (7)' Prose poem; nine lines. First line: 'Thubhairt fear rium, A bheil cuimhn agad an oidhch'

855 'An t-Eilean (8)' Prose poem; eight lines. First line: 'B'e siud a' chiad uair a chunna mi treàna,'

856 'An t-Eilean (9)' Ten lines. First line: 'Tha ghrian a' dol sìos air taobh siar eilean Leòdhais,'

857 'An t-Eilean (10)' Prose poem;seven lines. First line: 'Anns an sgoil tha a' Leadaidh Liath'

858 'An t-Eilean (11)' Prose poem; six lines. First line: 'Bha mi 'nam ruith troimh shràidean Lunnainn còmhla'

859 'An t-Eilean (12)' Prose poem; five lines. First line: 'Tha am bocsa anns a' chòrnair,'

860 'An t-Eilean (13)' Prose poem; ten lines. First line: 'Tha am peansail a' sgriachail air an sglèat.'

861 'An t-Eilean (14)' Prose poem; six lines. First line: 'Anns an taigh-dhealbh bha Errol Flynn'

862 'An t-Eilean (15)' Prose poem; six lines. First line: 'Cha leig e an cat a-steach don taigh.'

863 'An t-Eilean (16)' Prose poem; eight lines. First line: 'Bha an rèidio anns a' chòrnair le cuirtear oirre.'

864 'An t-Eilean (17)' Prose poem; five lines. First line: 'Cho brèagha 'na do chòta buidhe ...'

865 'An t-Eilean (18)' Prose poem; nine lines. First line: 'Tha e 'na shuidhe air seata ris an teine.'

866 'An t-Eilean (19)' Prose poem; five lines. First line: 'Shad an tidsear faclair oirnn: bhuail e air a' bhalla.'

867 'An t-Eilean (20)' Six lines. First line: 'Vodka, uisge-beatha, gin, Elvis Presley.'

868 'An t-Eilean (21)' Prose poem; nine lines. First line: 'Bha iad a' bàsachadh leis a' chaitheamh,'

869 'An t-Eilean (22)' Prose poem; eight lines. First line: 'De th'anns a' phaipear an-diugh.'

870 'An t-Eilean (23)' Seven lines. First line: 'Danns a' rathaid'

871 'An t-Eilean (24)' Five lines. First line: 'Dè th'anns a' phàipear an-diugh?'

872 'An t-Eilean (25)' Six lines. First line: 'An casg sinn na muirtearan le riaghailtean Dhè?'

873 'An t-Eilean (26)' Prose poem; eleven lines. First line: 'Thàinig thu dhachaigh às na States.'

874 'An t-Eilean (27)' Nine lines. First line: 'Nuair a bha mi dol dhachaigh air a' bhàta'

875 'An t-Eilean (28)' Prose poem; seven lines. First line: 'Reothadh is sneachd air an talàmh — gach nì geal.'

876 'An t-Eilean (29)' Prose poem; fourteen lines. First line: 'An latha bha seo anns an elevator'

877 'An t-Eilean (30)' Two pairs. First line: 'An Eala Bhàn.'

878 'An t-Eilean (31)' Two stanzas of two and five lines. First line: 'Bha "HBC" sgrìobhte air a van.'

879 'An t-Eilean (32)' Prose poem; fourteen lines. First line: 'Sheas sinn ann an gleann air latha fliuch,'

880 'An t-Eilean (33)' Prose poem; eight lines. First line: 'A bheil thu coimhead an tè sin a tha tighinn'

881 'An t-Eilean (34)' Prose poem; thirteen lines. First line: 'A' coimhead do ghnùis a-rithist an dèidh'

882 'An t-Eilean (35)' Prose poem; nine lines. First line: 'Tha mi cur litir dhachaigh, fliuch le sàl.'

883 'An t-Eilean (36)' Prose poem; nine lines. First line: 'Na h-Oganaich, Calum Kennedy, Pheigi a Ghràidh ...'

884 'An t-Eilean (37)' Prose poem; nine lines. First line: 'Togaidh tu clann ach cò thug ròsan dhut.'

885 'An t-Eilean (38)' Prose poem; eight lines. First line: 'Bha mi eadar òrain Uilleim Rois agus dàin Mhilton,'

886 'An t-Eilean (39)' Prose poem; eight lines. First line: 'Tha iad aig a' chleidh a' bruadrachadh.'

887 'An t-Eilean (40)' Prose poem; six lines. First line: 'Fhuair iad marbh thu ann an tenement ann an Glaschu.'

888 'An t-Eilean (41)' Prose poem; fourteen lines. First line: 'Tha dall anns a' bhaile.'

889 'An t-Eilean (42)' Prose poem; ten lines. First line: 'Tha cuimhn 'am aig àm a' chogaidh bha sinn a' lorg'

890 'An t-Eilean [42b]' This and the following poem have been misnumbered; both are numbered (43). Prose poem; six lines. First line: 'Anns an solas an Tilley bha mi cnuachasd geometry.'

891 'An t-Eilean [43]' Five lines. First line: 'An latha bha seo thug Rob cliop dhomh.'

892 'An t-Eilean (44)' Prose poem; eight lines. First line: 'Tha a chailleach a' fuireach 'na h-aonar.'

893 'An t-Eilean (45)' Eleven lines. First line: 'Aon latha bha mi ann a Halifax.'

894 'An t-Eilean (46)' Prose poem; thirteen lines. First line: '"Tha an t-eilean làn ceòl," mar a thubhairt an sgrìobhadair.'

895 'An t-Eilean (47)' Prose poem; eight lines. First line: 'Bha iad ag ràdh gu robh taibhsichean aig cladh Aignis.'

896 'An t-Eilean (48)' Prose poem; eight lines. First line: 'Dh'fhalbh na taibhsichean nuair a thàinig solas an dealain.'

897 'An t-Eilean (49)' Ten lines. First line: '"Fàsaidh smal air òr".'

898 'An t-Eilean (50)' Prose poem; fourteen lines. First line: 'Tha fear à Iapan a dh'ionnsaich a' Ghàidhlig.'

899 'An t-Eilean (51)' Prose poem; sixteen lines. First line: 'Thusa 'na do sheasamh aig Clachan Chalanais,'

900 'An t-Eilean (52)' Prose poem; ten lines. First line: 'Thusa ann a Hong Kong innis dhomh cò thu?'

901 'An t-Eilean (53)' Prose poem; nine lines. First line: 'Anns an t-Sìna, tha rickshaws a' ruith,'

902 'An t-Eilean (54)' Five lines. First line: 'Tha an saoghal mar orchestra, tha do phàirt fhèin agad-sa.'

903 'An t-Eilean (55)' Prose poem; sixteen lines. First line: 'Thog na saighdearan orra gu Waterloo, gu Majuba.'

904 'An t-Eilean (56)' Prose poem; thirteen lines. First line: 'Nach iad a rinn an t-amadan dhìot.'

905 'An t-Eilean (57)' Seven lines. First line: 'Tha am bocsa anns a' chòrnair.'

906 'An t-Eilean (58)' Prose poem; six lines. First line: 'Mo ruin, tha mi maol is reamhar.'

907 'An t-Eilean (59)' Prose poem; eight lines. First line: 'Aon latha bha mi air a' mhòintich.'

908 'An t-Eilean (60)' Prose poem; thirteen lines. First line: 'Aon turas anns a' bhliadhna bhiodh sinn a' dol suas am baile.'

909 'An t-Eilean (61)' Prose poem; fifteen lines. First line: 'Oidhche Shamhna a bh'ann.'

910 'An t-Eilean (62)' Prose poem; nine lines. First line: 'A' tighinn dhachaigh le peilichean bùrn,'

911 'An t-Eilean (63)' Prose poem; fifteen lines. First line: 'Dathan, dathan ùra, air an eilean'

912 'An t-Eilean (64)' Prose poem; ten lines. First line: 'A bheil Dia a' sùileachadh bron.'

913 'An t-Eilean (65)' Prose poem; seven lines. First line: 'Tha a' chnuimh ag èirigh às an talàmh,'

914 'An t-Eilean (66)' Ten lines. First line: 'A' chailleach a tha seo, tha i feitheamh ris a' bhas.'

915 'An t-Eilean (67)' Prose poem; twenty-two lines. First line: 'Bha mi thall ann a Germany, ars ise.'

916 'An t-Eilean (68)' Prose poem; seventeen lines. First line: 'Tha an eaglais ag èirigh as an talàmh,'

917 'An t-Eilean (69)' Prose poem; twenty-four lines. First line: 'Fichead taigh.'

918 'An t-Eilean (70)' Prose poem; eleven lines. First line: 'Vodka, gin? How are you keeping?'

919 'An t-Eilean (71)' Prose poem; twenty-eight lines. First line: 'Thugainn leam, thugainn leam,'

920 'An t-Eilean (72)' Prose poem; seven lines. First line: '"Cha bhi sneachd a' leanntainn an seo ann,"'

921 'An t-Eilean (73)' Prose poem; eight lines. First line: 'Chaidh thu sgiol Steòrnabhaigh.'

922 'An t-Eilean (74)' Prose poem; nine lines. First line: 'Feasgar agus ceò ann.'

923 'An t-Eilean (75)' Prose poem; thirteen lines. First line: 'Am fuaim a chluinneas tu air an eilean.'

924 'An t-Eilean (76)' Prose poem; eight lines. First line: 'Bha sinn air taobh a-muigh na sgoile:'

925 'An t-Eilean (77)' Prose poem; twenty-one lines. First line: 'Tha na pleunaichean a' fàgail Steòrnabaigh,'

926 'An t-Eilean (78)' Prose poem; fourteen lines. First line: 'Am balach a bha siud, air latha foghair,'

927 'An t-Eilean (79)' Prose poem; twelve lines. First line: 'Tha an telegram buidhe a' tuiteam mar dhuilleag foghair.'

928 'An t-Eilean (80)' Prose poem; seven lines. First line: 'Tha iad a' seasamh an coinneamh a chèile, Ruisia is Ameireaga.'

929 'An t-Eilean (81)' Prose poem; ten lines. First line: 'Eadar an dà sgàthan tha ifrinn ag èirigh.'

930 'An t-Eilean (82)' Prose poem; ten lines. First line: 'Tha iad a' giùlan a chiste-laighe gu Aignis.'

931 'An t-Eilean (83)' Prose poem; seventeen lines. First line: 'Thoir dhomh do làmh ... tha sinn mar shèine ceangailte ri chèile.'

932 'An t-Eilean (84)' Prose poem; fourteen lines. First line: 'Ifrinn, ifrinn, tionndaidh air falbh bhuainn.'

933 'An t-Eilean (85)' Eight lines. First line: 'Tha an t-earrach a' tighinn às ùr.'

934 'An t-Eilean (86)' Prose poem; ten lines. First line: 'An t-earrach a' tighinn às ùr. Na neòinein mun cuairt an taighe.'

935 'An t-Eilean (87)' Prose poem; twenty-six lines. First line: 'Tha an t-eilean a' seòladh air a' chuan.'

B

Introduction

The arrangement of this section differs slightly from that of section A. Iain Crichton Smith's novels and collections of short stories are listed here in chronological order, and if some material had appeared perviously in some form details are given. As with his verse, the main body of 'scholarship' to date consists of reviews, and I have tried to make the lists given here as full as possible. There have been a few translations of his work into other languages, and details of these are included in the hope that they will at least appeal to readers' curiosity.

Bùrn is Aran [Bread and Water], Clo-bhualaidhean Gairm, Leabhar 2 (Glasgow: Gairm, 1960 and 1974; second edition 1987. The second edition excludes the verse).

Poems and short stories; for verse, see Section A. Contents: 'Turus Dhachaidh — I'; 'An Coigreach'; 'An Fidheall'; 'Briseadh Cridhe'; 'Bùrn'; 'Clachan Chalanais'; 'Turus Dachaidh — II'; 'An Duine Dubh'; 'Am Bard'. 'An Coigreach' appeared in *Gairm*, 7 (1958/59), 29-32; 'An Fidheall' appeared in *An Gaidheal*, 55 (1960), 86-88.

Reviewed by *An Gaidheal*, 55 (1960), 130.

An Dubh is an Gorm [The Black and the Blue], Leabraichean ura Gaidhlig Oilthigh Obair-Dheadhain, aireamh 2 (Aberdeen, 1963); Leabhraichean ura Gaidhlig Oilthigh Glaschu, aireamh 2 (Glasgow, 1963; rep. 1969); and (Aberfeldy: Clo Chaillean, 1979).

ISBN 906623-02-2 (Clo Chaillean, 1979) Contents: 'An Solus Ur'; 'Is Agus Esan'; 'Am Maor'; 'An Cuan 's na Faoileagan'; 'A' Ghloine'; 'An Carbad'; 'E Fhein 's a Bhrathair'; 'Abraham is Isaac'; 'Jenkins is Marlowe'; 'A' Bhàn-Shoisgeulaiche'; 'Aig a' Chloich-Chuimhne'; 'An Tagadh'; 'An Còmhradh'; 'An Leine'; 'Anns a' Bhurn'; 'Anns an Uaimh'; 'Na h-Iudhaich'; 'Am Priosanach'; 'Na Facail air a' Bhalla'; 'An Dubh is an Gorm'. Several stories had appeared previously in *Gairm*. 'Am Maor' appeared in vol. 10 (1961/62), 41-46; 'An Cuan 's na Faoileagan', pp. 131-33; 'A' Ghloine', pp. 374-76; and 'A' Bhàn-Shoisgeulaiche', pp. 263-68. 'An Solus Ur' was published in *Gairm*, 9 (1960/61), 205-10; and 'Is Agus Esan', pp. 323-25. 'Am Maor' later appeared in *Feoil an Gheimridh*. 'An Solus Ur' appeared in *Rosg nan Eilean*. 'An Còmhradh' has been frequently anthologised.

Reviewed by Fionnlagh MacLeoid, *Gairm*, 11 (1962/63), 431-35.

A' Chuirt [The Trial], introduced by Domhnall MacThomais (Inverness: An Comunn Gaidhealach, 1966).

> One-act Gaelic play. Winner of four awards in the drama competition at the Mod, played by the Glasgow Skye Drama Club and produced by Donald B. MacLean.

> Reviewed by Domhnall Iain MacLeoid, *Gairm*, 15 (1966/67), 283-87; *An Gaidheal*, Oct. 1966, p. 111.

An Coilleach [The Cockerel]: *dealbh-chluich an Gaidhlig* (Inverness: An Comunn Gaidhealach, 1966).

> One-act Gaelic play. Winner of the Mod's best original play award and Premier award, performed by Na h-Eileanaich Drama Group.

> Reviewed by Domhnall Iain MacLeoid, *Gairm*, 15 (1966/67), 283-87.

Consider the Lilies (London: Victor Gollancz Ltd, 1968); published in America as *The Alien Light* (Boston: Houghton Mifflin, 1969). Edited by Evan Owen for Pergamon English Library (Oxford and New York: Athena Books, 1970); and by Isobel Murray for Canongate Classics (Edinburgh: 1987). Translated into Danish as *Se markens liljer* by E. Frandsen (Bogforlaget; VISION ApS, 1983).

> ISBN 0-575-000-35-X (Gollancz); SBN 08-016028-X (Pergamon); ISBN 0-86241-143-2 (Canongate) Novel. Short-listed for the 1969 SAC $1000 Literature Prize.

> Reviewed by Ruaraidh MacThomais, *Gairm*, 16 (1967/68), 285-86; P., *GH*, 9 Mar. 1968; Ian Hamilton, *Lsnr*, 79 (7 March 1968), 312; Robin Fulton, *NER*, Nov. 1969, pp. 7-8; David Wade, *New Stn*, 75 (Jan-June 1968), 307; C. Bermant, *Obs.*, 10 March 1968, p. 28; Henry Tube, *Spec.*, 220 (Jan-June 1968), 371-72; *TLS*, 4 Apr. 1968, p. 356.

Reviews of *The Alien Light* (American edition of *Consider the Lilies* included): *New York Times*, 23 Feb. 1969; *The Times* (Erie, PA), 10 Aug. 1969; *Advertiser* (Huntington, VA), 22 June 1969; *Appeal* (Memphis, Tenn.), 3 August 1969; *Advocate* (Baton Rouge, LA), 22 July 1969; *Sentinel* (Grand Junction, Col), 13 April 1969; *Blst*, 1 March 1969, p. 732; *Best Sellers*, 1 March 1969, p. 479; *Library Journal*, 15 March 1969, p. 1164; *Publishers' Weekly*, 20 Jan 1969, p. 267; *Saturday Review*, 8 March 1969, p. 129 Later editions reviewed by: 'The Century Column', *GH*, 23 August 1986; Gillian Somerville-Lang, *Irish Times*, 17 May 1986; Gwyneth Lewis, *Lit. Rev.*, 98 (August 1986), 22; Allan Massie, *Sctn*, 29 March 1986; Isobel Murray, *Sctn*, 30 May 1987; Frank Thompson, *WHFP*, 4 April 1986.

Iain am Measg nan Reultan [Iain amongst the Stars], illustrated by Linda NicEoghainn and Donnchadh MacAsgaill (Glasgow: Gairm, 1970; Clo-bhualaidhean Gairm, Leabhar 18).

Winner of award as best Gaelic book published in 1969, from SAC and the McCaig Trust, rept *Sctn*, 18 May 1970.

Reviewed by Donald MacAulay, *Sc. Int.*, 12 (Nov. 1970), 52-53; Donald MacAulay, *SGS*, 12 (1971/ 76), 131-32.

The Last Summer (London: Victor Gollancz, 1969). Reissued in Richard Drew Publishing's Scottish Collection (1986).

ISBN 0-575-00282-4 (Gollancz); 0-86267-163-9 and 0-86267-162-0 (pbk; Richard Drew). Novel.

Reviewed by Ruaraidh MacThomais, *Gairm*, 17 (1968/69), 375-77; Norman MacCaig, *Lines*, 29 (June 1969), 48-49; *Lsnr*, 29 May 1969, p. 761; J. Fenton, *New Stn*, 77 (Jan-June 1969), 777; *Obs.*, 1 June 1969, p. 28; Edwin Morgan, *Sc. Int.*, 7 (Sept. 1969), 61; *SLN*, 1, no. 1

(Oct. 1970), 29; Henry Tube, *Spec.*, 222 (Jan-June 1969), 756; *Sruth*, 26 June 1969; Alan MacGillviray, *Teaching English*, 20, no. 2 (Spr. 1987), 48-49 (p. 49); *TLS*, 12 June 1969, p. 629.

Dwr a bara: storiau gan Iain Mac a' Ghobhainn; wedi'u cyfiethu o'r Gaeleg gan Donald G. Howells (Aberystwyth: Canolfan Llyfrau Cymraeg, 1970)

ISBN 0-9500109-8-7

Maighisteirean is Ministeirean [Masters and Ministers] (Inverness: Club Leabhar, 1970).

Contents: 'Maighistirean is Ministearan'; 'Air an Trein'; 'An Duine Dubh anns a' Chubainn'; 'Air a' Bhus'; 'Pickering'. Reviewed by D. I. MacLeoid, *Gairm*, 19 (1970/ 71), 93-96; Donald MacAulay, *SGS*, 12 (1971/76), 131-32.

Survival without Error and other stories (London: Victor Gollancz Ltd, 1970).

ISBN 0-575-00423-1 Short Stories. Contents: 'The Ships'; Survival without Error'; 'The Exiles'; 'Close of Play'; 'Je t'Aime'; 'Goodbye John Summers'; 'The Black and the White'; 'Sweets to the S weet'; 'Murder without Pain'; 'The Adoration of the Mini'; 'Home'; 'On the Island'; 'Joseph'; 'The Idiot and the Professor and some Others'. 'Je t-Aime' is a version of a Gaelic story from *Sruth*, 30 Nov. 1967. 'On the Island' published *Sctn*, 1 July 1978. 'The Adoration of the Mini' and 'The Black and the White' appeared in the *Glasgow Herald* shortly before the book was published, on 21 and 14 Mar. 1970 respectively. 'Goodbye John Summers' later appeared in *Transatlantic Review*, 33/34, p. 73.

Reviewed by *Lsnr*, 9 Apr. 1970, p. 488; *New Stn*, 79 (Jan-June 1970), 482; Robert Nye, *Sctn*, 4 April 1970; Donald John MacLeod, *Sc. Int.*, 7 (Sept. 1969), 61.

My Last Duchess : a novel (London: Victor Gollancz Ltd, 1971).

ISBN 0-575-00702-8 The first chapter is a variant of the Gaelic story, 'Am Bàrd'.

Reviewed by *Books and Bookmen*, 16 (Sept. 1971), 57; *GH*, 17 July 1971; M. Sullivan, *Lsnr*, 15 July 1971, p. 89; David Haworth, *New Stn*, 82 (June-Dec 1971), 89; *Obs.*, 18 July 1971, p. 28; Derek Stanford, *Sctn*, 17 July 1971; Gavin Ewart, *TLS*, 16 July 1971, p. 825;.

An t-Adhar Ameireaganach is sgeulachdan eile [The American Sky and other stories] (Inbhirnis: Club Leabhar Limited, 1973).

SBN 902706-16-0 Gaelic short stories. Contents: 'A' Bhànrigh'; 'Oidhche air Cheilidh'; 'Bho Cheol gu Ceol'; 'Rudeigin Coltach ri Chekhov'; 'Aig a' Phairtidh'; 'An Deidh a' Chogaidh'; 'A' Dol Dhachaidh'; 'An Rionnag'; 'An Gaol'; 'Giuiainidh mi Fhìn do Leabhraichean'; 'Fear a' Rhodesia'; 'Na Guthan'; 'Latha nan Leumadairean'; 'An Tilleadh'; 'An Dealbh-chluiche'; 'Latha na Sabaid'; 'An t-Adhar Ameireaganach'; 'Robinson Crusoe'.

Reviewed by Domhnall Iain MacLeoid, *Gairm*, 1973/74, pp. 375-78.

The Black and the Red and other stories (London: Victor Gollancz Ltd, 1973).

ISBN 0-575-01705-8 Short stories. Contents: 'The Dying'; 'At the Party'; 'In the Station'; 'An American Sky'; 'After the Dance'; 'The Telegram'; 'The Wedding'; 'Getting Married'; 'The Little People';

'God's Own Country'; 'By the Sea'; 'The Black and the Red'; 'A Day in the Life of ...'; 'The Crater'; 'The Fight'; 'In Church'; 'Through the Desert'; 'The Return'; 'The End'; 'Journeying Westwards'; 'The Professor and the Comics'. 'The Telegram' is translated from 'An Telegram', published in *An Gaidheal*, 60 (1965), 38-39. 'The Fight' appeared in *London Magazine*, n.s. 2, no. 1 (Apr. 1962), 37-41; 'The Black and the Red' appeared in *New Saltire*, 7 (Mar. 1963), 42-57; 'The Dying' appeared in *Stand*, 13, no. 2 (1972), 13-14; and 'The Little People' previously appeared as 'The Small People' in *Sc. Int.*, 5, no. 3 (March 1972), 24-26.

Reviewed by C. Small, *GH*, 10 Nov. 1973; Lorn M. MacIntyre, *Glasgow Rev.*, 5, no. 1 (Smr 1974), 44; Robert Nye, *Gdn*, 13 Oct. 1975; *Irish Press*, 12 Jan. 1974; V. Cunningham, *Lsnr*, 8 November 1973, p. 638; Anthony Thwaite, *Obs.*, 30 Dec. 1973; Cuthbert Graham, *P&J*, 3 November 1973; Kay Dick, *Sctn*, 13 October 1973; M.D., *Scots Independent*, Apr. 1974; Leonard Barras, *ST*, 6 January 1974; Elizabeth Berridge, *DTel*, 11 October 1973; *TLS*, 19 October 1973, p. 1269.

Goodbye, Mr Dixon (London: Victor Gollancz Ltd, 1974).

ISBN 0-575-01875-5 Novel. Reviewed by Michael Maxwell Scott, *DTel*, 21 Nov. 1974; M. McCartney, *GH*, 23 November 1974; *Gdn Weekly*, 30 November 1974, p. 22; *Obs.*, 5 Jan. 1975; Derek Stanford, *Sctn*, 30 November 197; Ronald Blythe, *ST*, 24 November 1974; Susan Hill, *The Times*, 21 November 1974; Edwin Morgan, *TLS*, 17 January 1975, p. 48.

An t-Aonaran [The Hermit], Leabhraichean ura Ghàidhlig; aireamh 9 (Glasgow University: Department of Celtic, 1976).

SBN 0-903204-07-X Gaelic novel. Reviewed by Domhnall MacAmhlaigh, *Gairm*, 1975/76, pp. 373-78; William Gillies, *Lines*,

61 (June 1977), 47; Derick Thomson, *SGS*, 13 (1978/81), 137-39; John MacInnes, Sc. Rev., 7 (Smr 1977), 52-54; *WLT*, 51 (Aut. 1977), 665.

The Village (Inverness: Club Leabhar, 1976).

SBN 902706-30-6; 902706-41-1 (pbk) Short stories. Contents: 'Easter Sunday'; 'Sunday'; 'The Old Woman and the Rat'; 'The Delicate Threas'; 'The Conversation'; 'I'll Remember You'; 'The Ghost'; 'The Red Door'; 'The Blot'; 'The Vision'; 'The Phone Call'; 'The House'; 'The Painter'; 'The Existence of the Hermit'; 'Fable'; 'The Old Man'; 'The Prophecy'; 'The Letter'; 'Jimmy and the Policeman'; 'After the Film'; 'Moments'; 'Old Betsy'. 'The Ghost' was published in *Sctn*, 27 Aug. 1977; 'The Red Door' appeared in Eilean nan Fhraoich Annual (1974), 9-11.

Reviewed by Cuthbert Graham, *P&J*, 15 Jan. 1977; Allan Massie, *Sctn*, 19 January 1977; *ST*, 5 June 1977.

Tormod 's na Dolaichean [Norman and the Dolls] *agus Mairi 's an t-Each Fiodh* ['Mary and the Wooden Horse'], Clo-Bhualaidhean Gairm, Leabhar 45 (Glasgow: Gairm, 1976).

SBN 901771-55-4 Two Gaelic stories, illustrated by Donnchadh MacAsgaill.

Little Red Riding Hood agus An Dorus Iarùinn [The Iron Door], Clo-Bhualaidhean Gairm, Leabhar 46 (Glasgow: Gairm, 1977)

SBN 901771-56-2 Two stories. Illustrated by Donnchadh MacAsgaill.

The Hermit and other stories (London: Victor Gollancz, 1977).

ISBN 0-575-02340-6 Short stories. Contents: 'The Hermit'; 'The Impulse'; 'Timoshenko'; 'The Spy'; 'The Brothers'; 'The Incident'; 'Listen to the Voice'; 'The Exorcism'; 'Macbeth'; 'Leaving the Cherries'. A Gaelic version of the title story was pub lished by the Glasgow University Press in 1976.

Reviewed by David Gifford, *BiS*, 1 (Spr./Smr 1978), 11; Elizabeth Berridge, *DTel*, 13 Oct. 1977; *Economist*, 266, 4 Mar. 1978, p. 105; *Evening Times* (Glasgow), 8 October 1977; C. Small, *GH*, 22 Dec. 1977; J. Mellors, *Lsnr*, 15 December 1977, p. 806; Anthony Thwaite, *Obs.*, 18 December 1977; Allan Massie, *Sctn*, 2 October 1977; David Colledge, *Scottish Field*, 124, no. 917 (July 1978), 38; Norman Nicholson, *Sc. Rev.*, 11 (1978), 47-49; James Shaw Grant, *St. Gaz.*, 4 March 1978; A. Brien, *ST*, 30 October 1977; Edwin Morgan, *TLS*, 25 Novem ber 1977, p. 1373; Kay Dick, *The Times*, 1 December 1977; also among Allan Massie's best books of the year, *Sctn*, 17 Dec 1979.

An End to Autumn (London: Victor Gollancz, 1978)

ISBN 0-575-02563-8 Novel. Winner of a SAC book award, reported *Sctn*, 17 December 1979.

Reviewed by Lucy Hughes-Hallett, Books and Bookmen, 24 (Mar. 1979), 56; Brian Masters, *DTel*, 15 Feb. 1979; M. McCartney, *GH*, 8 February 1979; Christopher Wadsworth, *Gdn*, 8 February 1979; *Ilustrated London News*, 267 (Apr. 1979), 108; John Naughton, *Lsnr*, 15 February 1979, p. 266; B. McCabe, *NER*, 45 (February 1979), 31-32; B. Morrison, *New Stn*, 9 February 1979, pp. 189-90; *Obs.*, 11 March 1979; Allan Massie, *Sctn*, 10 February 1979; Norman Nicholson, *Sc. Rev.*, 14 (May 1979), 52-53; James Shaw Grant, *St. Gaz.*, 10 February 1979; Janice Elliott, *Sunday Telegraph*, 11

February 1979; *The Times*, 1 Dec. 1977; S. K., *TLS*, 30 Nov. 1979, p. 76; G. M. Brown, *Words,* 8 (1979), 6-7.

On the Island, illustrated by Carol Fowkes (London: Victor Gollancz Ltd, 1979; pbk edition Richard Drew Publishing, 1988)

ISBN 0-575-02689-8 (Gollancz) and 0-8267-226-0 (Richard Drew) Translated into Danish by E. Frandsen as Dreng og hans o ([Copenhagen]: Vision, 1985).

Reviewed by Douglas Gifford, *BiS*, 6 (Wtr 1979/80), 8-10 (p. 9); D. Craig, *Cenc.*, 2 (Spr. 1980), 39-40; D. Campbell, *NER*, 48 (Nov 1979), 36-37; *New Stn*, 9 Nov. 1979, p. 731; J. B. Caird, *North 7*, 38 (Mar./Apr. 1980), 28-29; *Obs.*, 2 Dec. 1979, p. 39; Cuthbert Graham, *P&J*, 10 November 1979; Ronald Black, *Sctn*, 16 Aug. 1979; Donald MacAulay, *SLJ* Supplement no. 12, pp. 136-38; Stewart Conn, *Words*, 10 (1980).

Am Bruadaraiche (Stornoway: Acair, 1980)

ISBN 0-86152-05-1 Gaelic stories. Contents: 'Hawkins agus One-Eyed Kelly'; 'A' sabaid ri na madaidh-allaidh'; 'Anns an tigh falamh'; 'Righ Harold'; 'Eilean an ionmhais'; 'A' cluich dha na Rovers'; 'A' sabaid ris na h-Apaches'; 'Anns an eathar'; 'Am measg nan daoine mora'; 'Anns a' gàradh'.

Murdo, and other stories (London: Victor Gollancz, 1981)

ISBN 0-575-02983-8 Short stories. Contents: 'In the Castle'; 'The Missionary'; 'At the Fair'; 'The Listeners'; 'Mr Heine'; 'The Visit'; 'Murdo'. An extract from 'Murdo' appeared in *Cenc.*, 5 (Smr 1981), 23. 'The Listeners' appeared in *Stand*, 20, no. 2 (1979), 66-68. 'In the Castle' was published in *Sctn*, 22 Mar. 1980.

Reviewed by D. Gifford, *BiS*, 10 (Spr. 1982), 10-14 (p. 12); *BBN*, Sept. 1981, p. 566; Andrew Lothian, *Cenc.*, 6 (Aut. 1981), 41; Stephen Glover, *DTel*, 21 May 1981; Deirdre Chmn, *GH*, 19 May 1981; Norman Shrapnel, *Gdn*, 14 May 1981; *Library Journal*, 15 Jan. 1982, p. 196; *Lsnr*, 14 May 1981, p. 652; Ian Bamforth, *NER*, 55 (Aug 1981), 30-31; James Campbell, *New Stn*, 15 May 1981, p. 21; Cuthbert Graham, *P&J*, 16 May 1981; *Publishers' Weekly*, 13 Nov. 1981, p. 74; Edwin Morgan, *SLJ* Supplement, no. 17, pp. 94-96; F. Urquhart, *Sc. Rev.*, 24 (Nov 1981), 39-40; Maurice Lindsay, *Sunday Standard*, 7 June 1981; John Mole, *TLS*, 26 June 1981, p. 730; *WLT*, 56 (Smr 1982), 558.

A Field Full of Folk (London: Victor Gollancz Ltd, 1982)

ISBN 0-575-03110-7 Novel.

Reviewed by *Books and Bookmen*, July 1982, p. 14; D. Gifford, *BiS*, 11 (Wtr 1982/ 83), 11-14 (p. 11); *BBN*, Aug. 1982, p. 513; Cairns Craig, *Cenc.*, 11 (New Year 1983), 44-45; Janice Elliott, *DTel*, 23 May 1982; Adam Mars-Jones, *FT*, 15 May 1982; *Kirkus Reviews*, 50 (1 Apr. 1982), 443; Iain Stephen, *NER*, 61 (Spr. 1983), 31-32; *New Yorker*, 16 August 1982, p. 89; *Obs.*, 16 May 1982, p. 30; *Publishers' Weekly*, 21 May 1982, p. 65; Allan Massie, *Sctn*, 8 May 1982; Iain Stephen, *St Gaz*, 28 August 1982; Alan Bold, *Sunday Standard*, 16 May 1982; Stuart Evans, *The Times*, 24 June 1982; *TLS*, 21 May 1982, p. 566.

Scottish Highland Tales (London: Ward Lock Educational, 1982)

ISBN 0-7062-3948-2 (school edn); 0-7062-3952-0 (net) Contents: 'The Battle of the Birds'; 'The Hoodie'; 'Silver Weed'; 'The Cat'; 'The Goldfinch'; 'Serpent's Stone'; 'The Sea Maiden'; 'The Dog'; 'The Salmon Trout'; 'The Speech of Birds'; 'The Three Shirts';

'Fables'; 'The Seal Woman'; 'The Brown Bear of the Green Glen';
'The Calfless Cow'; 'Lullaby'.

The Search (London: Victor Gollancz, 1983)

ISBN 0-575-03297-9 Novel.

Reviewed by *Blst*, 79 (1 June 983), p. 1263; D. Gifford, *BiS*, 13 (Aut.
1983), 11-16 (pp. 12-13); *BBN*, Sept. 1983, p. 81; Jamie Grant, *Cenc.*,
15 (New Year 1984), 53; *Contemporary Review*, 243 (Oct. 1983), 213;
Kirkus Reviews, 51 (15 Apr. 1983), 482; Marion Glastonbury, *New
Stn*, 14 May 1982, p. 25; *New Yorker*, 59 (27 June 1983), 99; *Obs.*, 5
June 1983; *Publishers' Weekly*, 29 April 1983, p. 45; *Punch*, 13 July
1983, p. 61; Allan Massie, *Sctn*, 28 May 1983; George Bruce, *Sc.
Rev.*, 32 (Nov. 1983), pp. 39-40.

Mr Trill in Hades and other stories (London: Victor Gollancz Ltd, 1984)

ISBN 0-575-03417-3 Short stories. Contents: 'What to Do About
Ralph?'; 'The Ring'; 'Greater Love'; 'The Snowballs'; 'The Play';
'In the School'; 'Mr Trill in Hades'. 'In the School' appeared in Sc.
Rev., 9 (1978), 19-26. 'What to Do About Ralph?' previously
appeared in *Shakespeare Stories* edited by Giles Gordon (Hamish
Hamilton).

Reviewed by *Blst*, 80 (15 Apr. 1984), p. 1153; D. Gifford, *BiS*, 15
(Smr 1984), 9-14 (pp. 11-12); *BBN*, Aug. 1984, p. 493; Elizabeth
Berridge, *DTel*, 16 Mar. 1984; Isobel Quigly, *FT*, 24 March 1984;
Dorothy Porter, *GH*, 14 April 1984; Norman Shrapnel, *Gdn*, 15
March 1984; Gillian Somerville-Lang, *Irish Times*, 31 March 1984;
Kirkus Reviews, 1 Feb. 1984, p. 110; Sheila MacLeod, *London
Evening Standard*, 25 April 1984; *New Yorker*, 30 April 1984, p. 120;
Cuthbert Graham, *P&J*, 31 March 1984; *Publishers' Weekly*, 2 March
1984, p. 85; Carole Mansur, *Punch*, 2 May 1984, p. 59; Isobel

Murray, *Sctn*, 17 March 1984; *TLS*, 13 July 1983, p. 61; Robert L. Kindrick, *WLT*, Spr. 1985.

The Tenement (London: Victor Gollancz, 1985)

ISBN 0-575-03669 Novel.

Reviewed by D. Gifford, *BiS*, 19 (Aut. 1985), 9-13 (pp. 10-11); Dilys Rose, *Chmn*, 43/44, pp. 182-83; Nina Bawden, *DTel*, 12 July 1985; Dorothy Porter, *GH*, 13 July 1985; Norman Shrapnel, *Gdn*, 2 Aug. 1985; Cuthbert Graham, *P&J*, 13 July 1985; Isobel Murray, *Sctn*, 6 July 1985; Andrew Sinclair, *The Times*, 1 August 1985; James Campbell, *TLS*, 9 August 1985, p. 874; shortlisted for Scottish Books of the Year (see *Sctn*, 18 Nov. 1985); included in Douglas Dunn's selectiion of the year's best books, *GH*, 28 Dec. 1985.

In the Middle of the Wood (London: Victor Gollancz, 1987)

ISBN 0-575-03967-1 Novel.

Reviewed by George Gunn, *Chmn* 50 [1987?], 179-80; Kenneth McLeish, *DTel*, 17 Apr. 1987; Alan Taylor, *GH*, 9 May 1987; Norman Shrapnel, *Gdn*, 10 April 1987; Isobel Murray, *Sctn*, 18 April 1987; Frank Thompson, *St Gaz*, 30 April 1987; Iain Bamforth, *TLS*, 5 June 1987, p. 611.

C

Introduction

Iain Crichton Smith's uncollected poems are listed here in chronological order, and in alphabetical order by title within years. Note that many titles are probably the editor's rather than the author's; poems from *Stand*, for example, are often headed 'untitled'; a different solution to the problem other organs solve by adopting a few words from the first line as a title.

This listing is intended to be complementary to the listing of collected verse in section A, so poems which have been collected at whatever stage do not appear here. Details of each poem are given only once, on its earliest appearance. Note I have allowed a degree of overlap with the list of anthologised poems in section E; though full details of each poem will only be given for its earliest appearance.

1   'Death of Poetry' by Eoin. Published in *Alba Mater*, Feb. 1946, [n.p.].
     Sonnet. First line: 'Methought I saw the men of violent eyes'

2   'Departure' Published in *North-East Review*, 91 (Oct. 1946). Unseen.
     No copy of this issue has been traced.

3   'Only the Sea Remains' by Iain Smith. Published in *AUR*, 32, no. 98
     (1947/48), 197. Two stanzas of fifteen lines. First line: 'Only the
     sea remains; the pinched faces'

4   'Bookworm' Published in *Alma Mater*, 59, no. 8 (Jan.1948), 17. Later
     appeared in *Scottish Student Verse 1937/47* (Edinburgh, 1948).
     Forty-six lines in four stanzas of seven to fourteen lines. First
     line: 'To know oneself is to face unexpected peril,'

5   'Epithalamion (For A.J.)' Published in *Alma Mater*, 59, no. 9 (June
     1948), 14. Twenty lines. First line: 'The maiden in the mirror'

6   'Orpheus and Eurydice' Published in *Alma Mater*, 59, no. 8
     (Jan.1948), 16. Seven quatrains. First line: 'The Greeks had a
     legend for it,'

7   'Sea Song' Published in *Alma Mater*, 59, no. 8 (Jan.1948), 17. Three
     quatrains. First line: 'The sea is the edge of the land'

8   'Sonnet' Published in *Alma Mater*, 59, no. 8 (Jan.1948), 12. First line:
     'I cannot look on childhood: I must not:'

9   'Symphony for Myself' Published in *Alma Mater*, 59, no. 9 (June
     1948), 14. Eighteen lines. First line: 'Singing here alone,'

10   'The Poet and the Castle' (Fragment of a Commentary on
     Macbeth) Published in *Alma Mater*, 59, no. 9 (June 1948), 15-16.
     A dramatic fragment of one hundred and twenty-two lines.

11   'Death: A Poem' by Iain Smith. Published in *AUR*, 33, no. 102
     (1949/50), 278. Sonnet. First line: 'The earth revolves with tree
     and man and stone,'

12   'On a Photograph of —' Published in *Alma Mater*, 60, no. 1 (Spr.
     1949), 14. Fourteen lines. First line: 'The background dark
     distinguishes your face,'

13   'Song for Cowper' by Iain Smith. Published in *AUR*, 33, no. 100 (1949/50), 29. Four quatrains. First line: 'The devil was in your tangled head,'

14   'Vision' Published in *Alma Mater*, 60, no. 1 (Spr. 1949), 44. Nine quatrains and one rhymed six-line stanza. First line: 'The woman was a little gnome'

15   'Gach latha geal a' sioladh' Published in *Gairm*, 1, no. 4 (An Samhradh 1953), 63. Three eight-line stanzas. First line: 'Gach latha geal a' sioladh'

16   'Autobiographical' Published in *Saltire Rev.*, 1, no. 1 (Apr. 1954), 49. Eight pairs. First line: 'Every poem a stone,'

17   'Poem' Published in *Lines*, 4 (Jan. 1954), 24-26. Seventy-five lines. First line: 'I do not know who or what I am.'

18   'With Burnt, Broken Knees' Published in *Lines*, 5 (June 1954), 20. Six rhymed five-line stanzas. First line: 'With burnt, broken knees'

19   'On Such a Night as This' Published in *Lines*, 9 (Aug. 1955), 26. First line: 'On such a night as this'

20   'The House is Listening' Published in *Poet*, 12 [1956]. Seven pairs. First line: 'The house is listening to your absence:'

21   'Burn Liath a' Dòrtadh' Published in *Gairm*, 5 (1956/57), 356. Four five-line stanzas. First line: 'Burn liath a dòrtadh'

22   'The Iolaire' Published in *Saltire Rev.*, 4, no. 13 (Wtr 1957), 54-56. Sequence of three poems, of three to forty-two lines. The second is in three-line and the third in seven-line stanzas. First lines: (1) 'The war over.' (2) 'Shark-headed God snaps from his gardened calm.' (3) 'The chart-house heaved. Out through the windward door'

23   'Airson Deorsa Caimbeul Hay' Published in *Gairm*, 6 (1957/ 58), 308. Six six-line stanzas. First line: 'A neart do bhàrdachd dh'ionnsaich mi'

24 'Dog' Published in *Lines,* 14 (Spr. 1958), 15. Eight quatrains. First line: 'Dog sniffing grass in the early showery day'

25 'Aig a' Chladh' Published in *Gairm,* 8 (1959/60), 157. Five four-line stanzas. First line: 'Chunna mi aig a' chladh an de iad,'

26 'Am Fear a Dh'fhalbh 's a Thill' Published in *Gairm,* 8 (1959/60), 157. Four four-line stanzas. First line: 'De chunna tu 'n ceann eile 'n t-saoghail,'

27 'An Deidh Blàr Chulodair' Published in *An Gaidheal,* 54 (1959), 95. Four four-line stanzas. First line: 'Tha mi a' tuigsinn mar a thill aid uile'

28 'The Idiot' Published in *GH,* 7 Nov. 1959. Four quatrains. First line: 'They kept the idiot indoors'

29 'Asking for Criticism' Published in *Gambit,* Spr. 1960, p. 24. Three rhymed eight-line stanzas. First line: '"What do you think of them?" she said,'

30 'At Midnight' Published in *Sctn,* 22 Oct. 1960. Two quatrains. First line: 'As I walk home at midnight, half-afraid,'

31 'Beyond the Emblems' Published in *Sidewalk,* 1, no. 1 [1960], 41. Five pairs. First line: 'At the heart of the emblem is the wilful fox'

32 'Bonnie Prince Charles' Published in *Lines,* 16 (Wtr 1960), 36-37. Four quatrains. First line: 'Moidart, Glenfinnan, Edinburgh, then'

33 'For Edwin Muir' Published in *New Stn,* 59 (Jan.-June 1960), 258. Six rhymed five-line stanzas. First line: 'You were a hero of a new kind'

34 'Highland Landscape with Girl' Published in *Saltire Rev.,* 6, no. 22 (Aut. 1960), 14. Five quatrains. First line: 'Inanities of rock,'

35 'Leopardi' Published in *Gambit,* Spr. 1960, p. 24. Four quatrains. First line: 'A trick of camels, poems filled his pack,'

36   'On a Bare Moor' Published in *Poetry and Audience*, 8, no. 8 (25 Nov. 1960), 4-5. Eleven rhymed five-line stanzas. First line: 'Sitting here on a bare moor'

37   'Scholar' Published in *Outposts*, 46 (Smr 1960). Later appeared in *Best Poems of 1960: Borestone Mountain Poetry Awards 1961*. Four quatrains. First line: 'In the hour of pale triangles he is happy.'

38   'That Suffering is Not Noble' Published in *Lines*, 16 (Wtr 1960), 37. Four rhymed six-line stanzas. First line: '"To suffer much, my friend, is not noble."'

39   'Do Bhan-Sgoilear' Published in *Gairm*, 9 (1960/61), 251. Two four-line stanzas. First line: 'Co dh'iarr ortsa bhith, 'nad sgoilear'

40   'Loch Lomond' Published in *Poetry and Audience*, 8, no. 13 (27 Jan. 1961), 5. Three quatrains. First line: 'Not different, this loch, from any other,'

41   'Spring' Published in *Spec.*, 206 (1961), 564. Four stanzas of three and four lines, alternating. First line: 'Over the tingling seas it came'

42   'The Lilac Hills' Published in *GH*, 10 June 1961. Six quatrains. First line: 'The lilac hills were gossiping together'

43   'For Carol' Published in *Outposts*, 52 (Spr. 1962), 13. Five quatrains. First line: 'For you this poem, as you sail away'

44   'Paolo and Francesca in Scotland' Published in *Lines*, 18 (Spr. 1962), 25-26. Fourteen lines. First line: 'You mustn't think ... because I bring you here'

45   'Tolstoy' Published in *Lines*, 18 (Spr. 1962), 25. Twenty-four lines in couplets. First line: 'In days of the green hum he heard'

46   'A Bible Class with Film-strip' Published in *Lsnr*, 70 (July-Dec. 1963), 21. Eight rhymed six-line stanzas. First line: 'It is so far away, this narrow country.'

47 'Highland Landscape' Published in *Outposts*, 58 (Aut. 1963), 10. Thirty-one lines rhymed in couplets. First line: 'Here where the fences slouch and buzzards hound'

48 'The Wind and the Stone' Published in *Scotland's Magazine*, 59, no. 3 (Mar. 1963), 40. Five half-rhymed pairs. First line: 'The good-luck heather makes my worn coat smile.'

49 'Eadar a' Ghàidhealtachd 's a' Galltachd' Published in *Gairm*, 12 (1963/64), 377. Sequence of four poems, of six to twelve lines. First lines: 'A-nochd a' tighinn a Helensburgh' 'Anns na coilltean uaine chuala mi isean' 'Transistors, cùbhraidheachd, gainmheach, bagh,' ''S gach fear a dh'fhalbhas leis an deoch air'

50 'Goodbye' Published in *Glasgow Rev.*, 1, no. 4 (Wtr 1964/65), 9. Two quatrains. First line: 'Goodbye Iona's heather bells'

51 'Seachd Orain Airson Nam Fogarrach' Published in *Gairm*, 13 (1964/65), 66-68. Seven poems of four to twenty lines, mainly in quatrains. First lines: (1) '"A ribhinn, a bheil cuimhna agad?"' (2) '"Mairi Nighean Alas' Caoidh"' (3) 'A Phadraig Sellar chunna mi' (4) 'Soraidh slan do Leòdhas' (5) 'Bha sinn an oidhch' ud air a' laimrig.' (6) 'Soraidh slan leat, a Thiumpain,' (7) 'Thig e a Canada dhachaidh,'

52 'The Stranger in the Islands' Published in *Lsnr*, 71 (Jan. -June 1964), 534. Nine half-rhymed quatrains. First line: 'They told him to leave the island —'

53 'Aeneas' Published in *An Gaidheal*, 60 (1965), 66. Fifteen lines. First line: 'Le m'athair air mo dhruim dh'fhàg mi àm bail' ud.'

54 'Far an Robh mi 'n Raoir' Published in *Gairm*, 13 (1964/65), 373-74. Fourteen three-line stanzas, closed by a pair. First line: 'Far an robh mi 'n raoir,'

55 'Òran' Published in *An Gaidheal*, 60 (1965), 99. Two stanzas of six and sixteen lines. First line: 'A MhicChoinnich a Siadair'

56   'Poem' Published in *P. Rev.*, 56 (1965), 157. Later appeared in *Three Regional Voices*. Three six-line stanzas. First line: 'From London you came to see me.'

57   'The End' Published in *Outposts*, 64 (Spr. 1965), 17. Fourteen lines. First line: 'On the seventh day the hard sickness wore off.'

58   'The Idiot' Published in *Sctn*, 27 Nov. 1965. Nineteen lines in four half-rhymed stanzas. First line: 'The idiot at the window'

59   '"Turas a' Chriosdaidh' ùr —' Published in *Gairm*, 13 (1964/65), 259-60. Sequence of eight poems, of two to thirteen lines. First lines: (1) 'Dh'fhàg e air sgàth an teine.' (2) 'Chunnaic e sgiolear beag a' leugadh' (3) 'O Uilleim Rois, dh'eigh mo chuairtear,' (4) 'Thachair a rithist ri cailleach aosd' (5) 'Uilleim Rois, gaoth na buaireas,' (6) ''S chunnaic mimu dheireadh te' (7) 'O Uilleim Rois, iutharn a' ghaoil,' (8) 'Sud na facail bha e seinn'

60   '1965' Published in *Sctn*, 17 July 1965. Nine lines. First line: 'To plod on, inch by inch, is best,'

61   'In the Wax-works' Published in *Sctn*, 27 Nov. 1965. Four four-line stanzas. First line: 'In the waxworks Marat lies in his bath'

62   'Anns an Oilthigh' Published in *Gairm*, 14 (1965/66), 276-77. Forty-seven lines in eleven stanzas of three to seven lines. First line: 'Anns an oilthigh'

63   'Goya' Published in *Lines*, 22 (Wtr 1966), 39-40. Four quatrains. First line: 'The wicked eye of the cat, the wicked eyes of love,'

64   'Na Càit' Published in *Gairm*, 14 (1965/66), 277, 279. Four four-line stanzas. First line: 'Air oidhche fhuair chuala mi na càit a' mialaich,'

65   'Nollaig' Published in *Gairm*, 14 (1965/66), 279. Four four-line stanzas. First line: 'Chi mi mìltean air thoiseach orm.'

66   'Poem' Published in *Outposts*, 69 (Smr 1966), 14. Eight rhymed five-line stanzas. First line: 'Love is helplessness as I have known it'

67   'Poem (after Lorca)' Published in *Lsnr*, 76 (July-Dec. 1966), 662. Thirty-five lines. First line: 'Green, I love you, green,'

68   'Tha an Samhradh air Tighinn' Published in *An Gaidheal*, Oct. 1966, p. 111. Four four-line stanzas. First line: 'Tha an samhradh air tighinn mar is abhàist dha.'

69   [untitled] Published in *Sruth*, 29 June 1967. Two stanzas of ten and twenty lines in couplets. First line: 'Let us rise early and praise'

70   'Army Days' Published in *Poet* (Scottish Number; Nov 1967), 16. First line: 'On the hard square the sergeant evolved aesthetics.'

71   'Carol and Hamlet' Published in *CQ*, 9 (1967), 230-33. A sequence of eleven sonnets said to be taken from a longer sequence, but according to Iain Crichton Smith there were only eleven. Seven were collected in *Hamlet in Autumn*, the first five and the last two of those published here. Those not collected begin: First line: 'Language won't give itself to evil men.' 'Language is a just society,' 'Our language feeling outwards tells us where' '"Absent thee from felicity awhile"'

72   'Cowper' Published in *Outposts*, 72 (Spr. 1967), 4. Fifty-eight lines in eleven stanzas of one to seven lines. First line: 'Incapable'

73   'Dain: Cha leig mi mo shoraidh leat a shaoghail' Published in *Gairm*, 15 (1966/67), 320-22. Sequence of three poems, of four or five quatrains. First lines: (1) 'Cha leig mo shoraidh leat a shaoghail' (2) ''Sann a talamh aosd a ghinear àm flùran' (3) 'Os cionn talamh donn tha a' ghealach ag eirigh'

74   'Farewell' Published in *Agenda*, 5, no. 4: 6, no. 1 (Aut./Wtr 1967/68), 83. Eighteen lines in four stanzas of four and five lines. First line: 'We were gone from each other'

75   'Farewell to God' Published in *Lines*, 24 (Smr 1967), 8. Four four-line stanzas. First line: 'Let you now be dismissed from the universe'

76   'Fishermen's Cliff Houses' Published in *Poet* (Scottish Number; Nov. 1967), 13. Sixteen lines in three stanzas of two to ten lines. First line: 'Blind backs to the blind sea;'

77   'For K' Published in *Akros*, 2, no. 4 (Jan.1967), [n.p.]. Five half-rhymed quatrains. First line: 'Hair cropped, you're like a boy actor'

78   'Gathering Blaeberries' Published in *Akros*, 2, no. 4 (Jan. 1967), [n.p.]. Twenty-two lines in six three and four-line stanzas. First line: 'Those days'

79   'Glaschu' Published in *Gairm*, 15 (1966/67), 322. Twenty-two lines. First line: 'Smaoinich'

80   'Haig' Published in *Akros*, 2, no. 4 (Jan.1967), [n.p.]. Five four-line stanzas. First line: 'You belonged to Walter Scott country,'

81   'Highland Exiles' Published in *Lsnr*, 77 (Jan.-June 1967), 315. Nineteen lines. First line: 'These sailed where no daffodils are.'

82   'Iago' Published in *Lines*, 24 (Smr 1967), 9. Three eight-line stanzas, rhymed in couplets. First line: 'A pure intelligence playful, unextended,'

83   'Landscapes and Figures' Published in *Poet* (Scottish number; Nov. 1967), 13-15. Sequence of three poems, of fifteen to thirty-six lines. First lines: (I) 'Whinbrush, wind-beaten, flares summer.' (II) 'Present now an island with a multitude,' (III) 'All gone to rack-ruin; what with'

84   'Light' Published in *Poet* (Scottish number; Nov. 1967), 16. Five four-line stanzas. First line: 'How a new switch seems to come on each day'

85   'Lord Jim' Published in *Spec.*, 219 (July-Dec. 1967), 720. Seven three-line stanzas. First line: 'Dandyish perhaps and gay and brilliant'

86   'Mr Trill, Classics Master and ex-First World War Soldier, Receives his Presentation' Published in *Lines*, 25 (Wtr 1967/ 68), 16-17.

Fifty-four lines in half-rhymed couplets. First line: '"Grateful to Mr Trill." Tall vases poised'

87 'Now that the Wind' Published in *Lines,* 25 (Wtr 1967/68), 17-18. Five rhymed six-line stanzas. First line: 'Now that the wind is moaning in the chimney'

88 'Orain Ura bho Chatullus: air an cur ri cheile' Published in *Gairm,* 15 (1966/67), 224-27. Sequence of eight poems, of six to ten lines; except the last, which is further divided into seven lyrics, seven to fourteen lines long. First lines: (1) 'Tha mi 'nam laighe' (2) 'Lionn sinn cisteachan le litrichean.' (3) 'Chan eil dragh agam do'n Impìreachd Ròmanach' (4) 'Da Lesbia,' (5) 'An de bha mi aig uaigh mo bhrathar.' (6) 'A Lesbia, chunna mi ann àm bàta thu.' (7) 'Tha mi a' tionndadh air cuibhle.' (8) (A) 'A Lesbia, a bha cho dìreach ris a' bheithe' (B) 'Chunna mi sibh uile,' (C) 'Tha na saighdearan a' gabhail seachad' (D) 'Thubhairt mi rium fhìn:' (E) 'A Lesbia, tha an t-isean marbh fo do làmhan' (F) 'Chunna mi an diugh' (G) 'Bha mi smaoineachadh air Scipio as de'

89 'Sreathan Sgriobhte air Oidhche na Bliadhn' Uir, 1967' Published in *Gairm,* 15 (1966/67), 163/64. Seventy lines in nine stanzas of five to sixteen lines. First line: 'An diugh aig ochd bliadhna deug air fhichead'

90 'Supposing' Published in *Lines,* 24 (Smr 1967), 8. Seventeen lines. First line: 'Supposing there were a flower'

91 'The Hypocrite' Published in *Lines,* 25 (Wtr 1967/68), 15-16. Forty two lines in three stanzas of ten to sixteen lines, in couplets. First line: 'How can you live the way you are,'

92 'Two Worlds' Published in *Lsnr,* 78 (July-Dec. 1967), 121. Three rhymed stanzas of five lines and one of four. First line: 'The curtains change from green to silver'

93 'What is Imaginable is Possible' Published in *Poet* (Scottish number; Nov. 1967), 15. Fifty lines in five stanzas of eight to thirteen lines. First line: 'What is imaginable is possible,'

94 'An Deidh a' Bhoma' Published in *Sruth*, 24 July 1968, p. 5. Three stanzas of eight, four and nine lines. First line: 'Ghlas iad anns àm preas'

95 'Dear Sir' Published in *Sctn*, 17 Feb. 1968. Four six-line stanzas. First line: 'Dear Sir, what tires one out is this'

96 'Flowers for MacGonagall' Published in *Akros*, 3, no. 7 (Mar. 1968), 18-19. Seventy-four lines in ten half-rhymed stanzas of two to eighteen lines. First line: 'Pity is not enough'

97 'Not Different' Published in *Sctn*, 5 Oct. 1968. Four seven line stanzas. First line: 'No, you are not different, not really,'

98 'Scotland' Published in *Sc. Int.*, 3 (Aug. 1968), 22. Thirty-six lines. First line: 'The wind hones the stone of Cape Wrath.'

99 'Students' Published in *Sctn*, 17 Feb. 1968. Five four-line stanzas. First line: 'By their white flannels you shall know them,'

100 'Sundays' Published in *Sc. Int.*, 3 (Aug. 1968), 29. Four four-line stanzas. First line: 'The bells ring out.'

101 'The Road to Hospital' Published in *Sctn*, 17 Feb. 1968. Six half-rhymed quatrains. First line: 'Climbing the road to the hospital,'

102 'Artist Manque' Published in *Lines*, 28 (Mar. 1969), 16. Two rhymed five-line stanzas. First line: 'He came huge and singing into the small house'

103 'Early Film Actresses' Published in *Sctn*, 6 Dec. 1969. Fifteen lines. First line: 'How they pose in their warm white furs'

104 'Encounter' Published in *Chirico*, 3 (Mar. 1969), 18. Five rhymed six-line stanzas. First line: 'I descend the stairs to where your children are'

105 'Freud' Published in *Lines*, 29 (June 1969), 14-15. Thirty-three lines, in nine stanzas of one to six lines. First line: 'In spite of the interviewers,'

106 'Garbo' Published in *Sctn*, 6 Dec. 1969. Later appeared in *Scottish Poetry Five* (Edinburgh, [1970]). Eight lines. First line: 'She is walking away from somewhere in her long coat.'

107 'Hector' Published in *Lines*, 29 (June 1969), 10. Twenty-three lines. First line: 'Without hope to set out again and again'

108 'Here' Published in *Form*, 1 (Smr 1969), 15. Eight lines in five stanzas of one to three lines. First line: 'The rain falls without end.'

109 'How Far That Little Candle Throws its Beams' Published in *Lines*, 29 (June 1969), 11. Forty-nine lines in twelve stanzas of one to six lines. First line: 'It is nighttime.'

110 'Napoleon on St Helena' Published in *Lines*, 29 (June 1969), 12-13. Seven four-line stanzas. First line: 'Autumn and the leaves are growing yellow.'

111 'Pain' Published in *Lines*, 29 (June 1969), 3. Three pairs. First line: 'Thorny fish from the rotting rocks.'

112 'Poem' Published in *Lsnr*, 81 (Jan.-June 1969), 88. Seven pairs. First line: 'I consider Scotland's writers'

113 'Rabbits and a Dog' Published in *Lines*, 29 (June 1969), 4. Two stanzas, of nine and ten lines. First line: 'The skinned rabbits have small toad heads'

114 'Russian Poem' Published in *Sctn*, 17 May 1969. Fifteen lines. First line: 'Sonia, Oblomov, Sasha, come in from the garden.'

115 'The Mirror seen from the Bed' Published in *Lines*, 29 (June 1969), 7. Seven quatrains. First line: 'A towel (red) over a white-backed chair.'

116 'The Monster' Published in *Lines*, 29 (June 1969), 4. Two seven-line stanzas. First line: 'The ice breaks.'

117 'The Swan' Published in *Lines*, 28 (Mar. 1969), 14. Four part-rhymed three-line stanzas. First line: 'I stopped today by the loch on my way to visit'

118 'The Visit of the Inspectors' Published in *Lines*, 29 (June 1969), 18-19. Later appeared in *Scottish Satirical Verse*, edited by Edwin Morgan (Manchester: Carcanet, 1980). Sixty-one lines in nine stanzas of two to ten lines. First line: 'The inspectors come to inspect.'

119 'The White Air of March' Published in *Sc. Int.*, 7 (Sept. 1969), 28-34. Sixteen poems of seven to thirty-one lines. First lines: (1) 'This is the land that God gave to Andy Stewart' (2) 'The Cuillins tower' (3) 'Scottish Dance Music.' (4) 'She came one night' (5) 'March, and the sails fly seaward,' (6) 'Sundays.' (7) '(I speak now of those who told the truth.)' (8) 'The exiles have departed,' (9) 'There have been so many' (10) 'What, out of this place,' (11) 'They died' (12) 'The tall buses pass by.' (13) 'I speak (with a little water) of the MacMurrows.' (14) 'McGonagall' (15) 'The Cuillins tower high in the air —' (16) 'Excellence!' Republished in *Penguin Modern Poets 21* (1972).

120 'The Witches' Published in *Lines*, 29 (June 1969), 10-11. Six four-line stanzas. First line: '"All hail to you that shalt be king hereafter."'

121 'This is the Time of Darkness' Published in *Sctn*, 30 Aug. 1969. Later appeared in *Scottish Poetry Five* (Edinburgh, [1970]). Three five-line stanzas. First line: 'This is the time of darkness. Everything falls,'

122 'Toothache' Published in *Sctn*, 17 May 1969. Twelve lines. First line: 'Your tooth sings a pure aria of pain.'

123 'Why do I Feel so Guilty?' Published in *Sctn*, 17 May 1969. Seventeen lines. First line: 'Why do I feel so guilty? I have murdered no one.'

124 'A Violinist is Playing' Published in *Sc. Int.*, 10 (May 1970), 17. Thirteen lines in five stanzas of one to five lines. First line: 'A violinist is playing in a desert of stones and thistles.'

125 'Early Films' Published in *Sctn*, 20 June 1970. Later appeared in *Scottish Poetry Six* (Edinburgh, [1972]). Twenty-four lines in four stanzas of four to eight lines. First line: 'From the cinema these voices return,'

126 'For Donald Thomson, on being awarded the O.B.E. for his services to Gaelic' Published in *Sctn*, 4 Apr. 1970. Nineteen-line prose poem. First line: 'To preserve a language is a possible way to spend a life,'

127 'Supporting Actor' Published in *GH*, 31 Jan.1970. Six three-line stanzas. First line: 'You have a minor part. Keep out of the way of the lightning.'

128 'The Thistle' Published in *Sctn*, 20 June 1970. Four five-line stanzas. First line: 'The thistle is what we bow down to.'

129 'This Monotony' Published in *Sc. Int.*, 10 (May 1970), 45. One three-line, and five five-line stanzas. First line: 'This monotony!'

130 'Again and Again' Published in *Sc. Int.*, Sept. 1971, p. 26. Later appeared in New Poems 1972-1973; see E00. Seventeen lines. First line: 'Again and again we are selling everything,'

131 'All Our Grandmothers' Published in *Sctn*, 5 May 1971. Nine lines. First line: 'All our grandmothers, all those shops with bull's eyes,'

132 'Alone' Published in *Spirit*, 38, no. 2 (Smr 1971), 36. Three stanzas of two, three and four lines. First line: 'Sometimes when I'm alone I think of you'

133 'An Cogadh Mor'/'The Great War' Published in *Scotia*, 15 (Mar. 1971), 1. Four five-line stanzas. First line: 'Tha iomaighean a chogaidh mhoir'/'Images of the Great War'

134 'Ann a' Bhail' Ud'/'In That Town' Published in *Scotia*, 14 (Feb. 1971), 4. Four four-line stanzas. First line: 'Anns a' bhail ud'/'In that town'

135 'Annunciation' Published in *Spirit*, 38, no. 2 (Smr 1971), 37. Thirteen lines. First line: 'The angel settled on unshaken grass.'

136 'At Midnight' Published in *Sctn*, 5 June 1971. Nine lines. First line: 'At night I imagine in the park'

137 'At Waverley Station' Published in *Sc. Int.*, Sept. 1971, p. 24. Eighteen lines. First line: 'Alone, my dear, we are nothing, less than nothing.'

138 'Autumn of Experience' Broadcast in 'Autumn Poems', 15 May 1971, Radio Four Scotland. Eight three-line stanzas. First line: 'This is the autumn of experience.' Tape no. TGW 17/SD466S

139 'By Allan Water' Published in *Sctn*, 2 Oct. 1971. Six part-rhymed nine-line stanzas. First line: 'I stand in the morning here by Allan Water'

140 'Dead, of a Child' Broadcast in 'Autumn Poems', 15 May 1971, Radio Four Scotland, prod. Stewart Conn. Four four-line stanzas. First line: 'Dead,' Tape no. TGW 17/SD466S

141 'Girl in the Blitz' Published in *Akros*, 6, no. 16 (Apr. 1971), 59. Two six-line stanzas. First line: 'Easily,'

142 'Hunting for Apples' Broadcast in 'Autumn Poems', 15 May 1971, Radio Four Scotland. First line: 'Hunting for apples' Tape no. TGW 17/SD466S

143 'Poem' Published in *Sc. Int.*, Sept. 1971, p. 28. Ten lines. First line: 'Our lion-emblemed shirts always go down'

144 'Poem' Published in *Sctn*, 5 June 1971. Nine lines. First line: 'I am tired of this blackwheel. I want it to stop.'

145 'Poem' Published in *Spirit*, 38. no. 2 (Smr 1971), 37. Four four-line stanzas. First line: 'Dead'

146 'Scott' Published in *Sctn*, 14 Aug. 1971. Nineteen lines. First line: 'They say that you were kind, that you loved dogs,'

147 'She Goes off to be a Missionary' Broadcast in 'Autumn Poems', 15 May 1971, Radio Four Scotland. Eight three-line stanzas. First line: 'She goes off to be a missionary' Tape no. TGW 17/SD466S

148 'The Old are not Happy' Published in *Spirit*, 38, no. 2 (Smr 1971), 36. Four five-line stanzas. First line: 'The old are not happy'

149 'The Sea' Published in *Akros*, 6, no. 16 (Apr. 1971), 59. Twelve three-line stanzas. First line: 'There was a track we followed through the corn'

150 'At a Railway Station in Wales' Published in *Sc. Int.*, 5, no. 8 (Oct. 1972), 29. Three eight-line stanzas. First line: 'Let me see this station.'

151 'Do Sholzenitsyn' Published in *Gairm*, 20 (1971/72), 315. Five four-line stanzas. First line: 'Tha an samradh air tighinn —'

152 'The Place' Published in *Sc. Int.*, 5, no. 8 (Oct. 1972), 29. Three half-rhymed five-line stanzas. First line: 'You say to me: And this is where Thomas died'

153 'The Poetic Notebooks of Robinson Crusoe' (extract) Published in *Glasgow Rev.*, 3, no. 1 (Smr 1972), 30-32. First line: 'My heart lungs kidneys liver' Published with six other poems, which all appeared in the sequence as finally published.

154 'These Gaelic Songs' Published in *Sctn*, 25 Mar. 1972. Three stanzas of four, five and nine lines. First line: 'These Gaelic songs, how much they tell of us ...'

155 'When You Went Away' Published in *Aquarius*, 5 (1972), 75. Two stanzas of nine and eight lines. First line: 'When you went away I fell asleep'

156 'Busy' Published in *Aquarius*, 6 (Scottish issue, 1973), 24. Five lines. First line: 'Trying to find a minute to do this, do that,'

157 'It Feels Like Spring' Published in *Aquarius*, 6 (Scottish Issue; 1973), 24. Eight lines. First line: 'It feels like spring again.'

158 'It Was Strange to See You' Published in *Antaeus Rev.*, 12 (Wtr 1973), 117. Ten lines. First line: 'It was strange to see you just like Joan of Arc'

159 'Poem': A further excerpt from the recently completed
unpublished 'Poetic Notebooks of Robinson Crusoe' where the
poet explores themes of loneliness, time and language.
Published in *Glasgow Rev.*, 4, no. 1 (Jan/Mar. 1973), 36-37. One
hundred and fifty-two lines in a variety of stanzas. These
poems were omitted from the final sequence. First lines: 'Time
passes' 'I saw a picture' 'Duration' 'I remember a picture' 'The
sea flounces' 'From moment to moment' 'Love comes through
the door' 'The clock begins to sing' 'The whole earth is in
blossom'

160 'Robinson Crusoe' Published in *Gairm*, 22 (1973/74), 33-36.
Sequence of thirty-two three-line poems. First lines: (1) 'Tha an
cuan a' còmhradh ris fhein' (2) 'Tha mi a' cur soitheach-siùil
ann àm botal' (3) 'Tha mo phigheid ag radh:' (4) 'Cruthaich mi
isean de fhiodh.' (5) 'Tha a' phigheid atharraicht bho'n isein.'
(6) 'Chuala mi an t-slige ri mo chluais' (7) 'Tha mo theanga fàs
tioram.' (8) 'Nuair a thig an oidhche' (9) 'Tha an saoghal dubh
gu leir.' (10) 'An cuan gun sgur' (11) 'Crùbagan dubha'
(12) 'Tha mi faicinn' (13) 'O na siùil mhora' (14) 'Nuair a
dhùisgeas mi sa' mhadainn' (15) 'Tha eagal orm' (16) 'Tha a'
phigheid ag radh' (17) 'An raor fhein' (18) 'Ann àm bruadar de
fhiodh' (19) 'Chuala mi e a' seinn' (20) 'Sheinn mi fhìn'
(21) 'Òran do'n fhiodh' (22) 'Òran do na dathan' (23) 'Òran do'n
chuan' (24) 'Òran do'n phigheid' (25) 'Òran do'n ghleoca'
(26) 'Òran do'n ghleoca' (27) 'Òran do'n ghleoca' (28) 'Òran
do'n ghleoca' (29) "nan dreasaichean fiodha' (30) 'Òran do
Dhia —' (31) 'Òran do Dh ia —' (32) 'Coileach derg na maidne'

161 'Saints' Published in *Antaeus*, 12 (Wtr 1973), 119. Ten rhymed
lines. First line: 'How does one know a saint? By the holed
shoes?'

162 'The Carpet' Published in *Aquarius*, 6 (Scottish Issue, 1973), 25.
Five way. First line: 'Today you laid a blue carpet.'

163 'The End of an Era' Published in *Sctn*, 14 July 1973. Nineteen lines. First line: 'The classic detective has been smashed to pieces,' This poem opened his Crime Column that week.

164 'Transparencies' Published in *Sc. Int.*, 6, no. 5 (May/June/ July 1973), 22. Nine poems of four to eleven lines, titled as follows: 'Imagine' 'Sunday A fternoon' 'Breugel' 'Detective Story' 'Come In' 'Storm' 'Old Pot' 'Waitres s' 'Dog' First line: 'Imagine' 'Sunday afternoon' 'Some day' 'Who stole the apple?' 'Come in' ' Storm I love you' 'Old pot' 'Running about' 'Where are you setting off for, Dog? '

165 'Ag innse do'n chloinn' Published in *Gairm*, 22 (1973/74), 323. Twelve lines. First line: 'An diugh innsidh mi dhuibh mu dheidhinn Iosa.'

166 'Aig àm Foghair' Published in *Gairm*, 22 (1973/74), 225. Eight lines. First line: "Sann aig àm foghair a chàidh mi dh'fhaicinn mo dhaoine.'

167 'Air an Eilean Mhuileach' Published in *Gairm*, 22 (1973/74), 225. Eleven lines. First line: 'Nuair' a bhìos an ceilidh seachad'

168 'An t-Eilean Ma Thuath: 'A' Chuthag' Published in *Gairm*, 23 (1974/75), 69. Eight lines. First line: 'Tha e iongantach gun till i tuilleadh'

169 'An t-Eilean Ma Thuath: Air a' Ghàidhealtachd' Published in *Gairm*, 23 (1974/75), 71. Twelve lines. First line: 'Nuair a bhìos mi ann gleanntann na Ghàidhealtachd'

170 'An t-Eilean Ma Thuath: àm Feasgar' Published in *Gairm*, 23 (1974/75), 69. Eight lines. First line: 'Tha àm feasgar ciùin'

171 'An t-Eilean Ma Thuath: An Ceise-ball' Published in *Gairm*, 23 (1974/75), 68. Nine lines. First line: "Se seo an Talamh. Tha sinn ag iarra dh'ar ceise-ball air ais.'

172 'An t-Eilean Ma Thuath: 'An Nochd' Published in *Gairm*, 23 (1974/75), 70. Seven lines. First line: 'An nochd tha thu cluich air a' ghuitar'

173 'An t-Eilean Ma Thuath: 'An t-Eilean' Published in *Gairm*, 23 (1974/75), 70. Nine lines. First line: 'Tha an t-eilean a' snàmh thugann a rithist'

174 'An t-Eilean Ma Thuath: 'An Ubhall' Published in *Gairm*, 23 (1974/75), 69. Five lines. First line: 'Thianig e mach as a' choinneamh'

175 'An t-Eilean Ma Thuath: Brathair mo Mhathair' Published in *Gairm*, 23 (1974/75), 72. Eighteen lines. First line: 'Thubhairt brathair mo mhathair 's e aig an tigh air chuairt:'

176 'An t-Eilean Ma Thuath: 'Dearcagan' Published in *Gairm*, 23 (1974/75), 70. Twelve lines. First line: 'Chruinnich sinn dearcagan air feasgar foghair'

177 'An t-Eilean Ma Thuath: Esan a' Bruidhinn' Published in *Gairm*, 23 (1974/75), 71. Twenty lines. First line: '"Air an oidhche gheamhraidh seo"'

178 'An t-Eilean Ma Thuath: Feasgar' Published in *Gairm*, 23 (1974/75), 68. Nine lines. First line: 'Thàinig an cu chun an doruis.'

179 'An t-Eilean Ma Thuath: Obair' Published in *Gairm*, 23 (1974/75), 68-69. Two six-line stanzas. First line: 'Nuair a bhiodh daoine aig an obair fhein'

180 'Da Rathad' Published in *Gairm*, 22 (1973/74), 226. Eleven lines. First line: 'Ghabh mis' aon rathad' Published with a translation in *International Poetry Review*, 5, no. 1 (Celtic Issue; Spr., 1979), 54-55.

181 'Esan' Published in *Gairm*, 22 (1973/74), 322-23. Twelve lines. First line: 'Bliadhnachan ann an Canada'

182 'Fictional Autumn' Published in *Sctn*, 22 June 1974. Five five-line stanzas. First line: 'Even the clouds are fictional, even'

183 'News for Pilate' Published in *Sctn*, 22 June 1974. Eight stanzas of five lines and one of ten. First line: 'No, really, you can't go back to'

184 'Rìoghachdan' Published in *Gairm*, 23 (1974/75), 231-32.
     Sequence of fourteen two and three-line poems. First lines:
     (1) 'Isean a' seinn anns a' chamhanaich' (2) 'Isean dealbht air
     vase.' (3) 'Cuthag ag eirigh as an sgoth' (4) 'Iolaire' (5) 'Tha an
     iolaire a' dol air thoiseach,' (6) 'Sheall an da arm suas' (7) 'Ged
     nach gabh seabhag air iolaire' (8) 'Rìogachd.' (9) 'A-mach as a'
     cheò' (10) 'A bheil isean ann' (11) 'A bheil isean ann' (12) 'A
     bheil seabhag ann' (13) 'Tha an aon duine a' gal anns gach blàr.'
     (14) 'A righ a righ'

185 'Steòrnabhagh' Published in *Gairm*, 22 (1973/74), 225. Seven
     lines. First line: 'Air sràid Steòrnabhaigh air latha na Sàbaid'

186 'Tha Bingo Anns an tigh-dhealbh' Published in *Gairm*, 22
     (1973/74), 226. Eight lines. First line: 'Tha Bingo anns an
     tigh-dhealbh'

187 'An teid thu leam, a Mhairi'/'Will you go with me, Mary'
     Published in *GH*, 11 Oct. 1975. Four three-line stanzas, with
     prose translation. First line: 'An teid thu leam, a Mhairi'/'Will
     you go with me, Mary'

188 'Art' Published in *Prospice*, 20. Nineteen lines. First line: 'Art,'

189 'At the Seaside' Published in *Lines*, 54 (Sept. 1975), 23-29. Sections
     5 and 7 later appeared in *Scottish Poetry Nine* (Manchester,
     1976). Sequence of seven poems, from sixteen to forty lines.
     Only the sixth, 'At the Spiritualist Meeting', is separately titled.
     First lines: (1) 'Evening again and the pink lights are on.'
     (2) 'Let's not read the Sunday Papers,' (3) 'The Salvation Army
     welcomes you' (4) 'Jesus saves, Jesus saves.' (5) 'The gulls
     scream outside the window' (6) 'I seem to see a field' (7) 'In the
     Victorian Music Hall'

190 'Beethoven' Published in *Lit. Rev.*, 18, no. 3 (Spr. 1975), 333.
     Thirteen lines. First line: '"I love trees better than men," he said'

191 'Christmas Poem' Published in *GH*, 24 Dec. 1975. Six quatrains.
     First line: 'It is as usual: the star was in the sky'

192 'For L.' Published in *Lit. Rev.*, 18, no. 3 (Spr. 1975), 334. Six lines. First line: 'I loved you then playing your guitar.'

193 'Goddess of Change' Published in *Sc. Rev.*, 1 (1, no. 1: Wtr 1975), 16. Thirty-five lines. First line: 'Goddess of change, you are the commonest.'

194 'Honesty' Published in *Sctn*, 18 Jan.1975. Sixteen lines. First line: 'Sometimes when I hear your voice so clear again,'

195 'Let it Not End' Published in *Sctn*, 18 Jan.1975. Sixteen lines. First line: 'Let it not end. Let not that be possible.'

196 'Napoleon' Published in *Gairm*, 23 (1974/75), 360-62. Sequence of twenty-six three-line poems. First lines: (1) 'Ruisia' (2) 'Dh'fhairich e an reul ga fhàgail' (3) 'O na làithean gorma' (4) 'Càit na robh na brataich?' (5) 'Josephine' (6) 'Na sgàthanan' (7) 'An caisteal' (8) 'Fuachd Ruisia' (9) 'Daoine crochte' (10) 'Bha an saoghal a' teannacha' (11) 'Tchaikowsky.' (12) '"A' Fàgail Mhoscow ..."' (13) 'Each geal' (14) 'Each geal' (15) 'An rionnag a' derrsadh,' (16) 'Aodach flagach,' (17) 'A chorp trom' (18) 'An deigh a' briseadh,' (19) 'Rionnag an fhoghair,' (20) 'Sneach geal,' (21) 'A' ghaoth a' seideadh' (22) 'Gealach ùr ag eirigh' (23) 'A' ghealach ùr ag iarraidh' (24) 'Spiorad nan Ruiseanach' (25) 'Trompaidean' (26) 'Air feadh nan steppes'

197 'Neptune' Published in *Sctn*, 18 Jan. 1975. Six half-rhymed six-line stanzas. First line: 'Neptune, with your bony trident,'

198 'Poets' Published in *Sctn*, 14 June 1975. Four stanzas of two and three lines alternating. First line: 'Our poets appear above the water,'

199 'Reading Tacitus' Published in *Lit. Rev.*, 18, no. 3 (Spr. 1975), 333-34. Twenty-three lines. First line: 'Evil's a running sore that will not heal.'

200 'Still Life' Published in *GH*, 11 Oct. 1975. Five pairs, with prose translation. First line: 'Chaidh mi steach do rùm. '/'I went into a room.'

201 'The Exile' Published in *Akros*, 9, no. 27 (Apr. 1975), 83-84. One hundred and one lines. First line: 'Flown back from Canada to my house again,'

202 'The Island' Published in *Prospice*, 20 [n.d.]. Nine lines. First line: 'Everywhere I go'

203 'The Music' Published in *Prospice*, 20 [n.d.]. Three three-line stanzas. First line: 'Something I wish to tell you. It's not the content,'

204 'The Saying' Published in *Sctn*, 18 Jan.1975. Thirteen lines. First line: 'Tonight when I think of what you used to say,'

205 'At Ely Cathedral' Published in *Poetry Now*; broadcast on Radio Three, 24 Oct. 1976. Thirty-one lines. First line: 'Shaved grass beneath my hand'

206 'Botticelli's Primavera' Published in *Chmn*, 4, no. 3 (1976), 28. Twelve lines. First line: 'The Graces with brown curly hair'

207 'Bràthair Mo Mhathair'/'My Mother's Brother' Published in *Akros*, 11, no. 31 (Aug. 1976), 9. Eighteen lines. First line: 'Thubhairt bràthair mo mhathair 's e aig an tigh air chuart:'/'My mother's brother said when he was home on a visit:'

208 'Chair' Published in *Stand*, 17, no. 3 (1976), 43. Twenty-three lines in seven stanzas. First line: 'Chair, you are here.'

209 'Detail from the Triumph of Death by Breughel' Published in *Chmn*, 4, no. 3 (1976), 27. Eight half-rhymed pairs. First line: 'A skeleton horse droops forward. On it sits'

210 'Detail from the Triumph of Death by Breughel' Published in *Chmn*, 4, no. 3 (1976), 27. Ten half-rhymed pairs. First line: 'On the table with white table cloth there lies'

211 '"Don Quixote" by Daumier' Published in *Chmn*, 4, no. 3 (1976), 29. Seven lines. First line: 'On a ghostly roan'

212 'Goya' Published in *Chmn*, 4, no. 3 (1976), 28. Seven half-rhymed pairs. First line: 'The doll-like royal family looks out'

213 'Morality Play in Cambridge in the Open Air' Published in *Poetry Now*; broadcast on Radio Three, 24 Oct. 1976. Eight half-rhymed pairs. First line: 'We hear the devils hiss among the trees,'

214 'Mother' Published in *Stand*, 17, no. 3 (1976), 43. Seven three-line stanzas. First line: 'Mother, what is happening to your boy?'

215 'Poem' Published in *Sctn*, 23 Oct. 1976. Seven rhymed three-line stanzas, closed by a pair. First line: 'Tremblingly, they say, life came.'

216 'Poems about Canada' [Editor's title?] Published in *Sctn*, 28 Feb. 1976. Ten poems of eight to eighteen lines. Five are titled: (1) 'Going Over' (3) 'Canada' (4) 'Early Morning' (5) 'In Church' (10) 'Canada'. First lines: (1) 'After the film, the Glasgow-Irish play' (2) 'Down Oak Street the cars restlessly shift lanes' (3) 'I do not imagine death here nor the mind' (4) 'The sadness of early morning even here.' (5) 'The turkey-necked elder takes a bow' (6) 'A large picture of Burns on the lounge wall' (7) 'The moon low over Vancouver. In Elizabeth Park' (8) 'With my allowance I bring an aged eye' (9) 'Death isn't found here among these' (10) 'Maybe without history — who knows? —'

217 'Tha na làithean a' dol seachad' Published in *Crann*, Jan. 1976, p. 4. Twelve lines in four stanzas of two to four lines. First line: 'Tha na làithean a' dol seachad gun sgur,'

218 '"The Tiger" by Frank Marc' Published in *Chmn*, 15 (4, no. 3: 1976), 29. Five pairs. First line: 'The tiger curls among cubes'

219 '"There is going to be another Ice Age" — Robert Ardrey' Published in *Sctn*, 23 Oct. 1976. Seven half-rhymed quatrains. First line: 'Difficult to believe in a new Ice Age'

220 'Young Poet' Published in *Poetry and Audience*, 8, no. 4 (28 Oct. 1960), 6. Later appeared in *Twenty-one Years of Poetry and Audience*, ed. Tom Wharton and Wayne Brown, p. 35 (Breakish,

Isle of Skye: The Aquila Publishing Co. Ltd, 1976). Five rhymed four-line stanzas. First line: 'He scribbled at a green oilskinned table.'

221 'A' Chuibhle'/'The Wheel' Published in *Sc. Rev.*, 6 (2, no. 6; Spr. 1977), 9. Eleven lines in four stanzas of two and three lines, with verse translation. First line: 'Tha a' chuibhl' a tionndadh,'/'The wheel is turning,'

222 'A' Dìreadh 's a Dìreadh'/'Climbing and Climbing' Published in *Sc. Rev.*, 6 (2, no. 6: Spr. 1977), 10. One three-line and two four-line stanzas, with verse translation. First line: 'A' dìreadh 's a dìreadh'/'Climbing and climbing'

223 'As Rilke ...' Published in *Sctn*, 9 Apr. 1977. Ten lines. First line: 'Vast sorrows remember us. Vast autumns.'

224 'Dante' Published in *Sctn*, 17 Sept. 1977. Five triplets. First line: 'Dante fixed his enemies once for all,'

225 'Fairy Stories' Published in *Sctn*, 9 Apr. 1977. Nineteen lines in three stanzas of four to eight lines. First line: 'When religion dies fairy stories come into their own.'

226 'Godmother' Published in *Sctn*, 17 Sept. 1977. Eight three-line stanzas. First line: 'Godmother at the door'

227 'Helensburgh Revisited' Published in *Sctn*, 17 Sept. 1977; and *Beacon*, 93 (Nov 1977), 4 (magazine of the Free High Church, Dumbarton). Five three-line stanzas. First line: 'In this town I am again reminded of you —'

228 'Leaving' Published in *Sctn*, 17 Sept. 1977. Seven rhymed pairs. First line: 'When she left, the roses were all in bloom.'

229 'Nuair a bhìos mi leughadh'/'When I am reading' Published in *Sc. Rev.*, 6 (2, no. 6: Spr. 1977), 8. Five four-line stanzas, with a verse translation. First line: 'Nuair a bhìos mi leughadh'/'When I am reading'

230 'Tha mi sealltainn riut'/'I am looking at you' Published in *Sc. Rev.*, 8 (Wtr 1977), 36-37. Eighteen lines in seven stanzas of one

to four lines. With verse translation. First line: 'Tha mi
sealltainn riut.'/'I am looking at you.'

231 'The Abyss' Published in *Chmn*, 18 (5, no. 1: Smr 1977), 40. Six
four-line stanzas. First line: 'The abyss sits by itself'

232 'The Spirit of Kindliness' (extract), translated from the author's
Gaelic by Derick Thomson. Published in *Poetry Australia*, 63
(May 1977), 59-60. Six eight-line stanzas. First line: '... They
handed me over to the scribes' '... O tremble midst your
pleasures,'

233 'A Ghealaich'/'Moon' Published in *Sc. Rev.*, 12 (1978), 23.
Fourteen lines, with verse translation. First line: 'A
ghealaich,'/'Moon,'

234 'Aig Deireadh Mo Latha'/'At the End of My Days' Published in
Sc. Rev., 10 (1978), 8. Two three-line and two four-line stanzas,
with verse translation. First line: 'Aig deireadh mo latha'/'At
the end of my days'

235 'Am Bard' Published in *Crann*, Feb. 1978, p. 45. Eleven lines in
two stanzas. First line: 'Tha àm bard a' dannsa'

236 'Baird' Published in *Crann*, Feb. 1978, p. 45. Ten lines in four two
and four-line stanzas. First line: 'Tha Iain Lom 'na sheasamh air
cnoc'

237 'Child' Published in *Poets and Peasants* (1978). Thirty lines in
twelve stanzas of one to three lines. First line: 'From the desert
of newsprint, the open mouth condemns.'

238 'Child Why are You Crying?' Published in *Resurgence*, 9, no. 3
(July-Aug 1978), 19. Two quatrains. First line: 'Child why are
you crying. Have they said'

239 'Coisichidh Sinn'/'We Will Walk' Published in *Sc. Rev.*, 11 (1978),
30. Four pairs, with verse translation. First line: 'Coisichidh sinn
eadar da rann,'/'We will walk between two verses'

240 'From the Train' Published in *Resurgence*, 9, no. 3 (July-Aug 1978), 23. Sixteen lines. First line: 'As the train is almost entering Glasgow Station'

241 'Grace is a Field' Published in *Sctn*, 25 Nov. 1978. Seven quatrains. First line: 'Grace is a field of buttercups in the sun'

242 'In Church' Published in *Sctn*, 4 Nov. 1978. Seven rhymed pairs. First line: 'The minister paces in his cage'

243 'In the Library' (extracts') Published in *P. Rev.*, 68, no. 3 (Sept. 1978), 6-7. Two poems, of twenty-seven and nineteen lines. First lines: (1) 'If there should come' (2) 'Dear mother,'

244 'Like You, Horace' Published in *NER*, 43 (Aut. 1978), 25. Twenty-eight rhymed lines. First line: 'Like you, Horace, it would be very pleasant'

245 'My Companions' Published in *Sctn*, 25 Nov. 1978. Two eight-line stanzas. First line: 'Here my head is as thick as a block of salt.'

246 'Sunday Evening, Union Street' Published in *Northern Light* (1978), 7. Fourteen part-rhymed lines. First line: 'The linked and squealing girls on Union St.'

247 'Teacher' Published in *NER*, 43 (Aut. 1978), 25. Two stanzas of three lines and one of six. First line: 'All the children pass in front of her eyes.'

248 'Thoir Dhomh do Lamh' Published in *Sctn*, 7 Oct. 1978. Nine lines. First line: 'Thoir dhomh do lamh. Tha an cuan stoirmeil an diugh.'

249 'A Speech by Pericles' Published in *Sctn*, 18 Mar. 1978. Ten five-line stanzas. First line: '"What then?" said Pericles, "do you wish to do?"'

250 [untitled] Published in *Bananas*, 17 (Aut. 1979), 52. Fifteen lines. First line: 'Ill, dying, he goes for long walks.'

251 'Autumn Poem' Published in *Sctn*, 3 Mar. 1979. Twenty-two lines. First line: 'Today it is raining,'

252 'Four Lewis Poems' Published in *Aquarius*, 11 (1979), 58-59. Four poems of nine to eighteen lines. First lines: (1) 'Yesterday I stood near you,' (2) 'The sky is a churn' (3) 'Going to school the sky was a blink of blue' (4) 'You are saying grace'

253 'In the Castle' Published in *Sc. Rev.*, 14 (May 1979), 28-29. Twelve half-rhymed quatrains. First line: 'A black marble clock is ticking'

254 'In the Graveyard' Published in *Chmn*, 25 (6, no. 1: Aut. 1979), 25. Twenty-one lines. First line: 'In the graveyard'

255 'Incident' Published in *Sctn*, 29 Sept. 1979. Twelve lines in five stanzas of one to four lines. First line: '"I'll kill him," so he says, "next time we meet,"'

256 'Old Characters' Published in *Chmn*, 6, no. 1 (Aut. 1979), 24. Thirteen lines. First line: 'Where are all the "characters"'

257 'On seeing a Russian version of Richard III at the Edinburgh Festival' Published in *Sctn*, 29 Sept. 1979. Nine pairs. First line: 'Power is amazing theatre'

258 'On Watching Wimbledon' Published in *Sctn*, 29 Sept. 1979. Six triplets. First line: 'He raises his racket, crashes his service down.'

259 'The Lesson' Published in *Tablet*, 22-29 Dec. 1979, p. 1260. Sixteen lines in four stanzas of three to six lines. First line: 'Such bores they are — his operation, her'

260 'The Voices of the Children' Published in *Scrivener*, (1979). Two stanzas, of two and ten lines. First line: '"Today," they say, "we played magic."'

261 'Tragedy' Published in *Sctn*, 3 Mar. 1979. Sequence of three poems, one of thirteen and two of twelve lines. First lines: (1) 'During a tragedy the clouds pass slowly' (2) 'The wind blows mournfully in the chimney' (3) 'The swing doors of Tragedy are exits and entrances.'

262 'After the Storm' Published in *Words*, 7, p. 13. Ten lines. First line:
'It is calm today after the storm.'

263 'All Those Nights' Published in *New Poetry*, 51/52 (final issue;
Wtr 1980/81), 38. Four half-rhymed three-line stanzas. First
line: 'All those nights in the cinema long ago,'

264 'Between Aberdeen and Elgin' Published in *New Poetry*, 51/52
(final issue; Wtr 1980/81), 37. Two four-line stanzas. First line:
'Square green fields, seagulls, grey sheep,'

265 'Coronary' Published in *Stand*, 22, no. 3 (1980/81), 23. Fourteen
lines. First line: 'Where did this tremor come from?'

266 'For Peter Leaving for the RAF' Published in *Lsnr*, 104 (July-Dec
1980), 701. Five half-rhymed six-line stanzas. First line:
'Standing on the platform as you leave'

267 'In Autumn' Published in *Words*, 7, p. 13. Thirteen lines. First
line: 'Just now walking the street I saw an old woman'

268 'Lear' Published in *Sctn*, 16 Feb. 1980. Sixteen lines. First line:
'The holy fool snaps at the heels of Lear,'

269 'Napoleon' Published in *Logos*, 7/8, p. 24. Twenty-one lines. First
line: 'Since today no valet called for me and there are no letters'

270 'Shylock' Published in *Sctn*, 16 Feb. 1980. Four stanzas of three
lines and one of six. First line: 'Shylock on you in the house of
grey ledgers'

271 'The Alien' Published in *Lit. Rev.*, 13 (4-17 Apr. 1980), on back
cover. Seventeen lines in five stanzas of three and four lines.
First line: 'It comes out of the winds of space into the space
ship.'

272 'The Church' Published in *Stand*, 22, no. 3 (1980/81), 23. Ten
lines. First line: 'The church faces me with haggard windows'

273 'The Forest of Arden' Published in *Sctn*, 16 Feb. 1980. Five
three-line stanzas. First line: 'Forest of Arden, you outlast
everything,'

274 'The Journey' Published in *New Poetry*, 48 (Spr. 1980), 12. Four
three-line stanzas. First line: '"If it were not so we would not
have told you."' Published as 'Poem' in *Words,* 10, p. 30; and see
also 'If It Were Not So' in *Sctn*, 11 Dec. 1982 (C305).

275 'The Spider' Published in *Words*, 7, p. 13. Twenty-three lines.
First line: 'The spider's at the centre of his web'

276 'This Generation' Published in *New Poetry*, 51/52 (final issue: Wtr
1980/81), 38. Six pairs. First line: '"This generation ... how
dazzlingly selfish they are,"'

277 'Those Schooldays' Published in *Cenc.,* 4 (Wtr 1980/81), 4.
Seventeen lines. First line: 'Sometimes they come back to me,
those schooldays,'

278 'Toileachas'/'Happiness' Published in *Sc. Rev.*, 17 (Feb. 1980), 7.
Two stanzas of four lines and five, with verse translation. First
line: 'Toileachas gun chrioch'/'Happiness without end'

279 'Travelling on the Train' Published in *Cenc.*, 4 (Wtr 1980/ 81), 4.
Sixteen lines. First line: 'The sun is setting over
Dumbartonshire'

280 'A Bare Art' Published in *Sctn*, 17 Jan.1981. Eight pairs. First line:
'There is a bare severe art that I am searching for'

281 'A Meditation on Gaelic' (dedicated to Donald Thomson, who
died in in July 1980). Published in *Chmn*, 30 (6, no. 1: Smr 1981),
44-50; a 'Scottish Long Poem Issue'. A sequence of fifty-three
poems, of eight to thirty lines, written mainly in three-line
stanzas. First lines: (1) 'When you died it was as if a lighthouse
had gone out,' (2) 'Sunlight so bright this morning, a new
language' (3) 'Nothing dies, not even a language dies.' (4) 'The
cows are munching buttercups. In the bay' (5) 'The language of
the psalms, the embroidering grace notes,' (6) 'Bare-legged you
ran to school, the iron bell' (7) 'When the boat sails, butting the
Atlantic,' (8) 'What is a language? It is the shadows cast'
(9) 'The minister stands out black against the void,' (10) 'The
old lady lies in her bed. She is weeping.' (11) 'The wrinkled

ribbon in the typewriter.' (12) 'Lying silent at the crossroads
here,' (13) 'Look out to sea, sun's language on the bay,'
(14) 'Death has its pure and formal ceremony.' (15) 'What are
we without language? We are exiles.' (16) 'Internal refugees on
narrowing roads ... ' (17) 'Boulders and rocks of Harris in the
rain,' (18) 'Dizzied I stand among the varying objects,'
(19) 'Some sailed to Glasgow, some to Canada.' (20) 'You give
the old names to the new places,' (21) 'He has his language
too ... There were the others,' (22) 'Railroads and camps and
farms ... tramps of this nothing,' (23) 'My thoughts are greened
by the green waving grass,' (24) 'The dancers of the night, those
luminous ghosts ...' (25) 'What language should we use to talk
of this' (26) 'Always I come back to you. Who are you?'
(27) 'When did I know you, of your wanderings' (28) 'Not as in
a painting, but fixed here' (29) 'There were for instance the tall
dandyish lairds' (30) 'As who is writing from Australia,'
(31) '"More than my mother I loved you." The masts tilt'
(32) 'Exile hurt our language, hurt our poetry' (33) '"The gallant
heroes". For whom, then, did you fight?' (34) 'Language, a
language ... is there a consonance' (35) 'A real language in a real
place' (36) '"More than my mother I loved you". Yet history is'
(37) 'Lacking a past, lacking a future, both,' (38) 'To stand in the
present, in the necessary' (39) 'This is not a metal warfare, nor'
(40) 'His love, his death, the mouth's last whispered words'
(41) 'The languages of summer, lupins, hay,' (42) 'Even in rain,
though, you can be yourself,' (43) 'You have much less than this
other country has, ' (44) 'Assuming the burnt thatch, the
sheeplike rocks,' (45) 'For the cormorant that sinks is seen to
rise,' (46) 'Transform them, imagination, these smooth lochs'
(47) 'Donald, the lighthouse winks on and off,' (48) '"To be as
exiles in our own land".' (49) 'The island vanishes, becomes our
sad' (50) 'Mother, you lived in Glasgow, you were one' (51) 'I
keep these meditations with old bones' (52) 'And you my uncle
in Columbia' (53) 'I keep my rendezvous with you my friends'

282 'Am Fear a Dh'fhàg a Duthaich'/'The Man Who Left His Country' Published in *An Teachdaire Gàidhealach*, 10 (Dec. 1981), 3. Published with a verse transalation.

283 'Beginnings' Published in *Words*, 10, p. 30. Fourteen lines. First line: '"Absent thee from felicity awhile ..."'

284 'Calvin and the South' Published in *Sctn*, 17 Jan.1981. Unrhymed sonnet. First line: 'Cockatoos and pheasants, how you burst on my Calvinist mind'

285 'Edinburgh' Published in *Sc. Rev.*, 21 (Feb. 1981), 3. Sixteen lines. First line: 'This city bothers me, it being so old,'

286 'Fairy Stories' Published in *Lines*, 78 (Sept. 1981), 23-24. Five three-line stanzas. First line: 'The fairy stories'

287 'For Wordsworth, written in Australia' Published in *Sctn*, 17 Jan.1981. Five three-line stanzas. First line: 'Your strength, I think, is where you found it strange,'

288 'Glasgow' Published in *Sc. Rev.*, 21 (Feb. 1981), 3. Twenty lines. First line: 'City made of dirty bricks and smoke'

289 'Goodbye to You' Published in *Words*, 10, p. 30. Twenty-nine lines. First line: 'Goodbye to you, lawyers, accountants, bankers.'

290 'In the Town' Published in *Lsnr*, 105 (Jan-June 1981), 352. Five half-rhymed six-line stanzas. First line: 'Twenty years I've lived in this town.'

291 'Na Seòladairean' Published in *Gairm*, 1980/81, p. 160. Eight lines. First line: 'Sheòl iad a-steach do m'bhroilleach'

292 'On This Autumn Day' Published in *NER*, 55 (Aug. 1981), 29. Fifteen lines in four stanzas of one to six lines. First line: 'On this autumn day — all days — you are alone.'

293 'Reminder' Published in *Lsnr*, 106 (July-Dec 1981), 620. Seven three-line stanzas. First line: 'Today, receiving a letter from a friend'

294 'Sometimes' Published in *Lines,* 78 (Sept. 1981), 25. Ten lines in three and four-line stanzas. First line: 'Sometimes I hear you running towards the house'

295 'The Dream' Published in *Lines,* 78 (Sept. 1981), 25-26. Twenty-seven lines in three and four-line stanzas. First line: 'Last night I dreamed'

296 'The Poet' Published in *Sc. Rev.,* 21 (Feb. 1981), 45. Eight lines. half-rhymed. First line: 'There was a poet I knew who wrote of love,'

297 'Things' Published in *NER,* 54 (May 1981), 12. Ten lines. First line: 'Things take the touch of our hands,'

298 'Those Others' Published in *PN Rev.,* 24 (8, no. 4: Autummn 1981), 44. Seven three-line stanzas. First line: 'How can they survive the days,'

299 'We Twa Hae Paddilt' Published in *Lines,* 78 (Sept. 1981), 24. Three four-line stanzas. First line: 'River, I see my legs'

300 'At the Dingle Peninsula, Ireland' Published in *Lines,* 81 (June 1982), 19-20. Five three-line stanzas. First line: 'Such silence in the west, such sharp mountains.'

301 'Dain' Published in *Gairm,* 1981/82, p. 216-18. Sequence of five poems, of eight to twenty lines. First lines: (1) 'Nuair a dh'fhosgail mi an doras' (2) 'Sheas sinn aig a' chidhe' (3) 'Tha an buisaichean a' dol seachad,' (4) 'Innsidh mi seo dhut' (5) 'Air latha foghair'

302 'Fear' Published in *Lines,* 81 (June 1982), 21. Seven three-line stanzas. First line: 'It is a kind of exile I suppose'

303 'Her Story' Published in *Lsnr,* 107 (Jan-June 1982), 24. Four half-rhymed quatrains. First line: 'Garrulous from loneliness she stops me, says:'

304 'If in this Summer' Published in *Akros,* 17, no. 50 (Oct. 1982), 47. Five three-line stanzas. First line: 'If in this summer'

305 'If It Were Not So' Published in *Sctn*, 11 Dec. 1982. Sixteen lines in five stanzas of two to five lines. First line: 'If it were not so I would not have told you'

306 'In Those Days' Published in *P. Rev.*, 72, no. 2 (June 1982), 39; and *Echo Room*, 5 (Smr 1986), 3. Later appeared in *Pen New Poetry 1* ed. Robert Nye (1986). Sixteen lines. First line: 'In those days that are called free'

307 'Incident' Published in *Sc. Rev.*, 27 (Aug. 1982), 43. Two quatrains. First line: 'As we sit in the theatre a tall cloaked man'

308 'Journey' Published in *Sctn*, 31 Dec. 1982. Seven three-line stanzs. First line: 'Winding through Scotland'

309 'Karl Marx' Published in *Sctn*, 25 Sept. 1982. Eleven lines in four stanzas of two and three lines. First line: 'The ghostly superstucture reared up in front of you' Revised slightly as 'Marx', published in *Sctn*, 1 Oct. 1983.

310 'Lightning, Thunder' Published in *Sctn*, 11 Dec. 1982. Four four-line stanzas. First line: 'Lightning, thunder,'

311 'Poem' Published in *P. Rev.*, 72, no. 2 (June 1982), 39. Four three-line stanzas. First line: 'Stupidly we stared down at our own heads'

312 'Teachers' Published in *Sctn*, 25 Sept. 1982. Eleven lines. First line: 'I have met old teachers in strange places.' Re-printed as 'Old Teachers' in *Sctn*, 1 Oct. 1983.

313 'The Storm' Published in *Lines*, 81 (June 1982), 20-21. Seven three-line stanzas. First line: 'The storm peeled the slates from our roofs,'

314 'The Teacher' Published in *Lines*, 81 (June 1982), 20. Twelve lines in two and three-line stanzas. First line: 'He has taught for forty-three years.'

315 'Ulysses' Published in *TLS*, 6 Aug. 1982, p. 852. Five three-line stanzas. First line: 'After your salt adventures to come home,'

316 'Cleaning Out' Published in *Cenc.*, 12 (Spr. 1983), 27. Eleven three-line and two two-line stanzas. First line: 'All that day we cleaned out the shed'

317 'Exile' Published in *Sctn*, 5 Nov. 1983. Twenty-four lines. First line: 'Writing'

318 'Father and Son' Published in *Lsnr*, 109 (Jan-Apr. 1983), 31. Five five-line stanzas. First line: 'Listening to his son being witty, bright,'

319 'Hector of the Battles' Published in *Cenc.*, 14 (Aut. 1983), 32-38. Nine hundred line epic poem about Hector Macdonald. Based on the Gaelic biography *Eachunn nan Cath*, by Allan Fraser (Glasgow: *Gairm*, 1979).

320 'My Land' Published in *Chmn*, 7, no. 5/6 (July 1983), 49. Later appeared in Published with three others in *Sctn*, 18 May 1985. Sonnet. First line: 'My land I wished so violently to leave'

321 'People' Published in *Sctn*, 5 Nov. 1983. Fifteen lines. First line: 'They climb'

322 'Sea and Land' Published in *Cenc.*, 12 (Spr. 1983), 27. Four half-rhymed quatrains. First line: 'Cutting away the fern with a blunt sickle'

323 'Spring' Published in *Sctn*, 1 Oct. 1983. Six three-line stanzas. First line: 'This is the time for the teachers'

324 'The Loved Place' Published in *Malahat Rev.*, 64 (Fall483), 208. Three quatrains. First line: 'Strange to see a place we once have known'

325 'The Meeting' Published in *Sctn*, 5 Nov. 1983. Eighteen lines. First line: 'You return to this town and you call on me.'

326 'The Old Lady' Published in *Chmn*, 7, no. 5/6 (July 1983), 50. Nineteen lines. First line: 'The old lady walks through the field with a basket of wild raspberries.'

327 'There are Those' Published in *North*, 1 (Wtr 1983/84), 14.
Seventeen lines in eight stanzas of two to three lines. First line:
'There are those who live from day to day,'

328 'Through the Leaves' Published in *Sctn*, 5 Nov. 1983. Five
three-line stanzas. First line: 'Running through the leaves we
are not the leaves.'

329 'To Glasgow' Published in *Chmn*, 7, no. 5/6 (July 1983), 49.
Thirty-three lines. First line: 'I look out as the rails'

330 'Autumn' Published in *Lsnr*, 5 Jan.1984, p. 34. Thirty-three lines
in nine stanzas of two to four lines. First line: 'Now it is the first
ice of autumn'

331 'Consider the Lilies' Published in *Sctn*, 15 Dec. 1984. Five
three-line stanzas. First line: 'Consider the lilies how they grow.'

332 'Drunk' Published in *Verse*, 1 (1984), 13. Five three-line stanzas.
First line: 'When he gets drunk he sings Irish songs'

333 'In the Garden' Published in *Sctn*, 15 Dec. 1984. Nine lines. First
line: 'I am bitten by the thorns of the roses.' Also published in
Spec., 29 June 1985, p. 28.

334 'In the Russian Novels' Published in *NER*, 65 (Spr. 1984), 5. Seven
pairs. First line: 'In the Russian novels there is much written in
quotation marks,'

335 'Lecture' Published in *P. Rev.*, 74, no. 2 (June 1984), 28. Two
stanzas of ten and sixteen lines. First line: 'Last night'

336 'Listen' Published in *PN Rev.*, 37 (10, no. 5: Feb. 1984), 22. First
line: 'Listen, I have flown through darkness towards joy,'

337 'Love Song' (For Donalda) Published in *Verse*, 1 (1984), 13. Four
half-rhymed quatrains. First line: 'The swart strait'

338 'Man' Published in *P. Rev.*, 74, no. 2 (June 1984), 28-29.
Twenty-nine lines. First line: 'Our brains bulged'

339 'Memory' Published in *Sctn*, 15 Dec. 1984. Later appeared in
Stand, 26, no. 2 (Spr. 1985), 7 as 'Incident'. Sixteen lines. The

version in *Stand* also has sixteen lines, but in stanzas of two and three lines, instead of one to four. First line: 'It was a day of roses.'

340 'My Friends' Published in *Blind Serpent*, 2 (1984). Thirteen lines. First line: 'My friends, I know who you are.'

341 'Old Woman' Published in *Stand*, 26, no. 2 (Spr. 1985), 6-7. Sequence of four poems, of three to five three-line stanzas. First lines: (1) 'All your sap is thickened towards survival. ' (2) 'The sea stings. It is older than you are.' (3) 'The lumpy wooden ones who rose from the dead,' (4) 'To be human is to be a river'

342 'On an Emigration Photograph' Published in *PN Rev.*, 14, no. 4, p. 43. Two stanzas of eighteen lines and eleven. First line: 'Your faces cheerful, though impoverished,'

343 'Poems from an Asylum' Published in *Verse*, 1 (1984), 12. Sequence of three poems, of eight to ten lines. First lines: (1) 'And so you wave goodbye' (2) 'The tree's inside' (3) 'The rain is falling down. Poor Tom, poor Tom!'

344 'Profitable Spring' Published in *Blind Serpent*, 2 (1984). Two stanzas, of nine and ten lines. First line: 'Profitable spring, you return to us'

345 'Schoolgirls' Published in *NER*, 65 (Spr. 1984), 5. Five three-line stanzas. First line: 'In your mauve uniforms you are a bubble of giggles'

346 'Storm' Published in *Sctn*, 17 Mar. 1984. Four quatrains. First line: 'Again today it is raining.'

347 'The Cat' Published in *Clamjamfrie*, 2 (Sept. 1984). Four half-rhymed quatrains. First line: 'The cat is restless tonight. It seeks the moon'

348 'The Letter' Published in *P. Rev.*, 74, no. 2 (June 1984), 28. Twenty-two lines. First line: 'Today'

349 'Yesterday you Cried' Published in *Sctn*, 17 Mar. 1984. Fifteen lines in four stanzas. First line: 'Yesterday you cried'

350 'A' Chailleach' / 'The Old Woman' Published in *Strata*, 5 (Spr. 1985), 10. Eight lines in three stanzas. First line: 'Anns an lios' / 'In the garden'

351 'A' Ghaoth' / 'The Wind' Published in *Chmn*, 42 (8, no. 5: Wtr 1985), 69. Two stanzas of three and four lines. First line: 'Tha cudeigin a' feadalaich' / 'Someone is whistling'

352 'Aberdeen in the Fifties' Published in *Lines*, 94 (Sept. 1985), 5-8. Sequence of six poems, of eight to thirty lines. First lines: (1) 'In the after-the-war years' (2) 'Fish-face lectured on Anglo-Saxon.' (3) 'I said to you' (4) 'In the cafe' (5) 'The trams ran on rails,' (6) 'Ol d men played draughts'

353 'Aiserigh' / 'Resurrection' Published in *Chmn*, 42 (8, no. 5: Wtr 1985), 68-69. Fourteen lines in four stanzas of two to five lines. First line: 'Theab mi basachadh.' / 'I nearly died.'

354 'Àiteamh' / 'Thaw' Published in *Strata*, 5 (Spr. 1985), 9. Three three-line stanzas. First line: 'An diugh tha àiteamh ann.' / 'Today it is thawing.'

355 'Art' Published in *Sctn*, 17 Aug. 1985. Seven pairs. First line: 'Art is decided by those' Reprinted in *Blind Serpent*, 9 (1986), [n.p.].

356 'Doing Well' Published in *Verse*, 3 (1985). Four three-line stanzas. First line: 'The smiling old lady does not die.'

357 'Fad na h-Oidhche' / 'All Night Long' Published in *Chmn*, 42 (8, no. 5: Wtr 1985), 70. Five three-line stanzas. First line: 'Fad na h-oidhche' / 'All night long'

358 'Gach Madainn' / 'Every Morning' Published in *Chmn*, 42 (8, no. 5: Wtr 1985), 69-70. Nine lines in four stanzas of one to three lines. First line: 'Gach madainn' / 'Every morning'

359 'Lewis' Published in *Poetry Australia*, 102 (*Renewing Dialects: new poetry issue*, 1985). Fifty-two lines, in seven stanzas of four to sixteen lines. First line: 'It follows me, that black island without ornament,'

360 'Moment in Aberdeen' Published in *Prospice*, 20. Four three-line stanzas. First line: 'The girl's head is bowed onto his breast.' Re-published in *Alma Mater* (Wtr 1987), 19 as 'Incident on Union Street.

361 'My Desk' Published in *Echo Room*, 1 (Smr 1985), 12. Eight four-line stanzas. First line: 'My desk sparkles among things.'

362 'My Muse' Published in *Sctn*, 18 May 1985. Five three-line stanzas. First line: 'My Muse, I return to you periodically'

363 'Na Feidh' / 'The Deer' Published in *Strata*, 5 (Spr. 1985), 8. Eight lines in three stanzas. First line: 'Cha robh an t-àite a' cordadh rium:' / 'The place didn't please me.'

364 'Poem' Published in *Aristophanes Middle Finger*, 1 [u.d.], 46. Twenty-nine lines in seven stanzas of three to five lines. First line: 'Roger who used to ski in the Swiss mountains'

365 'Reflections on Crofting Life' Published in *Eilean an Fhraoich Annual*, 1985, [n.p.]. Sequence of poems accompanied by period photographs. First lines: 'Cut the earth and leave a wake behind.' 'Humorous spectacled lady in the cart,' 'The clothes must be punished and beaten' 'The immense water that's ahead of us,' 'Knitting, I leave the peatstack with my creel.' 'How young we were' 'One eye almost shut, the other open,' 'Someone said a wheelbarrow. Why not cart?' 'Look what we have, all this fish.' 'Always we are digging on the moor.' 'She seems to conduct them.' 'O what a Russian cabaret' 'Look at me with my experienced eyes.' 'Wild killing waters and abundant foam,'

366 'Sometimes' Published in Official Programme of the Edinburgh Book Festival, 1985, p. 10. Twelve lines in three stanzas of threee and six lines. First line: 'Sometimes in this pitiless age'

367 'The Dead' Published in *Lit. Rev.*, 79 (Jan.1985), 42. Six three-line stanzas. First line: 'On a frosty day the dead are hacking with picks.'

368 'The Drowned' Published in *TLS*, 1 Mar. 1985, p. 220. Six three-line stanzas. First line: 'It is true that the drowned return to us.'

369 'The Poor Relations' Published in Official Programme of the Edinburgh Book Festival, 1985, p. 10. Later appeared in *PEN New Poetry 1* (1986). Nineteen lines. First line: 'Sometimes I remember the poor relations'

370 'The Weeds' Published in Official Programme of the Edinburgh Book Festival, 1985, p. 10. Four three-line stanzas. First line: 'I have built a path through the weeds'

371 'There are Those' Published in *Echo Room*, 1 (Smr 1985), 13. Five three-line stanzas. First line: 'There are those who live in houses of snow' The poem was also published in *Stand*, 27, no. 4 (Aut. 1986), 22.

372 'Towards the Ordinary' Published in *Lit. Rev.*, 79 (Jan. 1985), 10. Six three-line stanzas. First line: 'To climb the ladder towards the ordinary,'

373 'Tutorial' Published in *Sctn*, 18 May 1985. Twenty-five rhymed lines. First line: 'I used to read to the professor in his house.'

374 'Villagers, in the Second World War' Published in *Stand*, 27, no. 4 (Aut. 1986), 22. Later appeared in *PEN New Poetry 1* ed Robert Nye (1986; see Section E. Seven three-line stanzas. First line: 'So many of those I once knew'

375 'Weeds' Published in *Honest Ulsterman*, 79 (Aut. 1985), 34. Four four-line stanzas. First line: 'Weeds everywhere,'

376 'Aberdeen' Published in *Stand*, 27, no. 4 (Aut. 1986), 23. Seven four-line stanzas. First line: 'Sparkling leaves ... I remember Aberdeen,'

377 'After Reading the Speech by the Rev. Angus Smith, Parts of Which were Reported in the *West Highland Free Press*' Published in *WHFP*, 6 June 1986; in response to a front-page report May

1986. Fifty-six lines. First line: 'Lord God, go with them so long as they have the Bible in their hands.'

378 'An Coinneachadh'/'The Meeting' Published in *Spec.*, 26 Apr. 1986. Six three-line stanzas, with verse translation. The final stanza of the translation was accidentally omitted, and published in the next issue. First line: 'Chuir thu do làmhan mu m'amhaich.'/'You put your arms round my neck.'

379 'Autumn' Published in *Spec.*, 18 Oct. 1986, p. 34. Four three-line stanzas. First line: 'Let me read again the autumn newspapers.'

380 'Friends' Published in *Sctn*, 5 July 1986. Four three-line stanzas. First line: 'Profound sky with its millions of stars'

381 'Frost and Snow' Published in *Lines*, 98 (Sept. 1986), 7-8. Three poems of nine to fifteen lines, in three and four line stanzas. First lines: (1) 'The frost' (2) 'White roofs,' (3) 'The snow on the ground'

382 'In Lewis' Published in *Sctn*, 5 July 1986. Thirteen lines, in five stanzas of two and three lines. First line: 'The wind moans'

383 'In the North' Published in *Dream* (1986), [n.p.]. Four three-line stanzas. First line: 'Up there in the north there is a high wind.'

384 'My Last Duchess' Published in *Lines*, 98 (Sept. 1986), 5. Ten three-line stanzas. First line: 'This is my last duchess painted on the wall.'

385 'Poem' Published in *Blind Serpent*, 9 (1986). Seven two-line stanzas. First line: 'Art is decided by those'

386 'Predestination' Published in *Sctn*, 6 July 1986. First line: 'The tram ran on rails'

387 'Repertoire' Published in *Dream* (1986), [n.p.]. Eight lines in three stanzas of two and four lines. First line: 'Repertoire of seasons'

388 'Roman Poems' Published in *New Writing Scotland*, 4 (Aberdeen: ASLS, 1986), 62-68. Sequence of three poems, of forty-eight to eighty-five lines. The first and last, 'The Invasion' and 'The

Atoms', are in rhymed eight-line stanzas; the second, 'Marcus Aurelius Speaks', is in rhymed five-line stanzas. First lines: '"When will the Gauls invade us?"' 'I have to leave insomniac Rome' 'The Lares and Penates by'

389 'Rose' Published in *Sctn*, 5 July 1986. Five pairs. First line: 'Your exclusive shine, rose,'

390 'Snow' Published in *Blind Serpent*, 9 (1986). Sixteen lines in three-line stanzas with one single line. First line: 'The snow'

391 'The Dime Novelettes' Published in *Lsnr*, 14 Aug. 1986, p. 25. Two half-rhymed quatrains. First line: 'Sweet smell of the dime novelettes, the Westerns and Black Mask,'

392 'The Fish Van' Published in *Lsnr*, 3 July 1986, p. 33. Three seven-line half-rhymed stanzas. First line: 'The blue van which sells fish stands at the door.'

393 'The Music' Published in *Dream* (1986), [n.p.]. Three stanzas of three lines and one of four. First line: 'The wind moans'

394 'The Storm' Published in *Lines*, 98 (Sept. 1986), 6-7. Sequence of three poems, of six to seventeen lines. First lines: (1) 'The house rocks in the wind. Maybe we shall die.' (2) 'The lightning touches my hands with blue.' (3) 'After the storm all is quiet.'

395 'Tragedy' Published in *Dream* (1986), [n.p.]. Twelve lines in five stanzas of one to three lines. First line: 'You who slide over the road, remember that tragedy'

396 'Two Seasons' Published in *Dream* (1986), [n.p.]. Two quatrains. First line: 'In summer the world is malleable, as once'

397 'Argyll' Fourteen lines. First line: 'This is the land'. A 'Poster Poem' produced by Book Trust Scotland, 1987. The background to the poem is a reproduction of William McTaggart's 'The Coming of St Columba'.

398 'Autumn Day' Published in *PN Rev.*, 14, no. 4, p. 43. Six three-line stanzas. First line: 'Autumn day of a profound stillness'

399 'Death' Published in *Verse*, 4, no. 2 (June 1987), 4. Thirty lines. First line: 'Death strides freely across the countryside'

400 'Even' Published in *Verse*, 4, no. 2 (June 1987), 3. Four pairs. First line: 'Even the pace of the leaves has accelerated,'

401 'Glance' Published in *Verse*, 4, no. 2 (June 1987), 4. Nine lines. First line: 'She glanced at me over her shoulder like a faun.'

402 'Lear' Published in *Alma Mater*, Spr. 1987, p. 9. Nine rhymed pairs. First line: 'He bore his head of bone like a thin vase.'

403 'Plane and Poet' Published in *Lines*, 100 (Mar. 1987), 45. Three three-line stanzas. First line: 'The hollow sound of a plane in the sky.'

404 'Return to Aberdeen University' Published in *AUR*, 52, no. 1 (Spr. 1987), 97-98. Eighteen rhymed stanzas of three lines and one of two. First line: 'Thirty six years afterwards I return.'

405 'Silence and Speech' Published in *Bad Seed*, 1 (Apr. 1987), 26. Five three-line stanzas. First line: 'There are so many clever people in the universities'

406 'Song of the Married Woman' Published in *Spec.*, 3 Jan. 1987, p. 27. Two six-line stanzas. First line: 'See, the clouds are travelling along towards the sunset,'

407 'Stubble' Published in *Verse*, 4, no. 2 (June 1987), 3. Fourteen lines. First line: 'The corn has been cut,'

408 'The Aesthetic and the Ethical' Published in *PN Rev.*, 14, no. 4 (1987), p. 43. Five three-line stanzas. First line: 'Slowly we are adopted by the words ... slowly we are other.'

409 'The Cry of the Woman' Published in *Gallimaufry*, 14 (1987), 5. Four three-line stanzas. First line: 'No, I do not wish my hair to go gray,'

410 'The English Teacher Remembers' Published in *Lines*, 100 (Mar. 1987), 46. Eight three-line stanzas. First line: 'Across the years'

411   'The First Freshness' Published in *Lines*, 100 (Mar. 1987), 44-45. Five quatrains. First line: 'The first freshness'

412   'The Kitten' Published in *Lines*, 100 (Mar. 1987), 47. Nineteen lines in four stanzas. First line: 'The kitten explores the garden, the house.'

413   'The Local' Published in *Bad Seed*, 1 (Apr. 1987), 26. Twenty-six lines in seven stanzas of three to four lines. First line: 'Tell me about the "local"'

414   'The Poem' Published in *PN Rev.*, 14, no. 4 (1987), 43. Three three-line stanzas. First line: 'If your poem is not a jewel, what is it?'

415   'The Poet' Published in *Gallimaufry*, 14 (1987), 4. Seven lines in four stanzas. First line: 'I have outdistanced the music'

416   'The Rose Tree' Published in *Lines*, 100 (Mar. 1987), 47. Nine lines in three stanzas. First line: 'The rose tree stands upright against the wall.'

417   'The Scholar and the Poet' Published in *Verse*, 4, no. 2 (June 1987), 3. Four lines. First line: 'The scholar sharpens the teeth of the poet.'

418   'The Vase' Published in *Lines*, 100 (Mar. 1987), 44. Two quatrains. First line: 'A night such as we have never known'

419   'Those' Published in *Scratchings*, 7 (Apr. 1987), [n.p.]. Six pairs. First line: 'Those who are given early retirement and the radiant handshake'

D

Introduction

This section like the previous is arranged first chronologically by year, and then alphabetically by title. Unpublished plays as well as stories are listed here.

1   'Mother and Son' Story. Appeared in *Alma Mater*, 60, no. 1 (Spring 1949), 45-48.

2   'Am Bodach' Story. Appeared in *Gairm*, 2 (1953-54), 113-15.

3   'Gammy' Story. Appeared in *An Gaidheal*, 60 (1965), 65.

4   'New Stockings for Young Harold' Story. Appeared in *GH*, 20 August 1960.

5   'An Maor' Story. Appeared in *Gairm*, 10 (1961/62), 41-46. Also appears in *Feoil an Gheimridh*.

6   'The Scream' Story. Appeared in *London Magazine*, o.s. 8, no. 1 (January 1961), 27-31.

7   'Kierkegaard' Story. Appeared in *Gairm*, 11 (1962/63), 103-08.

8   'Turas do 'n Fhiteach' Story. Appeared in *Gairm*, 11 (1962/ 63), 23-37.

9   'Ioseph' Story. Appeared in *Gairm*, 11 (1962/63), 277-79.

10   'A' Chailleach' Story. Appeared in *Gairm*, 12 (1963/64), 169-71.

11   'Facail air Clar' Play. Appeared in *Gairm*, 12 (1963/64), 212-15.

12   'The Angel of Mons' Story. Appeared in *Lines*, 19 (Winter 1963), 16-24.

13   'The Black and the Red' Story. Appeared in *New Saltire*, 7 (March 1963), 42-57.

14   'Incident in the Classroom' Story. Appeared in *GH*, 18 July 1964.

15   'The General' Story. Appeared in *New Saltire*, 11 (April 1964), 16-19.

16   'An t-Iomradh' Story. Appeared in *An Gaidheal*, 60 (1965), 14-15.

17   'An Telegram' Story. Appeared in *An Gaidheal*, 60 (1965), 38-39.

18   'Granny anns a' Chornair' Series of short stories. Appeared in *Gairm*, 14 (1965/66), 161-75. Also appears in *Dorcha Tro Ghlainne*, ed. D. Macleoid (Gairm, 1970).

19   'Air a' Bhus' Story. Appeared in *Gairm*, 14 (1965/66), 237-38.

20 'Maighstir Trill agus Vergil' Story. Appeared in *Gairm*, 14 (1965/66), 68-74.

21 'Anns a' Chafe' Story. Appeared in *Gairm*, 14 (1965/66), 329-30.

22 'The Hermit' A different story on a parallel subject to the final long story. Appeared in *Sruth*, 10 August 1967.

23 'Je t-Aime' Gaelic story. A later English version appears in *Survival Without Error*. Appeared in *Sruth*, 30 November 1967.

24 'The Long Happy Life of Murdina the Maid' Story. Appeared in *Ossian*, 1968, p. 6-8.

25 'Phones' Play. Premiered by the Mull Little Theatre Company; mentioned in two articles about the MLTC in *GH*, 22 June 1968, and by Michael Pye, *Sctn*, 13 April 1968.

26 'Sweets to the Sweet' Story. Appeared in *Stand*, 11, no. 1 (1969-70), 24-28.

27 'An Leanabh' Story. Appeared in *Gairm*, 21 (1972/73), 156-58.

28 'Comhradh' Story. Appeared in *Gairm*, 21 (1972/73), 249-50. Not the story of the same title that appears in An Dubh is an Gorm.

29 'In the Maze' Story. Appeared in *Lines*, 42/43 (Sept 1972-Feb 1973), 9-11.

30 'The Meeting' Story. Appeared in *Lines*, 42/43 (September 1972/ February 1973), 12-14.

31 'The Injustice to Shylock' Story. Appeared in *Lines*, 42/43 (September 1972/February 1973), 7-9.

32 'Tha Slighe Dhorch ...' Story. Appeared in *Gairm*, 22 (1973/74), 183.

33 'Waiting for the Train' Story. Appeared in *GH*, 27 July 1984.

34 'In the Cafe' Story. Appeared in *Scotia Rev.*, 8 (December 1974), 37-40.

35 'On the Road' Story. Appeared in *Scotia Rev.*, 8 (December 1974), 41-43.

36 'Brathair mo Mhathar' Story. Appeared in *Gairm*, 1975/76, pp. 69-70.

37 'Eilidh' Gaelic play; winner of the SCDA North Argyll District Drama Festival, 20 March 1975. Unpublished; a copy is available at the Mitchell Library in Glasgow (catalogue no. SD f891 6323 SMI 3/EIL).

38 'Murchadh' Novel. Appeared in *Gairm*, 1978/79: pp. 147-57, 250-64, 370-79; *Gairm*, 1979/80, pp. 75-87.

39 'The Button' Story. Appeared in *Helix*, 2 (August 1978), 27-28.

40 'On the Island' Story. Appeared in *Sctn*, 1 July 1978.

41 'Coigrich' Story Appeared in *Sctn*, 8 July 1978.

42 'The Snow' Story. Appeared in *NER*, 46 (May 1979), 27-28.

43 'A September Day' Story. Appeared in *North 7*, 32 (March/ April 1979), 28.

44 'An Coinneachadh' Story. Appeared in *Sctn*, 5 May 1979.

45 'In the Corridor' Story. Appeared in *Words*, 5, p. 6.

46 'An Litir' Story. Appeared in *Sctn*, 12 July 1980.

47 'Nach tusa bh'ann a Halifax' Story. Appeared in *Sctn*, 2 February 1980.

48 'Christine' Story Appeared in *Words*, 9, p. 2-3.

49 'Murdo and the Open University' Story. Appeared in *Eilean an Fhraoich Annual*, December 1981 (Stornoway Gazette Ltd), 38-39.

50 'The Maze' Story. Appeared in *Enc.*, 57, no. 6 (December 1981), 3-7.

51 'Tormod Reamhar 's an Taigh Geal' Story. Appeared in *Gairm*, 1981/82, pp. 111-14.

52 'A' Chroit' Story. Appeared in *Gairm*, 1981/82, pp. 25-27.

53 'Maireadh' Story. Appeared in *Gairm*, 1981/82, pp. 313-16. Also appears in *Eadar Peann is Paipear* (1985).

54   'Mad Murdo and Cunning Calvin' Story. Appeared in *Sc. Rev.*, 28 (November 1982), 27-32.

55   'The Black Halo' Story. Appeared in *Words*, 11/12, pp. 5-6.

56   'Tog Orm mo Speal' Won many prizes at the Mod Final Drama Competition in 1982, performed by the Oban Gaelic Drama Group; see *St. Gaz.*, 13 October 1982. The play has also been broadcast on Radio Scotland. There is also an English version, entitled 'Oblomov'.

57   'An Saor' Story. Appeared in *Gairm*, 1982/83, pp. 154-58.

58   'The Parade' Story. Appeared in *NER*, 59 (Autumn 1982), 4-5.

59   'The Kitten' Story. Appeared in *Sctn*, 17 July 1982.

60   'Kant' Story. Appeared in *2 Plus 2*, no. 1 (Autumn 1983), 72-77. Published later as 'A Night with Kant' in *Enc.*, 64 (April 1985), 3-6.

61   'The Yacht' Story. Appeared in *NER*, 63 (Autumn 1983), 10-12.

62   'Scruffy' Story, with a note by Raghnall Mac Ille Dhuibh. Appeared in *Sctn*, 22 October 1983.

63   'The Arena' Winner of the Sinclair/*Scotsman* short story competition. Appeared in *Sctn*, 27 August 1983.

64   'Na Gibhtean' Story, with a note by Raghnall Mac Ille Dhuibh. Appeared in *Sctn*, 3 December 1983.

65   'An t-Ubhal' Story. Appeared in *Sctn*, 13 October 1984.

66   'Record of Work' Story. Appeared in *Stand*, 25, no. 3 (Summer 1984), 47-48.

67   'In the Asylum' Story. Appeared in *Chmn*, 42 (1985), 63-64.

68   'The Black Halo' Story. Appeared in *Chmn*, 42 (1985), 65-67.

69   'The Crossing' Story. Appeared in *Chmn*, 42 (1985), 67-68.

70   'Turas Beatha' Story. Appeared in *Gairm*, 1985/86, pp. 151-63, pp. 276-84, and pp. 358-69; 1986/87, pp. 82-90.

71   'Napoleon and I' Story. Appeared in *Glasgow Magazine*, 6 (Summer 1985), 40-44.

72   'The Survivor' Story. Appeared in *Radical Scotland*, 16 (Aug/Sept 1985), 32-33.

73   'Am Profeasair' Story. Appeared in *Gairm*, 1986/87, pp. 129-31.

74   'An Turas' Story. Appeared in *Gairm*, 1986/87, pp. 371-73.

75   'Air an Eilean' Story. Appeared in *St. Gaz.*, 23 August 1986.

76   'An Gunfighter' Story. Appeared in *Gairm*, 1987/88, pp. 13-15.

77   'At Jorvik Museum' Story. Appeared in *PN Review*, 55 (13, no. 5: 1987), 72-73.

E

Introduction

Iain Crichton Smith's early poems in particular have often been anthologised. There are also a significant number of poems which have been anthologised but not published elsewhere (or at least not more accessibly). Anthologies are listed here in chronological order of publication, then alphabetically by title. Iain Crichton Smith's poems (or stories) in each anthology are listed with an abbreviated reference to the collection they can be found in, or fuller details for uncollected items.

Abbreviations

The Long River	*LgR*
The White Moon	*WhM*
Bùrn is Aran	*BA*
Thistles and Roses	*ThR*
Biobuill is Sanasan-reice	*BSr*
The Law and the Grace	*LG*
Three Regional Voices	*3RV*
From Bourgeois Land	*FBL*
Selected Poems (1970)	*Sel* (1970)
Hamlet in Autumn	*HA*
Love Poems and Elegies	*LPE*
Eadar Feala-dha is Glaschu	*EFG*
Orpheus and other poems	*Orp.*
The Notebooks of Robinson Crusoe	*NRC*
Poems for Donalda	*Don.*
The Permanent Island	*PI*
In the Middle	*IM*
River, River	*RR*
The Exiles	*Ex*
Selected Poems 1955 — 1980	*Sel 1955 — 1980*
An Dubh is an Gorm	*DG*
Survival without Error	*SwE*
The Black and the Red	*BR*
The Village	*Vge*
The Hermit	*Hmt*
Murdo	*Mdo*
Mr Trill in Hades	*MTH*

Scottish Student Verse 1937-47 edited by I. F. Holroyd (Edinburgh and London: by the Ettrick Press for the Scottish Union of Students, 1948)

'Bookworm' Forty-six lines in four stanzas. First line: 'To know oneself is to face unexpected peril,'

'Burial' Sixteen rhymed lines. First line: 'Bury him in silence' First published in *North-East Review*, 91 (Oct. 1946).

'Elegy' Three stanzas of seventeen to twenty-four lines. First line: 'I have come home to an unheroic people'

Best Poems of 1956: Borestone Mountain Poetry Awards 1957 (Stanford, CA: Stanford University Press, 1957)

'False Summer Leans' *WhM*

Criochan Ura: Trusadh de rosg is de bardachd o'n raitheachan Gairm air achur ri cheile le Iain A. MacDhomhnaill (Glasgow: Gairm, 1958).

'Tha thu air aigeann m'inntinn' *BA*

Honour'd Shade: An anthology of new Scottish poetry to mark the bicentenary of the birth of Robert Burns edited by Norman MacCaig (Edinburgh: Chambers, 1959).

'A Note on Puritans' *ThR*

'Darwin' Four rhymed six-line stanzas. First line: 'So much to have removed,'

'Old Woman' ['And she, being old, ...'] *ThR*

Best Poems of 1960: Borestone Mountain Poetry Awards 1961. A compilation of Original Poetry published in Magazines of the English-speaking World in 1960 (Palo Alto, Ca.: Pacific Books, 1962)

'The Scholar' Four quatrains. First line: 'In the hour of pale triangles he is happy.' *Outposts,* 46 (Smr 1962)

Best Poems 1961: Borestone Mountain Poetry Awards 1962 (Pacific Books, 1962)

[No copy of this anthology was available.]

New Poets of England and America: second selection edited by Donald Hall and Robert Pack (World Publishing Co., c. 1962)

'A Young Highland Girl Studying Poetry' *ThR*

'End of the Season on a Stormy Day: Oban' *WhM*

'Old Woman' ['And she, being old, ...'] *ThR*

'Schoolgirl on Speech-day in the Open Air' *ThR*

'The Window' *WhM*

Best Poems 1962: Borestone Mountain Poetry Awards 1963 (Pacific Books, 1963)

[No copy of this anthology was available.]

Poems on Poetry: The Mirror's Garland edited by Robert Wallace and James G. Taffe (E. P. Dutton, 1965)

'A Young Highland Girl Studying Poetry' *ThR*

Young Commonwealth Poets '65 edited by P. L. Brent (London: Heinemann in association with Cardiff Commonwealth Arts Festival, 1965)

'The Soldier's Wish' *LG* Originally the fourth part of the sequence 'World War One'.

Modern Scottish Poetry: an anthology of the Scottish Renaissance edited by Maurice Lindsay, 2nd edn (London: Faber and Faber, 1966)

'Lenin' *LG*

'Luss Village' *ThR*

'Old Woman' ['And she, being old, ...'] *ThR*

'The Cemetry near Burns's Cottage' *LG*

'The Temptation' *LG*

'The Witches' *LG*

'Two Girls Singing' *LG*

New Poems 1966: Critical Quarterly Poetry Supplement Number 7 (London: Critical Quarterly Society, [1966]), edited by C. B. Cox and A. E. Dyson.

'At the Firth of Lorne' *LG*

'Two Girls Singing' *LG*

New Poetry, The edited by A. Alvarez (Penguin, 1962, rvsd edn 1966)

'By Ferry to the Island' *ThR*

'For the Unknown Seamen ...' *WhM*

'Old Woman' ['And she, being old, ...'] *ThR*

'Statement by a Responsible Spinster' *WhM*

'Sunday Morning Walk' *ThR*

Oxford Book of Scottish Verse edited by John MacQueen and Tom Scott (Oxford University Press, 1966).

'Culloden and After' *ThR*

'For Angus MacLeod' *ThR*

'For My Mother' *ThR*

'John Knox' *ThR*

Rosg nan Eilean edited by A. J. MacAsgaill (Glasgow University, Department of Celtic, 1966).

'An Solus Ur' *DG*

Scottish Poetry One, edited by George Bruce, Maurice Lindsay and Edwin Morgan (Edinburgh University Press, [1966])

'Old Woman' Three stanzas of four to seven lines. First line: 'Overwhelmed with kindnesses and you have nothing.' *3RV* (1968)

'She Teaches Lear' Thirteen rhymed six-line stanzas. First line: 'Much to have given up? Martyr, one says?' *3RV* and *Sel* (1970)

'Wedding' Four three-line stanzas. First line: 'With a great working of elbows'

All Sorts and Conditions of Men: an anthology edited by Mary Sullivan, Use of English Pamphlet no. 5 (London: Chatto and Windus, 1967)

'Rythm' *LG*

'Two Girls Singing' *LG*

'Luss Village' *ThR*

Book of Peace, A edited by Elizabeth Goudge (Coward-MacCann, 1967)

'By Ferry to the Island' *ThR*

'For the Unknown Seamen ...' *WhM*

Book of Scottish Verse, A edited by R. L. Mackie; 2nd edn, the selection revised with a new introduction by Maurice Lindsay (London: OUP, 1967)

'At the Firth of Lorne' *LG*

'Old Woman' ['And she, being old, ...'] *ThR*

'Two Girls Singing' *LG*

Commonwealth Poems of Today edited by Howard Sergeant (London: John Murray for the English Association, 1967)

'A Note on Puritans' *ThR*

'The Law and the Grace' *LG*

Poems Addressed to Hugh MacDiarmid and presented to him on his seventy-fifth birthday edited by Duncan Glen (Preston: Akros Publications, 1967)

'For MacDiarmid' Nine three-line stanzas. First line: 'A world in yourself you have persuaded us'

Scottish Poetry Two edited by George Bruce, Maurice Lindsay and Edwin Morgan (Edinburgh University Press, 1967)

'Lament for Adlai Stevenson' One two-line and five three-line stanzas. First line: '"Thought," says one, "is the index of failure."'

'Shepherds' Two stanzas of eleven and twelve lines. First line: 'The shepherds on the hills'

Scottish Literary Revival, The: an anthology of twentieth century poetry edited by George Bruce (London: Collier-Macmillan, 1968)

'A Note on Puritans' *ThR*

'Johnson in the Highlands' *LG*

'Luss Village' *ThR*

'Old Highland Lady Reading Newspaper' *LG*

'Old Woman' ['And she, being old, ...'] *ThR*

'Schoolgirl on Speech-day in the Open Air' *ThR*

'Two Girls Singing' *LG*

Scottish Poetry Three, edited by George Bruce, Maurice Lindsay and Edwin Morgan.

'By the Sea' Sequence of fourteen poems, of ten to twenty-seven lines, mostly in short rhymed stanzas. Some of the poems are separately titled: (4) 'In the Cafe' (6) 'Dumbarton' (7) 'The Gale' (8) 'After the Gale' (9) 'Young Girl' (10) 'Dunoon and the Holy Loch' (11) 'Tourist Driver' (12) 'In the Park' (14) 'At the Silent Films' First lines: (1) 'Sitting here by the foreshore day after day' (2) 'At Helensburgh the tide is out again —' (3) 'These hundred-year-olds preserved in glazed' (4) 'The leaf-fringed fountain' (5) 'Milk jugs, cups,' (6) 'They're pulling down the Bingo hall today.' (7) 'Out of the grey the white waves mouth at the shore.' (8) 'The stunned world stops on its axis.' (9) 'Nothing more impermanent, it appears' (10) 'The huge sea widens from us mile on mile.' (11) 'He tells us there's a cow and there's a cow.' (12) 'Over the shoes in pebbles I sit here.' (13) 'Days when the world seems like an old French film' (14) 'O Chaplin with your little black moustache'

Three Regional Voices (London: Poet and Printer, 1968)

'By the Great War Memorial' Six half-rhymed quatrains. First line: 'Gulls squabble in a sea blindingly blue.'

'Money-man Only' Five part-rhymed five-line stanzas. First line: 'Money man only, yes I pity you'

'Old Woman' ['Overwhelmed with kindnesses ...'] *Scottish Poetry One* ; *Sel 1955—1980*

'Poem' Three six-line stanzas. First line: 'From London you came to see me.' *P. Rev.*, 56 (1965), 157

'Returning Exile' Twenty-four lines. First line: 'Home he came after Canada' *Lsnr*, 77 (Jan-June 1967), 135. *The Exiles*

'She Teaches Lear' *Scottish Poetry One Sel* (1970)

'The Departing Island' Three half-rhymed six-line stanzas. First line: 'Strange to see it — how as we lean over' *Saltire Rev.*, 6, no. 22 (Aut. 1960), 51; *Sel 1955—1980*

'Two Voices' Eighty-four line dialogue, between Calvin and Freud. Originally broadcast on the Third Programme.

'Two Worlds' Four rhymed five-line stanzas. First line: 'The curtains change from green to silver.' *Lsnr*, 78 (June to Dec 1967), 121

Scottish Poetry Four edited by George Bruce, Maurice Lindsay and Edwin Morgan (Edinburgh University Press, 1969).

'Not Different' Four seven-line stanzas. First line: 'No, you are not different, not really,' *Sctn*, 5 Oct. 1968

'Remember Me' Nine rhymed pairs. First line: '"Remember me in honour," was what he said'

Contemporary Scottish Verse edited by Norman MacCaig and Alexander Scott (London: Calder and Boyars, 1970).

'A' dol dachaidh' Printed with a translation. *BA*

'Aberdeen' ['Mica glittered ...'] *Sel 1955—1980*

'Highland Portrait' *ThR*

'In the Cafe' Five four-line stanzas. First line: 'The leaf-fringed fountain'

'In the Time of Useless Pity' *HA*

'Meeting' *LG*

'Old Highland Lady Reading Newspaper' *LG*

'Old Woman' ['Your thorned back ...'] *LG*

'Poem: "Some move others"' *Sel 1955—1980*

'Schoolroom' *LG*

'Tha thu air aigeann m'inntinn'/'Your are at the Bottom of my Mind' Printed with a translation. *BA*

'Those Who Act' *Sel 1955-1980*

'To Have Found One's Country' *Sel 1955—1980*

'Two Girls Singing' *LG*

Dorcha Tro Ghlaine: tagadh de sgeulachdan-goirid edited by Domhnall-Iain MacLeoid (Glasgow: Gairm, 1970).

'An Comhradh' Story. *DG*

'Granny anns a' chornair' *Gairm*, 14 (1965/66), 161-75

Poems of the Sixties edited by F. E. S. Finn (London: Murray 1970).

'At the Highland Games' *Sel* (1970)

'Rythm' *LG*

Akros Anthology of Scottish Poetry 1965-70, The edited by Duncan Glen (Preston: Akros Publications, 1970).

'For Ann in America in the Autumn' *HA*

'Iona' Five stanzas of four lines and one of five. First line: 'The green light began here'

Twelve Modern Scottish Poets edited by Charles King (London: Hodder and Stoughton, 1971)

'A Young Highland Girl Studying Poetry' *ThR*

'By Ferry to the Island' *ThR*

'Culloden and After' *ThR*

'Envoi' *LG*

'For the Unknown Seamen ...' *WhM*

'From Bourgeois Land: 12' *FBL*

'In Luss Churchyard' *WhM*

'John Knox' *ThR*

'Old Woman' ['Your thorned back ...'] *LG*

'Poem of Lewis' *LgR*

'Seagulls' (extract) First line: 'There is nothing anyone can do with these' *WhM*

'Some Days were Running Legs' *LgR*

'The Visit of the Inspectors' *Lines*, 29 (June 1969), 18-19

Voices of Our Kind edited by Maurice Lindsay (Edinburgh: The Saltire Society, 1971).

'Culloden and After' *ThR*

'Luss Village' *ThR*

'Old Woman' ['And she, being old, ...'] *ThR*

'Two Girls Singing' *LG*

Penguin Modern Poets 21: Iain Crichton Smith, Norman MacCaig, George Mackay Brown (Harmondsworth: Penguin, 1972)

'At the Firth of Lorne' *LG*

'At the Sale' *FBL*

'By Ferry to the Island' *ThR*

'By the Sea' *Sel* (1970) and *Scottish Poetry Three*

'Deer on the High Hills: A Meditation' Published by Giles Gordon, 1962.

'Envoi' *LG*

'For the Unknown Seamen ...' *WhM*

'Home' *ThR*

'If You Are About to Die Now' *Sel* (1970)

'Jean Brodie's Children' *Sel* (1970)

'Kierkegaard' *ThR*

'Lenin' *LG*

'Old Woman' ['And she, being old, ...'] *ThR*

'Old Woman' ['Your thorned back ...'] *LG*

'Schoolgirl on Speech-day ...' *ThR*

'She Teaches Lear' *3RV Sel* (1970)

'Statement by a Responsible Spinster' *WhM*

· 'Sunday Morning Walk' *ThR*

'The White Air of March' *Sc. Int.*, 7 (September 1969), 28-34

'The Witches' *LG*

'Two Girls Singing' *LG*

'World War One' *LG*

Scottish Poetry Six edited by George Bruce, Maurice Lindsay and Edwin Morgan (Edinburgh University Press, [1972]).

'Early Films' Twenty-four lines in four stanzas of four to eight lines. First line: 'From the cinema these voices return,' *Sctn*, 20 June 1970

'Everything is Silent' *HA*

'Russian Poem' Five poems, of twenty-two to eighty-six lines. Only the last, 'Lenin', is separately titled.
First lines: (1) 'Sometimes one feels like Chekhov, waiting for something to happen, ' (2) 'Ivanov, to marry your Sonia was tempting,' (3) 'And then there was you Tolstoy aristocrat of the

body' (4) 'Dostoevski, you taught us the power of humiliation,'
(5) 'So you came and everything exploded.'

Machars '73 edited by Alastair S. Macmillan, Roderick Sharp and Janet
Shepperson (Aberdeen, 1973)

'Written after the Aberdeen Teach-in, 1971' Ninety-nine lines in
seven stanzas of twelve to seventeen lines. First line: 'We sat on
the floor, all of us, towards morning.'

New Poems 1972-1973: A PEN Anthology of Contemporary Poetry edited by
Douglas Dunn (London: Hutchinson and Co. Ltd, 1973).

'Again and Again' Seventeen lines. First line: 'Again and again we
are selling everything.' *Sc. Int.*, Sept. 1971, p. 26

'At Waverley Station' *Sc. Int.*, September 1971, p. 24

'Poem' First line: 'Dipping your spoon in the mash of TV' *HA* and
Oxford Book of Twentieth Century Verse edited by Philip Larkin
(Oxford: Clarendon Press, 1973).

'Old Woman' ['And she, being old, ...'] *ThR*

Poetry Dimension1: A Living Record of the Poetry Year edited by Jeremy
Robson (London: Robson Books, 1973)

'Do Not Put On That Wig' *LPE*

'The World's a Minefield' *LPE*

'You Lived in Glasgow' *LPE*

The House that Jack Built: Poems for Shelter edited by Brian Patten and Pat Krett (London: George Allan and Unwin, 1973)

'Speech for a Poor Man' Thirty-two lines in four stanzas of five to eleven lines. First line: 'If God is our landlord he has left us now ...'

Living Poets edited by Michael Morpurgo and Clifford Sinmons (London: John Murray, 1974)

'Rythm' *LG*

Modern Poetry: a selection edited by John Rowe Townsend (J. B. Lippincott, 1974)

'By Ferry to the Island' *LG*

Scottish Poetry Seven edited by Maurice Lindsay, Alexander Scott and Roderick Watson (University of Glasgow Press, 1974)

'Leaving the Island' Two stanzas of five and thirty-six lines. First line: 'We leave the island. And the sea accompanies us.'

'Search' Two half-rhymed six-line stanzas. First line: 'You search for a four-leafed clover in a field'

'The Workmen' *NRC*

For Sydney Goodsir Smith (Loanhead: MacDonald, 1975).

'Sydney Goodsir Smith' Nineteen lines. First line: 'You said once, in one of your joyous flights,'

Poems Since 1900: an anthology of British and American Verse in the Twentieth Century edited by Colin Falck and Ian Hamilton (London: Macdonald and Jane's, 1975)

'Old Woman' ['And she, being old, ...] *ThR*

Poetry Dimension Annual 3: The Best of the Poetry Year edited by Dannie Abse (London: Robson Books, 1980)

'Journey' *NRC*

'The Sound of Music' *NRC*

Scottish Love Poems: a personal anthology edited by Antonia Fraser (Canongate, 1975; Penguin, 1976)

'Farewell' *Agenda*, 5, no. 4: 6, no. 1 (Aut./Wtr 1967/68), 83

'The Shadows' *Don.*

'Tonight' *Orp.* and *Don.*

Scottish Poetry Eight edited by Maurice Lindsay, Alexander Scott, and Roderick Watson (Cheadle: Carcanet/Scottish Arts Council, 1975)

'Return to Lewis, 4 and 5' The fourth and fifth sections of a sequence. *Sel 1955—1980*

Trees: an anthology edited by Angus Ogilvy (Stirling: Stirling Gallery, 1975)

'Trees' Eleven lines in five stanzas of two and three lines. First line: 'When the trees rustle, it's the voices of the dead speaking,'

Modern Scottish Poetry: an anthology of the Scottish Renaissance, 1925-1975 edited by Maurice Lindsay (Manchester: Carcanet, 1976)

'Highland Portrait' *ThR*

'Old Woman' ['Your thorned back ...'] *LG*

'Young Girl' *BA* (Gaelic) and *BSr* (Gaelic and English)

Nua-bhardachd Ghaidhlig /Modern Scottish Gaelic Poems: a bilingual anthology edited by Donald MacAulay (Edinurgh: Southside, 1976)

'At the Cemetry'/'Aig a' Chladh' *BA*. Translated in *BSr* and *The Permanent Island*

'Da Oran Airson Ceilidh Uir'/'Two Songs for a New Ceilidh' First lines: 'Nuair a thug i 'n cuan mor oirr'/ 'When she took the great sea on her' '"Thoir Lunnain ort," thubhairt iad rium.'/'"Go to London," they said to me.' *BSr*, and translated in *The Permanent Island*. These are the second and seventh poems of the original sequence.

'Give Me Your Hand'/'Thoir Domh do Lamh' Based on 'Give Me Your Hand' from *HA*. Also appears in *Cerddi Gaeleg Cyfeloes*.

'Going Home'/'A' Dol Dachaidh' *BA* and *BSr*, and translated in *The Permanent Island*

'Oban' *BSr*, and translated in *The Permanent Island*

'Tha thu air aigeann m'inntinn'/'You are at the Bottom of my Mind' *BA*. Translated in *BSr* and *The Permanent Island*.

'The Exiles' *The Exiles*

'The Letter' /'An Litir' First line: 'Here is my letter to you out of the mirror'/'So mo litir thugad as an sgathan,' *HA* (English text only)

'The Old Woman' / 'A' Chailleach' *BA* and *BSr*; translated in *The Permanent Island*.

'To Derick Thomson: Selection' / 'Do Ruaraidh MacThomais: Tagadh' First lines: 'We were reared in Bayble together' / 'Thogadh sinn am Pabail comhla' 'The cuckoo is in the mouth of the hawk' / 'Tha chuthag ann am beul na seabhaig.' *BSr*

'Young Girl' / 'A Nighean Og' *BA*. Translated in *BSr* and *The Permanent Island*.

Scottish Poetry Nine edited by Maurice Lindsay, Alexander Scott amd Roderick Watson (Manchester: Carcanet / Scottish Arts Council, 1976)

'At the Seaside', 5 and 7 (extract) Orig. from *Lines*, 54 1975)

'Finding a Nest' Five six-line stanzas. First line: 'The oyster catcher of long red beak'

'Goddess of Change' Thirty-five lines. First line: 'Goddess of change you are the commonest.' *Sc. Rev.*, 1 (1, no. 1: Wtr 1975), 16

'In Ireland' *IM*

'When Day is Done' *IM*

Twenty-one Years of Poetry and Audience edited by Tom Wharton and Wayne Brown (Breakish, Isle of Skye: Aquila Publishing, 1976)

'Young Poet'

Birds: an anthology of New Poems edited by Angus Ogilvy, George Sutherland and Roderick Watson (Stirling: Stirling Gallery, [1977])

'The Birds' Three quatrains. First line: 'They leave us always in the autumn when'

'The Crows' Eleven lines. First line: 'The crows showed us the way. The battle was over.'

'Two Birds' Two quatrains. First line: 'A single note, the cuckoo's, in the spring.'

Modern Scottish Short Stories 1978 edited by Fred Urquhart and Giles Gordon (London: Faber and Faber, 1978; pbk edn 1982)

'Timoshenko'

Scottish Stories edited by John L. Foster. WLE Short Stories 9 (London: Ward Lock Educational, 1978)

'Home' *SwE*

Amannan: Sgialachdan Goirid (U & R Chambers, 1979)

'Murchadh' Short story. *Gairm*, 1978/79, pp. 147-57, 250-64, 370-79; 1979/80, pp. 75-87

Poetry of Scotland, The edited by Douglas Dunn (London: B. T. Batsford, 1979)

'Luss Village' *ThR*

Scottish Short Stories 1979 edited by Valerie Gillies (London: Collins, 1979)

'The Visit'

Short Stories from Scotland edited by John Blackburn (Exeter: Wheton, 1979)

'Jimmy and the Policeman' *Vge.*

'The Blot' *Vge.*

Feoil an Gheimhridh edited by Colm o Baoill (Baile Atha Cliath 1: FNT, 1980); an anthology of translations from Scots Gaelic into Irish.

'Am Maor' *BA*

'An Comhra' *DG*

'La Na Saboide' *An t-Adhar Ameireaganach*, as 'Latha na Sabaid'

'Na Focail ar an Bhalla'

Scottish Satirical Verse: an anthology edited by Edwin Morgan, (Manchester: Carcanet, 1980)

'The Visit of the Inspectors' *Lines*, 29 (June 1969), 18-19. Translated into Chinese in *Poetry*, 90 (Oct. 1981), edited by Wong Wai-ming (Honk Kong). Translated into Polish in *Litteratura na Swiecie*, 10 (1982), 135 by Andrzej Szuba.

Scottish Short Stories 1980 edited by Alan Massie (London: Collins, 1980)

'On Christmas Day' Story.

Scottish Comic Verse: an anthology edited by Maurice Lindsay (London: Robert Hale, 1981)

'The Rev. R. MacLeod Gives his Advice' Twenty-one lines. First line: '"What must you do to be saved?"'

'The Visitors' First line: 'The bell rings.' *Orp.*

Scottish Short Stories 1981 edited by Willis Pickard, Alan Massie, and Hilary Davies (Collins, 1981)

'Chirico's Return'

Seven Poets: Hugh MacDiarmid, Norman MacCaig, Iain Crichton Smith, George Mackay Brown, Robert Garioch, Sorley MacLean, Edwin Morgan. With Paintings and Drawings by Alexander Moffat and Photographs by Jessie Ann Matthew. Iain Crichton Smith interviewed by Marshall Walker. (Glasgow: Third Eye Centre, 1981)

'Accident Prone' Two four-line stanzas. First line: 'If it's not his leg that limps, then his face is cut.'

'Childhood and Adulthood' Four stanzas of three lines and one of one. First line: 'The window opened. Two small boys were playing. '

'Islander' Twenty-four lines in four stanzas of two to eleven lines. First line: 'Ash on an old man's sleeve —'

'Lenin' *LG*

'Near Oban' Fifteen lines. First line: 'Morning and the sea calm'

'Old Woman' ['And she, being old, ...'] *ThR*

'Problem' Four five-line stanzas. First line: 'We listen to your story of the bully.'

'Self-portrait' Eleven lines. First line: 'Whose is this Free Church face?'

'Sunday Morning Walk' *ThR*

'The Ghost' Eight lines. First line: 'Dead, she swam towards me in the light.'

Akros Verse: an anthology from 'Akros' no.s 1-49 edited by Duncan Glen (Nottingham: Akros, 1982).

'For Ann in America in the Autumn' *HA*

How Very Different the Tastes: A Selection of British Poetry 1970-1981 edited by Ben Bal (Amsterdam: Stichting Workshop Amsterdam School Press, 1982)

'The Church' Ten lines. First line: 'The church faces me with haggard windows' *Stand*, 22, no. 3 (1980/81), 23

Mehr Gespenster: Gespenstergeschlichten aus England, Schottland und Irland edited by May Hottinger (Zurich: Diogenes Evergreen, 1 982).

'Die Bruder' Story. *Hmt*

Poems of the Scottish Hills edited by Hamish Brown and with a foreword by Norman MacCaig (Aberdeen University Press, 1982)

'Ben Dorain' (extract) First line: 'Yestreen, I stood on Ben Dorain'

'Deer on the High Hills' (extract) [2] Deer on the High Hills

Shakespeare Stories edited by Giles Gordon (London: Hamish Hamilton, 1982)

'What to do about Ralph?' Story.

Third Poetry Book, A edited by John L. Foster (OUP, 1982)

'Halloween' *RR*

'Reflection' *RR*

'Shadows' Four quatrains. First line: 'The boy walks with his shadow'

'The Dinosaur' *RR*

'The Sea' Two quatrains. First line: 'Today the sea is playful and'

Poetry of Motion: an anthology of Sporting Verse edited by Alan Bold (Edinburgh: Mainstream, [u.d.]

'School Sports; At the Turnstile' *Lines*, 29 (June 1969), 8 *Sel 1955—1980*

Scottish Poetry Book, A edited by Alan Bold (OUP, 1983)

'Robin' Two quatrains. First line: 'If on a frosty morning'

'Spelling Game' Three quatrains. First line: 'If the plural of house is houses' *Hippo Book of Funny Verse*

'The Moon' Four rhymed lines. First line: 'The moon is a boat that drifts in the sky'

'The Rainbow' Four rhymed lines. First line: 'The rainbow's like a coloured bridge'

Scottish Short Stories 1983 edited by Joan Lingard (London: Collins, 1983)

'Greater Love'

Standpoints: an anthology of Contemporary Poetry edited by John L. Foster (London: Harrap, 1983)

'In the Youth Club' Sixteen lines in four stanzas of three to five lines. First line: 'It's like this, I want to talk to her and I can't.'

'Interview' Twenty-seven lines in six stanzas of one to three and fifteen lines. First line: 'When I went for this interview'

'Love' Four quatrains. First line: 'They always go on about Love'

'My Dad' Three quatrains. First line: '"Walk tall," said my Dad'

'Westerns' Nineteen lines in four stanzas of three to seven lines. First line: 'Sometimes when I see a Western'

'What's In the Paper' *RR*

Britain: A World By Itself. Reflections on the landscape by eminent British writers (London: Aurum Press, 1984)

'Argyll' Thirty-four lines in five stanzas of two to thirteen lines. First line: 'Rowan trees, birches, roses, and calm lochs,'

'The Mountain' Thirty-four lines in seven stanzas of three to seven lines. First line: 'In summer the deer are questionmarks on the mountains'

Core English: Out of this World (London: Heinemann Educational Books, 1985)

'Two Girls Singing' *LG*

Danevellou gouezeleg a Vro-Skos edited by **Mikael Madeg** (Brest: Brud Nevez, 1984). A volume of translations from Scottish Gaelic into Breton.

'An Comhradh' Story. *DG*

Rapunzel, las dein Haar herunter: Erzahlungen aus GroBhritannien translated by Reinhild Bohnke (Berlin: Verlag Neues Leben, 1984).

'Die Schwarzen und die Roten' Short story. *BR*

Scottish Short Stories 1984 edited by Anne Smith (London: Collins, 1984)

'The Tour' Story.

Seagate II: an anthology of Dundee Writing edited by Brenda Shaw (Dundee: TAXVS, 1984)

'Let Us Be Grateful' Six pairs. First line: 'Let us be grateful'

'Running Through the Leaves' Five three-line stanzas. First line: 'Running through the leaves we are not the leaves.'

Very First Poetry Book, A edited by John L. Foster (Oxford University Press, 1984)

'Launderama' Two quatrains. First line: 'The clothes go bouncing up and down'

'Robin' *A Scottish Poetry Book* (1983)

Core English: Out of This World edited by Ronald Caie *et al* (London: Heinemann Educational, 1985)

'The Planets' Two quatrains. First line: 'All the planets have been named'

Eadar Peann is Paipear edited by Domhnall Iain MacIomhair (Glasgow: Gairm, 1985); an anthology of Gaelic stories.

'Aig a' Chloich-chuimhne' *DG*

'An Coigreach' *BA*

'An Comhradh' *DG*

'An Duine Dubh' *BA*

'An Tagadh' *DG*

'Burn' *BA*

'Ioseph' *Gairm*, 11 (1962/63), 277-79; see D00

'Mairead' *Gairm*, 1981/82, pp. 313-16 (see D00)

Foundation English Anthology (London: Heinemann Educational Books, 1985)

'Rythm' *LG*

Nonsense Poems edited by John L. Foster (London: Robert Royce, 1985)

'Miss Twiss' *Lines*, 29 (June 1969), 30 (part 36 of the sequence 'Transparencies')

'Spelling Game' *A Scottish Poetry Book*, edited by Alan Bold

Scottish Short Stories 1985 edited by Stewart Conn (London: Collins, 1985)

'The Old Woman, the Baby; and Terry'

Seccond Scottish Poetry Book, A edited by Alan Bold (Oxford University Press, 1985)

'A Summary of Midsummer Night's Dream' Four half-rhymed pairs. First line: 'Some stuff about the moon'

'At School' Three pairs. First line: 'Millions and millions of stars'

'TV' Six rhymed pairs. First line: 'Sometimes when I watch TV'

'When I Leave School' Five rhymed pairs. First line: 'When I leave school I want to be'

Spaceways edited by John L. Foster (OUP, 1985)

'In the Late Evening'

'Retired'

'Strangers'

'The Children'

'Towards the Stars'

Anyone for Tennis? A Collection of Poems about Sport edited by Caroline Sheldon and Richard Heller (London: Hutchinson, 1986)

'Rythm' *LG*

Appreciating Poetry edited by R. K. Sadler, T. A. S. Hayllar and C. J. Powell (Hampshire: Macmillan Educational, 1986. First published by Macmillan Co. of Australia)

'Rythm' *LG*

Book of School Poems, A edited by John L. Foster (OUP, [1986])

'August Poem'

'Day-dreaming'

Cerddi Gaeleg Cyfoes, edited by John Stoddart (Cardiff: Gwasg Prifysgol Cymru, 1986); an anthology of Gaelic poems translated into Welsh.

'I hen wraig' ['Do Sheana-bhoireannach'] *BSr*

'Merch ifanc' ['A Nighean Og'] *BA*

'Mynd adref' ['A' Dol Dhachaidh'] *BA*

'Pregeth' ['Searmon'] Twenty lines.

'Rho imi dy law' ['Thoir domh do lamh'] Twenty-four lines in six stanzas of one to five lines. *Nua-Bhardachd Ghaidhlig/Modern Scottish Gaelic Poems*. The poem is based on 'Give Me Your Hand' from *HA*.

''Rwyt ti'n eigion fy meddwl' ['Tha thu air aigeann m'inntinn'] Three six-line stanzas. *BA*

'Wrth feini Calanais' ['Aig clachan Chalanais'] *BA*

'Y ffwl' ['An t-amadan'] *BSr*

'Y llythyr' ['An litir'] *BSr*

'Y mab afradlon' ['Am Mac Strodhail'] *BSr*

'Y Pabi Coch' ['An Crom-lus'] *BSr*

'Yn y fynwent' ['Aig a' Chladh'] *BA*

'Yr alltudion' ['Na h-eilthirich'] *Na h-Eilthirich*

'Yr hen wraig' ['A' chailleach'] *BA*

From January to December: Through the Year in Poems (London: Bell and Hyman, 1986)

'Robin' *A Scottish Poetry Book*, edited by Alan Bold

Inward Eye, The: A Poetry Anthology edited by Frank Ormsby (Sligo: Half Moon Press for Sligo Community Arts Group and Omagh Arts Committee, 1986)

'Against Death' Twelve lines in five stanzas of one to three lines. First line: 'Let us not sleep in the green.'

PEN New Poetry 1 edited by Robert Nye (London: Quartet Books, 1986)

'In Those Days' *P. Rev.*, 72, no. 2 (June 1982), 39; and *Echo Room*, 5 (Smr 1986)

'Not in Heaven' Six pairs. First line: 'No, it is not in heaven that we find the dry'

'The Poor Relations' *Official Programme of the Edinburgh Book Festival, 1985.*

'The Story' Seven four-line stanzas. First line: 'This is the story that I've always loved.'

'Villagers' *Stand*, 27, no. 4 (Aut. 1986); as 'Villagers, in the Second World War'

Portraits of Poets by Christopher Barker, edited by Sebastian Barker (Manchester: Carcanet, 1986)

'Reflection' *RR*

Scottish Short Stories 1986 edited by Deirdre Chapman (London: Collins, 1986)

'The Travelling Poet'

Tales to Tell edited by Donald Campbell (Edinburgh: St Andrews Press, 1986)

'The Beautiful Gown'

Wild Ride, The, and Other Scottish Stories edited by Gordon Jarvie (Harmondsworth: Viking Kestrel, 1986)

'Do You Believe in Ghosts?'

'The Blot' *Vge.*

Another Third Poetry Book edited by John L. Foster, Oxford Poetry Anthologies for Juniors (New Series) (OUP, 1987)

'Water and Ice'

Hippo Book of Funny Verse edited by Beverley Mathias (London: Hippo Books, Scholastic Publications, 1987)

'Spelling Game' *A Scottish Poetry Book* edited by Alan Bold

Leopardi: A Scottis Quair: A volume of poems presented to Francesco Cossiga President of the Italian Republic in commemoration of his admission to the honorary degree of Doctor honoris causa of the University of Edinburgh ([n.d.])

'A se stesso' / 'Thugam Fhin' Twenty-two lines. First line: "S a-nis, mo chridhe claoidht,'

'A Sylvia' / 'Sylvia' Sixty lines in seven stanzas of five to thirteen lines. First line: 'Sylvia, a bheil cuimhn' agad'

'Il Sabato del Vilaggio' / 'Oidche Shathuim Anns a' Bhaile' Fifty-two lines in six stanzas of five to thirteen lines. First line: 'Tha a' chaileag a' tllleadh bho na raointean'

Leopardi's Italian texts are accompanied by translations in English, Scots, and Gaelic; Iain Crichton Smith and Derick Thomson both supplied Gaelic translations.

Poetry Book Society Anthology 1987/88 edited by Gillian Clarke (London: Hutchinson, 1987)

'Snow' Four stanzas of four lines and two of eight. First line: 'Snow, you create a country of ghosts.'

'The Cat' Nineteen half-rhymed lines. First line: 'You were eighty-five when the cat appeared'

Quest 7B (New York: Scholastic Inc., 1987)

'Two Girls Singing' *LG*

Scottish Cat, The: an anthology edited by Hamish Whyte (Aberdeen University Press, 1987)

'The Cat' *Poetry Book Society Anthology*

Under Another Sky: The Commonwealth Poetry Prize Anthology edited by Alastair Niven (Manchester: Carcanet, 1987)

'Aberdeen University 1945-49 (1)' *A Life* U.K. and Europe Area Winner, 1986.

Another Third Poetry Book edited by John L. Foster, in Oxford Poetry Anthologies for Juniors (New Series) (OUP, 1987)

'The Rainbow' *A Scottish Poetry Book*, edited by Alan Bold

Little White Rose: an anthology of Scottish Poetry translated and edited by Yair Hurvitz (Tel Aviv, 1988)

[Six poems translated into Hebrew; the original titles are not given.]

Sunken Well, The [edited by Keith Murray] (Aberdeen: Keith Murray Publications, 1988)

'Crofter' Three pairs. First line: 'It is strange how like a bull you look'

'Winter Sun' Six lines. First line: 'The sun is a low pale helmet in the sky.'

Thirty Years of the Poetry Book Society edited by Jonathan Barker and introduced by Blake Morrison (London: Hutchinson, 1988)

'Remembering' *Sel 1955—1980*

F

Introduction

Most readers of Iain Crichton Smith in either tongue will know of his translations of Duncan Ban MacIntyre and Sorley MacLean: successful attempts to bring the great poets of the Gaelic tradition, past and present, to a wider readership. Fewer will know of his translations from other languages into Gaelic. His translations work alongside his work as editor and essayist, propagandising for the value of Gaelic, both language and literature, as 'another window on the world'. A chronological arrangement was not thought appropriate for this section, and it is arranged alphabetically by author. Details of the volume publications of his translations are given in an introductory section.

Books

Ben Dorain: translated from the Gaelic of Duncan Ban MacIntyre
(Preston, Akros, 1969; reprinted from *Akros*, 3, no. 9 (January
1969). 2nd edn 1969). Also by Northern House (Newcastle,
1969; reprinted 1988).

ISBN 0-900570-35-0 (Northern House 1988)

Poems to Eimhir by Sorley MacLean. Poems from 'Dain do Eimhir'
translated from Gaelic (Newcastle upon Tyne: Northern House,
and London: Victor Gollancz, 1971).

Reviewed by Ruaraidh MacThomais, *Gairm*, 19 (1970/71), 379-84 ;
Christie Mitchell, *NER*, 19 (1972), 40.

Poems

Anonymous

'Allan, I would go with you', translated from 'Ailein Duinn
shiubhlainn leat'. *An Gaidheal*, 56 (1961), 94. Thirty-seven lines, in
seven stanzas of one to ten lines. First line: 'I feel no joy tonight,
but pain,'

'Love Song' *An Gaidheal*, 57 (1962), 34. Six eight-line stanzas. First
line: 'Three things will come without seeking,' Author and date
not given.

'And if our language says that love' *Poetry Australia*, 63 (May
1977), 98. Eight three-line stanzas. First line: 'And if our language
says that love'

'Gregor Roy's Lament: by his widow' *Poetry Australia*, 63 (May 1977), 38-40. Seventeen four-line stanzas. First line: 'One morning of October'

'Never was I so tormented' *Poetry Australia*, 63 (May 1977), 99. Three four-line stanzas. First line: 'Never was I so tormented'

'Shores' *Poetry Australia*, 63 (May 1977), 102-03. Three half-rhymed eight-line stanzas. First line: 'If we were in Talisker on the shore'

'The knife of my intellect' *Poetry Australia*, 63 (May 1977), 100-01. Twelve half-rhymed quatrains. First line: 'The knife of my intellect made a cut'

'The Inheritance' *Ellery Queen's Mystery Magazine*, 1980 [unseen]. Translation of Gaelic tale.

Anonymous (MacDonald Collection)

'A Sister's Lament' *Lines*, 62 (Sept. 1977), 5-6. Fifteen half-rhymed pairs. First line: 'It is I who am sad,'

'Love Song' *Lines*, 62 (Sept. 1977), 7. Thirteen half-rhymed lines. First line: 'My love for you was deeper, dearer'

'Lullaby' *Lines*, 62 (Sept. 1977), 7. Seven half-rhymed quatrains. First line: 'Many a night of wet and dryness'

Auden, W. H.

'An Seacharanaiche' ('The Wanderer') *Gairm*, 17 (1968/69), 75. Thirty lines in three stanzas of seven to fourteen lines. First line: 'Tha Dan nas duirche 's nas doimhne na glaic na mara.'

'Cha bhi Sith ann' ('There Will Be no Peace') *Gairm*, 17 (1968/ 69), 74. Four six-line stanzas. First line: 'Ged a thig aimsir chiuin a rithist'

Brecht, Bertolt

[Untitled] *Gairm*, 19 (1970/71), 114. Twenty lines in four stanzas of three to six lines. First line: 'A bhith teagasg gun sgoilearan,'

Cavafy, C. P.

'A' Feitheamh ris na Barbarians' ('Expecting the Barbarians') *Gairm*, 16 (1967/68), 116-17. Thirty-six lines in eleven stanzas of two to six lines. First line: 'Cia ris a tha sinn a' feitheamh, cruinn ann am meadhon a' bhaile?'

'Am Baile' ('The City') *Gairm*, 16 (1967/68), 116. Two eight-line stanzas. First line: 'Thubhairt thu: "Theid mi gu duthaich eile, gu cuan eile,"'

'Am Faochadh a Fhuair Nero' ('Nero's Term') *Gairm*, 16 (1967/68), 117-18. Two stanzas of six lines and one of three. First line: 'Cha do chuir e dragh air Nero nuair a chual e'

'Ithaca' *Gairm*, 16 (1967/68), 118-19. Thirty-five lines in five stanzas of three to twelve lines. First line: 'Nuair a thogas tu ort gu Ithaca'

Derick Thomson

'When Tender and Mild' *Saltire Rev.*, 6, no. 22 (Aut. 1960), 28. Thirty-six lines in five stanzas of three to fourteen lines. First line: 'When, tender and mild,'

Donn, Rob

'Lament for Iain MacEachainn' *Poetry Australia*, 63 (May 1977), 44-6. Twelve rhymed eight-line stanzas. First line: 'Iain Mhic Eachainn since your dying'

Dunn, Douglas

'Roghainn' ['Warning'] *Gairm*, 20 (1971/72), 351. Four lines. First line: 'An t-samhachd am an sporan struidhear.'

Hamilton, Ian

'Clag Smalaidh' ['Fire Alarm'] *Gairm*, 20 (1971/72), 354. Six lines. First line: 'Meadhon oidhce,'

'Dachaigh' ['Home'] *Gairm*, 20 (1971/72), 353. Two stanzas of three and four lines. First line: 'Tha an tide dona gun sgur. Os cionn ar cinn'

'Dusgadh' ['Wakening'] *Gairm*, 20 (1971/72), 353. Six lines. First line: 'Tha do cheam, cho tinn, ag aomadh ri mo cheann-sa.'

'Nadur' ['Nature'] *Gairm*, 20 (1971/72), 354. Five lines. First line: 'Tha mi 'nam shuidhe fo'n chreig dhealrach so'

'Naidheachd' ['News'] *Gairm*, 20 (1971/72), 353. Seven lines. First line: 'Tha cogadh Vietnam 'na shlaod bith-bhuan'

'Seana Dealbh' ['Old Picture'] *Gairm*, 20 (1971/72), 353. Seven lines. First line: 'Tha thu air iomrall anns an raon dhomhainn'

Herbert, Zbigniew

'A' Chlach' ['The Stone'] *Gairm*, 18 (1969/70), 143. Seventeen lines in seven stanzas of two to four lines. First line: ''Se creutair coimhliont'

'Coignear' ['Five'] *Gairm*, 18 (1969/70), 140-41. Sequence of three poems, of seven to twenty-eight lines. First line: (1) 'Bheir iad a-mach iad sa' mhadainn' (2) 'Nuair a chuimsicheas na gunnairean an gunnachan' (3) 'Cha do dh'ionnsaich mi so an diugh'

'Fortinbras a' Bruidhinn' ['Fortinbras Speaking'] *Gairm*, 18 (1969/70), 139-40. Forty-eight lines in five stanzas of seven to thirteen lines. First line: 'Seach gu bheil sinn nar n-aonar a phrionnsa'

'Sioda Aon Anam' ['There is One Soul': 'I never spoke to her ...'] *Gairm*, 18 (1969/70), 142-43. Forty lines in ten stanzas of three to seven lines. First line: 'Cha do bhruidhinn mi rithe riamh'

Iku, Takenaka

'Rionnagan' ['Stars'] *Gairm*, 18 (1969/70), 31. Eighteen lines if four stanzas of one to ten lines. First line: 'Os cionn Iapan tha rionnagan,'

Kunert, Gunter

'Film a ruth air ais' ['Film Running Backwards'] *Gairm*, 19 (1970/71), 117. Eighteen lines. First line: 'Nuair a dhuisg mi' Larkin, Philip

'A' Falbh' ('Going') *Gairm*, 17 (1968/69), 76. Ten lines in four stanzas of one and three lines. First line: 'Tha feasgar a' tarraing a-steach'

'Laithean' ('Days') *Gairm*, 17 (1968/69), 76. Two stanzas of four and six lines. First line: 'Ciod brigh nan laithean?'

Lom, Iain

'Lament for his Chief' *Poetry Australia*, 63 (May 1977), 43. Ten rhymed three-line stanzas. First line: 'Lord, low is my spirit,'

Lorca, Garcia

'Ballad an t-Sail' ['Ballad of the Sea': 'The sea is laughing ...']
Gairm, 18 (1969/70), 30. Twelve lines. First line: 'Tha am muir a'
gaireachdainn fad air falbh.'

'Amhran a' mharcaiche' *Gairm*, 19 (1970/71), 113. Eight lines. First
line: 'Cordoba fad as 's na aonar'.'

Lowell, Robert

'An Deicheamh Te de'n Cheolraidh' ['The Rider's Song': 'Cordoba
far off ...'] *Gairm*, 17 (1968/69), 260-61. Five five-line stanzas. First
line: 'An deicheamh te de'n Cheolraidh, a Leisg, a Leisg,'

'Meadhon Aois' ('Middle Age') *Gairm*, 17 (1968/69), 260.
Twenty-three lines in four stanzas of five to seven lines. First line:
'Tha mi air mo bhleith aig meadhon geamhraidh.'

'Tilleadh' ('Returning') *Gairm*, 17 (1968/69), 259-50. Forty-two
lines in seven stanzas of four to eight lines. First line: 'A' tighinn
dhachaidh chon a' bhaile bhig fhasgaicht so'

MacIntyre, Duncan Ban

'Ben Dorain 1: Urlar' *Akros* 3, 9 (Jan. 1969), 11-12. Ten stanzas of
four lines and one of eight, rhymed. First line: 'Honour to all past
bens'

'Ben Dorain 2: Siubhal' *Akros* 3, 9 (Jan. 1969), 12-14. Seventy-four
lines, mainly in quatrains, with six and ten-line st First line: 'The
hind that's sharp-headed'

'Ben Dorain 3: Urlar' *Akros* 3, 9 (Jan. 1969), 14-16. Twenty-four
quatrains. First line: 'Pleasant to me rising'

'Ben Dorain 4: Siubhal' *Akros* 3, 9 (Jan. 1969), 16-18. Seventy-two lines in fifteen rhymed stanzas of four, six and eigh First line: 'Luxuriant mountain'

'Ben Dorain 5: Urlar' *Akros* 3, 9 (Jan. 1969), 18-19. Twelve quatrains. First line: 'Volatile the hind'

'Ben Dorain 6: Siubhal' *Akros* 3, 9 (Jan. 1969), 20-21. Seventy-four lines, mainly in quatrains with three six-line stanz First line: 'That troupe was beloved'

'Ben Dorain 7: Urlar' *Akros* 3, 9 (Jan. 1969), 22-23. Thirteen quatrains. First line: 'The wide and empty moor'

'Ben Dorain 8: An Crunluath' *Akros* 3, 9 (Jan. 1969), 23-25. Twenty-three quatrains. First line: 'When the hind is in this solitude'

MacLean, Sorley

'Poems to Eimhir: I' One five-line and four four-line rhymed stanzas. First line: 'Girl of the gold-yellow hair,'

'Poems to Eimhir: II' *Stand*, 12, no. 2 (1971), 9. Eight rhymed three-line stanzas. First line: 'And if our language says that love'

'Poems to Eimhir: III' Three quatrains. First line: 'Never was I so tormented'

'Poems to Eimhir: IV' Six quatrains. First line: 'Girl of the yellow, heavy-yellow, gold-yellow hair,'

'Poems to Eimhir: VIII' Two quatrains. First line: 'I thought I understood from you'

'Poems to Eimhir: XI' Four rhymed lines. First line: 'Often walking quite alone'

'Poems to Eimhir: XIV' Four rhymed five-line stanzas. First line: 'Poet struggling under strain,'

'Poems to Eimhir: XVII' Three half-rhymed quatrains. First line: 'Tumultuous plenty in the heavens,'

'Poems to Eimhir: XVIII' Seventeen half-rhymed five-line stanzas. First line: 'Now that the ivory towers are down'

'Poems to Eimhir: XIX' Five half-rhymed eight-line stanzas. First line: 'I gave you eternity'

'Poems to Eimhir: XX' Seventeen half-rhymed lines. First line: 'If my capacity were such'

'Poems to Eimhir: XXI' Eight rhymed lines. First line: 'What is my place to me'

'Poems to Eimhir: XXII' Seven half-rhymed quatrains. First line: 'I walked with my intelligence'

'Poems to Eimhir: XXIII' Fourteen half-rhymed quatrains. First line: 'Deaf and restless the rage,'

'Poems to Eimhir: XXIV' Six lines. First line: 'When you have remarked that beauty'

'Poems to Eimhir: XXVII' *Stand,* 12, no. 2 (1971), 10. Seven rhymed lines. First line: 'The reader told me my imagination'

'Poems to Eimhir: XXVIII' Three half-rhymed stanzas of seven, twelve and two lines. First line: 'Perhaps if I had won your love'

'Poems to Eimhir, XXIX: Dogs and Wolves' Twenty-four half-rhymed lines. First line: 'Across eternity, across her snows,'

'Poems to Eimhir: XXX' Fifteen lines rhymed in couplets. First line: 'Though I'm a Bolshevik who would never sing'

'Poems to Eimhir: XXXI' Six half-rhymed lines. First line: 'William Ross, what would we say'

'Poems to Eimhir: XXXII' *Stand*, 12, no. 2 (1971), 10. Eight lines rhymed in couplets. First line: 'Let me lop from my verse every grace'

'Poems to Eimhir: XXXIII' *Stand*, 12, no. 2 (1971), 10. Five rhymed lines. First line: 'Not different from the fate of bards'

'Poems to Eimhir: XXXIV' Twelve lines rhymed in couplets. First line: 'When I speak of a loved face'

'Poems to Eimhir: XXXV' Thirteen lines in half-rhymed couplets. First line: 'Come to me tranquil night and you'

'Poems to Eimhir: XXXVII' *Stand*, 12, no. 2 (1971), 10. Eight half-rhymed lines. First line: 'It was not your body's beauty,'

'Dain do Eimhir' XLII *An Gaidheal*, 61 (1966), 28. Two stanzas of ten lines and one of nine. First line: 'If we were in Talisker on the shore'

'Poems to Eimhir: XLIII' Five half-rhymed quatrains. First line: 'If it weren't for you, the Cuillin'

'Poems to Eimhir: XLV' Twelve half-rhymed quatrains. First line: 'The knife of my intellect made a cut'

'Poems to Eimhir: XLVIII' Four quatrains. First line: 'With you my humility'

'Poems to Eimhir: XLIX' Three half-rhymed quatrains. First line: 'My boat was sailing on the Clarach'

'Poems to Eimhir: L' Six half-rhymed quatrains. First line: 'Grief is scaled to zero and'

'Poems to Eimhir: LII' *Stand*, 12, no. 2 (1971), 10-11. Six half-rhymed quatrains. First line: 'To my scrutiny you were a star'

'Poems to Eimhir: LIV' Three four-line stanzas. First line: 'You were a daybreak on the Cuilthionn,'

'Poems to Eimhir: LV' Eight half-rhymed lines. First line: 'I cannot see the sense'

'Poems to Eimhir: LVI' Four lines. First line: 'In my ten years of striving'

'Poems to Eimhir: LVII' *Stand*, 12, no. 2 (1971), 11. Eighteen quatrains with two longer stanzas of fourteen and twenty-six lines in couplets. First line: 'I'm haunted by a face'

Mairi Nighean, Alastair Ruaidh or Mary MacLeod (17 c.).

'The Song for the Chief of the MacLeods' *An Gaidheal*, 54 (1959), 65-66, 78. Thirteen eight-line stanzas. First line: 'Sitting her[e] on this hillock'

Montale, Eugenio

'An t-Easgann' ('The Eel') *Gairm*, 18 (1969/70), 29. Thirty-one lines. First line: 'An t-easgann, maighdeann na mara,'

'Xenia (do mo bhean)' ('Xenia: Songs of Hospitality') *Gairm*, 17 (1968/69), 327-30. Sequence of fourteen poems, of two to twenty lines. First line: (1) 'Mo Mhosca beag phriseil' (2) Mosca bhochd gun speuclairean, gun sgiathan,' (3) 'Anns an tigh-osda am Paris' (4) 'Bha sinn a' cruasachd na siorruidheachd:' (V) 'Cha do thuig mi riamh an e mise' (VI) 'Cha tainig e steach ot' (VII) 'Fein-thruas, pian gun dheireadh, is amhghar' (VIII) 'Do theanga bacach 's neo-chealgach' (IX) 'B'e eisdeachd do mhodh-seallaidh.' (X) '"An d'rinn i urnuigh?"' (XI) 'A' cuimnheachadh do dheoirean ('s bha m'fheadhainnsa dubailt')' (XII) 'Tha an t-earrach a' briseadh a-mach mar bhall-dorainn.' (XIII) 'Bhasaich do bhrathair og.' (XIV) 'Tha iad ag radh'

Quasimodo, Salvatore

'An t-soitheach-siuil ard' ['The Sailing-ship is Tall'] *Gairm*, 16 (1967/68), 225. Twenty-three lines in four stanzas of four to ten lines. First line: 'Nuair a thainig na h-eoin, 'n gluasad duilleagan'

'Tha mi air mo chur fodha aig do sholus' *Gairm*, 16 (1967/68), 225-26. Twenty lines in seven stanzas of two to four lines. First line: 'Tha mi air mo chur fodha aig do sholus'

Queneau, Raymond

[Untitled] *Gairm*, 19 (1970/71), 116. Eighteen lines in three stanzas of five to eight lines. First line: 'Ma tha thu de'n bheachd, ma tha thu de'n bheachd a nighneig,'

Rimbaud, Arthur

'Soraidh' ('Farewell': from A Season in Hell) *Gairm*, 18 (1969/70), 311-12.

Ros, Uilleam

'One Monday Evening' *Poetry Australia*, 63 (May 1977),47-49. Eleven eight-line stanzas. First line: 'One Monday evening, as I was walking,'

Seferio, Seoras

'Tha ar Tir' ['Our Land Is ...'] *Gairm*, 19 (1970/71), 113-14. Two stanzas of seven and eleven lines. First line: 'Tha ar tir air a cuartachadh le beanntann,'

Soloukhin, Vladimir

'Dearcag' *Gairm*, 18 (1969/70), 31-32. Twenty-nine lines. First line: 'Ann an glasach na coille, tri ceumannan bho'n fhrith-rathad,'

Spender, Stephen

'Do Nighean' ('To My Daughter') *Gairm*, 17 (1968/69), 75. Five lines. First line: 'Greim soillier aig a laimh timcheall m'ordaig,'

Stevens, Wallace

'Tri Doighean Deug a bhi meorachadh air lon-dubh' ('Thirteen Ways of Looking at a Blackbird') *Gairm*, 20 (1971/72), 351-53. Sequence of thirteen poems of two to seven lines. First line: (1) 'Am measg fhichead bheann shneachdach' (2) 'Bha mi de thri smaointean,' (3) 'Bha an lon-dubh a' tionndadh ann an gaoitean na foghair.' (4) 'Tha duine is boireannach' (5) 'Chan eil fhios am de's fhearr leam,' (6) 'Lion caisean-reodhta an uinneag fhada' (7) 'A dhaoine thana a Haddam,' (8) 'Tha fhios am air cananan morair,' (9) 'Nuair a chaidh an lon-dubh air iteig' (10) 'A' coimhead nan lon-dubh' (11) 'Mharcaich e tarsain air Connectitcut' [sic] (12) 'Tha an abhainn a' gluasad.' (13) "Se bial na h'oidhche bh'ann fad feasgar.'

Traditional

'Seathan Son of the King of Ireland' *Stand*, Spr. 1987, p. 50-53. One hundred and ninety lines, in twenty stanzas. First line: 'Pity who heard and didn't speak of it.' Presented by Alexander Carmichael and printed in his *Carmina Gadelica*, vol. 5.

'Did You See the Modest Girl' *Stand*, Spr. 1987, p. 50. Two stanzas, of five and seven lines. First line: 'Did you see the modest girl'

Waulking song, from *Folk Songs of South Uist*, presented by
Margaret Fay Shaw.

'Pity That I was Not Born Blind' *Stand*, Spr. 1987, p. 49. Three
four-line stanzas. First line: 'Pity that I was not born blind without
language or seeing'

Voznesensky, Andrei

'Talamh' ['Soil' /'Land'] *Gairm*, 18 (1969/70), 32-33. Thirty-two
lines in four stanzas of six to nine lines. First line: "S caomh leinn
a bhith coiseachd'

Gairm, 19 (1970/71), 114-16. Forty-three lines in ten stanzas of four
to five lines. First line: 'Tha cuideigin a' bualadh boireannach'
('Someone is hitting a woman')

Williams, William Carlos

'Faoileagan' ['Seagulls': 'My friends, out in the wide world,']
Gairm, 18 (1969/70), 30-31. Twenty-nine lines, in four stanzas of
four to ten lines. First line: 'Mo chairdean, a-muigh anns an
t-saoghal mhor,'

G

Introduction

As the first entries in this chapter show, Iain Crichton Smith has been publishing reviews for almost as long as he has been publishing verse. Some of his best critical writing has been collected in *Towards the Human,* — the relevant citations are indicated. Once again citations are arranged chronologically, then alphabetically by title. Though published titles are included for ease of reference most are of course editorial.

1   'Two Book Reviews' In *Alma Mater*, 59, no. 8 (Jan. 1948), 31-33. Review of *Sea and Sardinia* by D. H. Lawrence, and *The Lawless Roads* by Graham Greene.

2   'The Noun and the Adjective', by Eoin. In *Gaudie*, 15, no. 14 (11 Feb. 1948), 5. Article on the language and imagery of modern poetry.

3   'One Aspect of Graham Greene' In *Alma Mater*, 60, no. 1 (Spr. 1949), 31-32.

4   'Notes from a Journal' by Eoin. In *Alma Mater*, 60, no. 2 (Smr 1950), 65-66. Philosophical essay.

5   'Modern Scottish Gaelic Poetry' In *SGS*, 7, no. 2 (1953), 199-206.

6   'Homage to Sorley MacLean' In *Saltire Rev.*, 5, no. 15 (Smr 1958), 37-40.

7   'A Note on Modern Gaelic Poetry' In *An Gaidheal*, 54 (1959), 46-47.

8   'The Poetry of Norman MacCaig' In *Saltire Rev.*, 6, no. 19 (Aut. 1959), 20-23.

9   'A Note on Feasgar Luain' In *SGS*, 9, no. 1 (1961), 80-83.

10   'The Future of Gaelic Literature' In *TGSI* , 43 (1960/63), 172-80.

11   Untitled review in *New Saltire*, 3 (Spr. 1962), 79-81; of *The Wisdom of the Scots: A Choice and a Comment* by Morag McLaren (Michael Joseph, [1962]).

12   Untitled review in *New Saltire*, 3 (Spr. 1962), 79-81; of *The Wisdom of the Scots* by Moray MacLaren.

13   'Kierkegaard' In *Gairm*, 11 (1962/63), 103-08.

14   'On Being Contemporary' In *An Gaidheal*, 58 (1963), 8-9. 15 Untitled article in *Scottish Field*, Mar. 1963, p. 67. Article on writing in Scotland today.

16   'An t-Iarunn is an Ros' In *Gairm*, 12 (1963/64), 260-63. Article on Nathaniel Hawthorne's *The Scarlet Letter*. 17 'Oiteagan o'n Ear (1) Singapore' In *Gairm*, 13 (1964/65), 114-23.

18   'Oiteagan o'n Ear (2) Ceylon' In *Gairm*, 13 (1964/65), 206-16.

19 Untitled review in *Gairm*, 13 (1964/65), 87-93 of *Orain Iain Luim* deas. le Anna NicCoinnich (Comunn nan Text Gaidhlig).

20 'A Poem by Donald MacAulay' In *An Gaidheal*, 60 (1965), 128-29. Commentary on 'Iain a-measg na reultan'.

21 'A Note on the Poetry of Iain Lom' In *An Gaidheal*, 60 (1965), 80-81.

22 'Superego versus ID' In *Sctn*, 3 July 1965. Interview with John Horder.

23 *Modern Gaelic Verse* (Glasgow: An Comunn Gaidhealach, 1966) Eight-page pamphlet, the third in a series. Discusses work by a range of poets, including himself.

24 'Two Poems by Derick Thomson' In *An Gaidheal*, 61 (1966), 52-54. Commentary on Thomson's poems 'Tilleadh' and 'Clann-nighean an Sgadain'.

25 'Air an Eilean' In *An Gaidheal*, 61 (1966), 75. Essay. 26 'Turus Mhurchaidh' In *An Gaidheal*, 61 (1966), 86-87. Essay.

27 'Not Much About Lewis' In *GH*, 28 May 1966. Review of *The Islanders: A Hebridean Experience* by Rosemary Millington (Hutchinson).

28 'New Verse: Virtues of Care' In *GH*, 11 June 1966. Review of poetry by Charles Tomlinson, R. S. Thomas, Seamus Heaney, Brian Higgins, Johannes Bobrowski, W. Price Turner and Charles Senior; plus a selection of pamphlets and periodicals.

29 'A Note on Andrew Young' in *Lines*, 22 (Wtr 1966), 28-32. 30 'The Golden Lyric: an essay on the poetry of Hugh MacDiarmid' (Preston: Akros, 1967) Also appeared in *Hugh MacDiarmid: a Critical Survey*, edited by Duncan Glen (Edinburgh and London: Scottish Academic Press, 1972); and *Towards the Human*.

31 'On *Scottish Field*' In *Sruth*, 15 June 1967. Article.

32 'Signals Across the Years' In *GH*, 15 July 1967. Review of *Eadar Samhradh is Foghar* [Between Summer and Autumn] by Ruaraidh MacThomais (Gairm).

33 'On Translation' In *Sruth*, 28 Nov. 1967.

34   'Modern Gaelic Poetry' In *Akros*, 2, no. 6 (Dec. 1967), 27-41. Also appeared in *Towards the Human*.

35   'New Verse: Some Random Samples' In *GH*, 2 Dec. 1967. Review of *A Look Around the Estate* by Kingsley Amis (Jonathan Cape); *To Find the New* by Alan Bold (Phoenix Living Poets); and *Landscapes and Figures* by George Bruce (Akros Publications).

36   'Bardachd W. B. Yeats' [Yeats and the Profession of the Poet] In *Gairm*, 16 (1967/68), 363-72.

37   'Dour Demotic' In *Spectator*, 220 (Jan-June 1968), 708. Review of *The Ploughing Match* by Fred Urquhart (Hart-Davis).

38   'The MacAulay World' In *Sruth*, 22 Feb. 1968 (Part One: 'The Austere Visionary') and 7 Mar. 1968 (Part Two: 'Gaelic Triumphant'). Review of *Seobhrach as a' Chlaich* by Donald MacAulay.

39   'On Modern Scottish Literature' In *S.S.T.A. Magazine*, 23, no. 1 (May 1968), 40-41.

40   'Childhood in Lewis' In *Scottish Field*, June 1968, pp. 33-35.

41   'Iain Crichton Smith on his Poetry' In *Chirico*, 2, no. 1 (1969), 1-4.

42   'The House with Green Shutters' In *SSL*, 7, no. 1/2 (July/Oct. 1969), 3-10.

43   Untitled review in *Akros*, 4, no. 11 (Aug. 1969), 72-75. Review of *This Business of Living* by Maurice Lindsay (Akros, 1969).

44   'Crime Fiction' In *GH*, 25 Oct. 1969 and 6 Dec. 1969. Review column.

45   'New Verse: Too Much Talk' In *GH*, 13 Dec. 1969. Review of *The Opening of the Field* by Robert Duncan (Jonathan Cape); *Letters to Five Artists* by John Wain (MacMillan); *Fifteen Poems and a Play* by Sydney Goodsir Smith (Edinburgh: Southside); *On Pain of Seeing* by Erich Fried (Rapp and Whiting); *The Way of the World* by Charles Tomlinson (OUP); *Darker Ends* by Robert Nye (Calder and Boyers); and *Old World, New World* by David Holbrook (Rapp and Whiting).

46 'A Bard of Uist' In *GH*, 20 Dec. 1969. Review of *The Poems and Songs of Donald Macdonald* by Domhnall Ruadh Choruna (Gairm).

47 'Norman MacCaig: Colours of Happiness' In *GH*, 27 Dec. 1969. Review of *A Man in My Position* (Chatto and Windus).

48 'Highlander in Glasgow' In *GH*, 8 Aug. 1970. Review of *The Serpent* by Neil M. Gunn (Club Leabhar).

49 'Hugh MacDiarmid: "Sangschaw" and "A Drunk Man Looks at the Thistle"' In *SSL*, 7, no. 3 (1970), 169-79. Also appeared in *Towards the Human*.

50 'Three Scottish Poets' In *GH*, 3 Oct. 1970. Review of *Collected Poems* by Burns Singer, *The Moral Rocking Horse* by W. Price Turner, and *Lines Review*, 34.

51 'The World of the Wind [sic - Mind?]' In *Sruth*, 8 Jan. 1970. Article about pschychology.

52 'Modern Gaelic Poetry' In *Scotia*, 2 (Feb. 1970), 2-4.

53 'The Laureate, and Others' In *GH*, 11 Apr. 1970. Review of new verse by C. Day Lewis, Ezra Pound, Michael Dennis Brown, and John Toronto [Dr Strachan].

54 'The Roman Destiny and Moral Passion' In *GH*, 27 June 1970. Review of novels by William MacIllvaney, David Jones, Ted Walker and W. S. Graham.

55 'Writing in Gaelic' In *Lines*, 33 (July 1970), 3-9 , and reprinted in *Planet*, 13 (Aug./Sept. 1972), 15-21 ed. Ned Thomas.

56 'Put Gaelic to the Test' In *Sruth*, 6 Aug. 1970.

57 'Government by Pure Thought' In *GH*, 22 Aug. 1970. Review of *The Glass Bead Game* by Herman Hesse. Translated by Richard and Clara Wilson (Jonathan Cape).

58 'A Note on Sorley MacLean's *Dain do Eimhir*' In *Stand*, 12, no. 2 (1971), 8. Introducing a selection of his own translations.

59 Untitled review in *Lines*, 36 (Mar. 1971), 39-40. Review of *Collected Poems 1939-1970* by George Bruce (Edinburgh UP, 1971).

60   Untitled review in *Akros*, 6, no. 16 (Apr. 1971), 57-58. Review of
     The MacDiarmids: A Conversation by Hugh MacDiarmid and
     Duncan Glen.

61   'Writer in the Market-place' In *Sctn*, 22 May 1971. Interview with
     David Gow, after winning an SCA Spring publication award.

62   'Gaelic Without Tears' In *Sctn*, 28 Aug. 1971. Review of *Gaelic* by
     Roderick MacKinnon.

63   'Poet in Bourgeois Land' In *Sc. Int.*, Sept. 1971, p. 22-27. Interview
     with Lorn MacIntyre. The interview took place in Oban on
     5 March 1 971, and was prepared as part of project on Iain
     Crichton Smith in completion of her Honours degree at Stirling
     University. The tape is held at the Library there, and is available
     on application to the librarian.

64   'Islefolk at the Top: Iain Crichton Smith; Prizewinning Poet,
     Novellist, and Playwright' In *St. Gaz.*, 4 Sept. 1971. Interview.

65   'The Problems of the Gaelic Writer' In *Ossian*, 1972, pp. 37-40.

66   'Writing in Gaelic' In *Planet*, 13 (Aug./Sept. 1972), 15 and 21.

67   Untitled review in *Lines*, 41 (June 1972). Review of *The Spaces
     Between the Stars* and *The Man with the Surbahar* by Robin Fulton.

68   'Scotland's Sunny Side' In *Sctn*, 24 June 1972. Review of *Alistair
     MacLean Introduces Scotland*, edited by Alastair M. Dunnett
     (London: Dunnett, 1972).

69   'Writing in Gaelic' In *Planet*, 13 (Aug/Sept 1972), 15-21. Article.

70   'Crime' In *Sctn*, 19 Aug.; 14 Oct.; 2, 30 Dec. 1972; 27 Jan.; 10, 24
     Feb.; 17 Mar.; 7, 21 Apr.; 5 May; 2, 30 June; 14 July 1973. Review
     column.

71   'Spy File' In *Sctn*, 19 Aug.; 7 Oct.; 11 Nov. 1972. Review column.

72   In *Poetry Book Society Bulletin*, 74 (Aut. 1972). Note published
     when *Love Poems and Elegies* was a Society Recommendation.
     Published with 'On Looking at the Dead'.

73   'MacDiarmid the Visionary' In *GH*, 7 Oct. 1972. Review of *The
     Hugh MacDiarmid Anthology: Poems in Scots and English*, edited

by Michael Grieve and Alexander Scott, The Scottish Series (London and Boston: RKP, 1972).

74   Untitled review in *Gairm*, 1972/73, 186. Review of *Mu'n Cuairt an Cagailte: Sgealachdan* (Club Leabhar).

75   'Gael Force' In *Sctn*, 27 Sept. 1972. Interview with Raymond Gardner.

76   'The Poetry of Sorley MacLean' In *Glasgow Review*, 4, no. 3 (1973), 38-41.

77   'Major Gaelic Poet in a European Context' In *GH*, 27 Oct. 1973. Article on Sorley MacLean. Preface to *Poems 1932/82* by Sorley MacLean (Philadelphia: Iona Foundation, 1987).

78   Untitled review in *GH*, 16 Feb., 1974. Review of Derick Thomson, *An Introduction to Gaelic Poetry* (London, 1974).

79   'Duncan Ban MacIntyre' In *Sctn*, 20 Mar. 1974. Also appeared in *Towards the Human*.

80   'The Moment that made MacIntyre a Genius' In *Sctn*, 25 May 1974.

81   'Home-Grown' In *Sctn*, 20 July 1974. Review of *Scottish Short Stories, 1974* [ed. Scottish Arts Council] (London: Collins, 1974).

82   'Scottish insight' In *Sctn*, 28 Sept. 1974. Review of *Hawkfall and Other Stories* by George Mackay Brown (Hogarth, 1974).

83   'Writers and Education: Iain Crichton Smith' In *Scottish Educational Journal*, 31 Oct. 1975, pp. 1010-1011.

84   'The Appreciation of the Golden Lyric: early Scots Poems of Hugh MacDiarmid' In *SLJ*, 2, no. 1 (1975), 41-66. Errata: 2, no. 2 (1975), 63-64; comment by Iain Crichton Smith, supp. no. 3 (1976), 55-6.

85   'Writers and Education: Iain Crichton Smith' In *Scottish Educational Journal*, 31 Oct. 1975, p. 1010-11.

86   Untitled review in *GH*, 11 Dec. 1975. Review of Sydney Goodsir Smith, *Collected Poems, 1941-1975*.

87   Untitled review in *GH*, 29 Apr. 1976. Review of *Odusseia Homair: Homer's Odyssey translated into Gaelic verse* by John MacLean (Glasgow, 1976).

88   Untitled essay on 'poetry and the muse'. In *Chmn*, 4, no. 4 (Smr 1976), 12-18.

89   'Scotland: the facts for all to see' In *Sc. Rev.*, 4 (1, no. 4; Aut. 1976), 3-7. Article.

90   Untitled review in *Akros*, 11, no. 32 (Dec. 1976), 107-110. Review of *Catacomb Suburb* by Alastair Fowler (Edinburgh, 1976).

91   'The Golden Lyric: opinion' In *SLJ*, Supp. no. 3 (Wtr 1976), 55-56. Note on Kenneth Buthlay's analysis of the Golden Lyric, esp. 'The Bonnie Brouckit Bairn'.

92   Untitled review in *Gairm*, 1976/77, 189-91. Review of *Calum Tod* by Norman Malcolm Macdonald (Club Leabhar, 1976).

93   'Scottish Poetry in English' In *Scottish Writing and Writers*, edited by Norman Wilson (Edinburgh: The Rams ay Head Press, 1977), 29-37.

94   'The Highland Element in my English Work' In *SLJ*, 4 (May 1977), 47-60. Paper read at the annual conference of the Association for Scottish Literary Studies on 'The Highlands in Lowlands Literature', at Glasgow University on 8 May 1976.

95   Untitled review in *GH*, 30 June 1977. Review of Norman MacCaig's *Tree of Strings*, Phoenix Living Poets (London: Hogarth, 1977).

96   Untitled review in *GH*, 30 June 1977. Review of *Walking Without an Overcoat: Poems 1972-76* by Maurice Lindsay (London: Hale, 1977).

97   Untitled review in *GH*, 30 June 1977. Review of *Elegies for the Dead in Cyrenaica* by Hamish Henderson (Edinburgh: EUSPB, 1977).

98   Untitled review in *GH*, 30 June 1977. Review of *A Sense of Belonging: Six Scottish Poets of the Seventies* by B. Murray and S. S. Smyth.

99   Untitled review in *BiS*, 1 (1978), 26. Review of Nan Shepherd, *The Living Mountain* (Aberdeen: AUP, 1977).

100 Untitled review in *Sc. Rev.*, 11 (1978), 44-45. Review of *Some Walk a Narrow Path* by Janet Caird (Ramsay Head Press); *A Lamentation for the Children* by Walter Perrie (Canongate); and *Each Bright Eye* by Valerie Gillies (Canongate).

101 Untitled review in *Words*, 6 (1978), 57-58. Review of Stewart Conn, *Under the Ice* (London: Hutchinson, 1978).

102 Untitled review in *Sc. Rev.*, 9 (Spr. 1978), 38-39. Review of James Burn Singer, *Selected Poems* edited by A. Cluysenaar (Manchester: Carcanet, 1977).

103 Untitled review in *Lines*, 65 (June 1978), 27-30. Review of *Saorsa agus an Iolaire* by Derick Thomson (Gairm, 1978).

104 Untitled review in *BiS*, 2 (Aut. 1978), 30. Review of *Weathering: poems and translations* by Alastair Reid (Edinburgh: Canongate, 1978).

105 Untitled review in *BiS*, 2 (Aut. 1978), 31. Review of *Each Bright Eye*, by Valerie Gillies (Canongate).

106 Untitled review in *BiS*, 3 (Wtr 1978/79), 30. Review of *Raasay: a study in island history* by R. Sharpe (London, 1978).

107 'English as a Function for Gaelic' In *BiS*, 3 (Wtr 1978/79), 6-8. Discussion with Frank Thompson and Angus Nicholson.

108 Untitled review in *GH*, 7 Dec. 1978. Review of *The Complete Poems of Hugh MacDiarmid*, edited by M. Grieve and W. R. Aitken (London, 1978). Also appeared in *Towards the Human*.

109 Untitled review in *Gairm*, 1978/79, 182-83. Review of *'S Fheairrde Duine Gaire le Tearlach MacLeoid* (University of Glasgow, Roin nan Canan Ceilteach, 1978).

110 'What it feels like to be a Scottish poet' In *Aquarius*, 11 (1979), 74-77. Iain Crichton Smith was one of several respondents to this question, asked by Douglas Dunn.

111 'Between Sea and Moor' In *As I Remember: Ten Scottish authors recall how writing began for them*, edited by Maurice Lindsay (London: Hale, 1979), 107-22. Also appeared in *Towards the Human*.

112 'Night the Iolaire Went Down' In *GH*, 6 Jan. 1979. Review article about *The Loss of the Iolaire* by Norman Macdonald (Stornoway: Acair).

113 'Betwixt the Devil and the Deep Blue Sea' In *GH*, 3 Mar. 1979. Interview with Raymond Gardner.

114 Untitled review in *GH*, 26 Apr. 1979. Review of *The Ministers* by Fionn MacColla (London: Souvenir Press, 1979).

115 Untitled review in *Sc. Rev.*, 14 (May 1979), 54-55. Review of *Saorsa Agus an Iolaire* by Derick S. Thomson (Glasgow: Gairm, 1977.

116 Untitled review in *BiS*, 4 (Smr 1979), 17. Review of new poetry by Stewart Conn, Naomi Mitchison and others.

117 Untitled review in *BiS*, 4 (Smr 1979), 18. Review of new poetry by George MacBeth, J. F. Hendry and others.

118 'The Poetic Experience' In *BiS*, 4 (Smr 1979), 19. Review of *Poetic Truth* by Robin Skelton (Heinemann Educational Books).

119 Untitled review in *NER*, 47 (Aug. 1979), 26-27. Review of *Scottish Journey* by Edwin Muir (Edinburgh: Mainstream, 1979).

120 'Spontaneous and Fluent' In *BiS*, 5 (Aut. 1979), 10-11. Interview with Frank Thompson.

121 Untitled review in *Sc. Rev.*, 16 (Nov. 1979), 55-57. Review of Maurice Lindsay's *Collected Poems* (Edinburgh: Paul Harris).

122 'Candidates for the Pantheon' In *BiS*, 6 (Wtr 1979/80), 14. Review of new poetry by Douglas Dunn (*Barbarians*), W. S. Graham (*Collected Poems*) and others.

123 'Ossian Twilight' In *BiS*, 6 (Wtr 1979/80), 16. Review of *Fragments of Ancient Poetry* by James MacPherson (Dundee: Clarsach, 1979, reprint of 2nd edn, 1760).

124 Untitled review in *GH*, 6 Dec. 1979. Review of *Collected Poems* by Maurice Lindsay (Edinburgh: P. Harris, 1979).

125 Untitled review in *GH*, 6 Dec. 1979. Review of *Collected Poems 1942-77* by W. S. Graham (London: Faber, 1979).

126 'The True Dance' In *Lit. Rev.*, 14 Dec. 1979, p. 13. Review of *The Poems of Stanley Kunitz 1972-1978* (Secker).

127 'A Poet in Scotland' In *Aquarius* (1979). Article. Also appeared in *Best of the Poetry Year: Poetry Dimension Annual 7* edited by Dannie Abse (London: Robson Books, 1980).

128 'A Poet in Scotland' In *Poetry Dimension Annual: The Best Poetry of the Year*, ed. Danny Abse (1980). Also appeared in *Towards the Human*.

129 'MacDiarmid and Ideas, with special reference to "On a Raised Beach"' In *The Age of MacDiarmid*, edited by P. H. Scott and A. C. Davies (Edinburgh: Mainstream, 1980), 157-62. Also appeared in *Towards the Human*.

130 Introduction to *The Cone Gatherers*, by Robin Jenkins, Scottish Fiction Reprint Library (Edinburgh: P. Harris, 1980).

131 'Scots Master' In *GH*, 3 Jan. 1980. Review of *Gillespie* by John MacDougall Hay (Einburgh: Canongate, 1979; orig. 1914).

132 'Screams from Behind the Curtain' In *NER*, 49 (Feb. 1980), 34-37. Review of *Cruel in the Shadow* by Lorn MacIntyre (Collins) and *The Captive Summer* by Jeremy Bruce-Watt (Chambers).

133 'From Scotland to Australia' In *Sc. Rev.*, 19 (Aug. 1980), 4-8. Essay.

134 Untitled review in *BiS*, 8 (Aut./Wtr 1980), 10-11. Review of poetry by Duncan Glen, Robin Fulton and others.

135 'The Artist, the Individual and Excellence': an interview with Iain Crichton Smith, by Niall Brown. In *GUM: Glasgow University Magazine*, [1981?], 19-23.

136 'Luther: A Colossus' In *GH*, 19 May 1981. Review of *Luther: A Biography* by H. G. Haile (Sheldon Press).

137 Untitled review in *Sc. Rev.*, 23 (Aug. 1981), 52-53. Review of *A'
Mheanbhchuileag* by Feargas MacFhionnlaigh (Glasgow, Gairm).

138 'Sorley MacLean: The Passionate Voice of Gaelic Poetry' In *GH*,
24 Oct. 1981. Article.

139 'Search for an Image' In *Lit. Rev.*, 42 (Dec. 1981), 36-37. Article on
Australian poetry.

140 'Ath-sgrudadh, (1) Donnchadh Ban Mac an t-Saoir' In *Gairm*,
1981/82, pp. 177-83.

141 'The Lyrics of Robert Burns' In *The Art of Robert Burns*, edited by
R.D.S. Jack and Andrew Noble, Critical Studies Series (London:
Vision, and Totowa, New Jersey: Barnes and Noble, 1982), 22-35.

142 Untitled review in *Sc. Rev.*, 25 (Feb. 1982), 38-40. Review of *A Net
to Catch the Winds and other poems* by Maurice Lindsay (Hale).

143 Untitled review in *Sctn*, 10 Apr. 1982. Review of *Poor Tom* by
Edwin Muir.

144 'Poetic Energy, Language and Nationhood' In *Sc. Rev.*, May 1982.
Essay. Also appeared in *Towards the Human*.

145 'Smaointean air turus a' Bhrendain' In *Sctn*, 8 May 1982. Article.

146 'Ambiguous World of Quadruple Agents' In *GH*, 5 June 1982.
Review of recent spy fiction.

147 Untitled review in *Lines*, 81 (June 1982), 41-42. Review of *The
Vernacular Republic: Poems 1961-81* (Edinburgh: Canongate,
1982).

148 'Gaeldom's "Modern Consciousness"' In *Sctn*, 11 Sept. 1982.
Essay.

149 'Home and Away' In *Sctn*, 18 Sept. 1982. Review of *Scottish Short
Stories 1982* (Collins).

150 Untitled review in *Sc. Rev.*, 28 (Nov. 1982), 42-43. Review of *From
the Domain of Arnheim* by Alastair Fowler (Secker and Warburg),
and *The Vernacular Republic* by Les Murray (Canongate).

151 'Scottish Poetry Since 1945' In *Equivalencias*, 3-4 (Dec. 1982), 173-94.

152 'Critics' Choice' In *Sctn*, 31 Dec. 1982. Critics select their year's favourite; Iain Crichton Smith's was *Fields of Focus* by Robin Fulton (Anvil Press Poetry).

153 'Ath-sgrudadh (4) Suil Gheur: Sgeulachdan Iain Mhoirich' In Gairm, 1982/83, 170-73.

154 Untitled review in *Gairm*, 1982/83, pp. 187-88. *Camhanaich*, by Domhnall Iain Maclomhair (Stornoway: Buidheann-foillseach aidh nan Eilean an Iar, 1982).

155 Untitled review in *Gairm*, 1982/83, p. 283. *Suileabhan*, by Calum MacFhearghais, a rinn moran dhealbh dhan leabhar (Glasgow: Gairm, 1983).

156 'Poet with many Personae' In *GH*, 9 Apr. 1983. Review of *Complete Poetical Works* by Robert Garioch (Macdonald).

157 'Towards the Human: The Poetry of Stewart Conn' In *NER*, 62 (Smr 1983), 20-22. Also appeared in *Towards the Human*.

158 'Poetry in Scott's Narrative Verse' In *Sir Walter Scott: The Forgotten Melody* edited and introduced by Alan Bold (London: Vision, 1983. Totowa, N.J.: Barnes and Noble, 1983), 109-26.

159 In *Sc. Rev.*, 29 (Feb. 1983), 36-37. Review of *Scotch Passion: an anthology of Scottish erotic poetry*, edited by Alexander Scott (London: Robert Hale).

160 'Harpist and the Highland Way' In *Sctn*, 19 Feb. 1983. Review of *Creachadh na Clairsach* [Plundering the Harp] by Ruaraidh MacThomais (Macdonald, 1983).

161 'Another Window on the World' In *Sctn*, 26 Feb. 1983; and included in one a series of course books for young learners of Gaelic published by the Languages Dept, Islay High School, Bowmore, Islay (1984).

162 'Ciamar a tha e beo?' In *Gairm*, 1983/84, pp. 30-32. Article.

163 'Ath-sgrudadh. An Dotair Leointe: Bardachd Dhomhnaill MhicAmlaigh' ['The Modest Doctor: The Poetry of Donald MacAulay'] In *Gairm*, 1983/84, pp. 68-73. Printed in English in *Towards the Human*.

164 'North-west Passages' In *Sctn*, 2 July 1983. Review of *A Journey to the Western Isles: Johnson's Scottish Journey*, edited by Finlay J. Macdonald.

165 'Astrailia: aite air leth' ['Australia: A Place Apart'] In *Sctn*, 30 July 1983. Article, with a note by Raghnall Mac Ille Dhuibh.

166 'Derek Thomson's "Clann Nighean an Sgadain"' In *Akros*, 17, no. 51 (Oct. 1983), 42-44. One of twenty criticisms of twenty modern Scottish poems published as part of the last-issue celebrations.

167 In *Sc. Rev.*, 32 (Nov. 1983), 40-42. Review of *A World of Difference* by Norman MacCaig (Chatto and Windus; *Grafts and Takes* by Edwin Morgan (Marischat; *A Distant Urn* by Janet Caird (Ramsay Head); and *A Gathering of Poems* by Gael Turnbull (Anvil Press).

168 'An Deirceach' ['The Beggar'] In *Sctn*, 28 Feb. 1983. Essay.

169 In *Foreign Literatures*, 11 (Scottish no: 1984). Article translated into Chinese.

170 'The Puzzling Lure of Crime Stories' In *Sctn*, 28 Jan. 1984. Essay.

171 In *Sc. Rev.*, 33 (Feb. 1984), 48. Review of *Time Gentlemen: some collected poems* by Hamish Brown (Aberdeen University Press); and *Sireadh Bradain Sicir* [Seeking Wise Salmon] by Simon Fraser (Balnain Books).

172 Untitled review in *BiS*, 14 (Spr. 1984), 20. Review of *A World of Difference* by Norman MacCaig; *Poems and Prose* by David Rorie; and Robert Garioch's *Complete Poetical Works*.

173 'Eilthireachd is Duthas: a comhradh ri Iain Mac a' Gobhainn' In *Facal air an Fhacal*, 2 (Spr. 1984), 8-24 (published by the Gaelic Books Council). Gaelic interview, with English introduction, a selection of his work and a checklist of his Gaelic publications.

174 'Gaelic Master: Sorley MacLean' In *Sc. Rev.*, 34 (May 1984), 4-10. Article. Also appeared in *Towards the Human*.

175 Untitled review in *Sc. Rev.*, 34 (May 1984), 44-45. Review of *The Companion to Gaelic Scotland*, edited by Derick S. Thomson (Basil Blackwell, [1984]).

176 'Modest War' In *Lsnr*, 10 May 1984, pp. 30-31. Review of *Home and Dry: Memoirs III* by Roy Fuller (London Magazine).

177 'The Scarecrow from Geneva' In *Student*, 17 May 1984. Interview with Giles Sutherland.

178 'The True Story of Sir Hector Macdonald' In *Stand*, 25, no. 3 (Smr 1984), 44-46.

179 'George Campbell Hay: Language at Large' In *Sc. Rev.*, 35 (Aug. 1984), 45-50. Article. Also appeared in *Towards the Human*.

180 'The Heart of a Nationalist Poet' In *Sctn*, 11 Aug. 1984. Article on the Gaelic Poetry of George Campbell Hay.

181 'Books of the Year' In *Sctn*, 15 Dec. 1984. Iain Crichton Smith chose Seamus Heaney's *Station Island*.

182 Ath-sgrudadh (10): Bhardachd Mairi Mhor nan Oran' In *Gairm*, 1984/85, pp. 321-27.

183 Untitled review in *Gairm*, 1984/85, pp. 377-80. Review of *TGSI*, 53 (Inverness, 1 985).

184 'The Poetry of Derick Thomson' In *Sc. Rev.*, 37/38 (Feb./May 1985), 24-30. Article. Also appeared in *Towards the Human*.

185 Untitled review in *Chmn*, 8, no. 3 (Spr. 1985), 72-73. Review of Robert Garioch's *Collected Poems*.

186 'The Routine of Being a Robinson Crusoe' In *TES*, 14 June 1985, p. 4. Interview with Aonghas MacNeacail.

187 'Spirit of Place' In *Sctn*, 22 Aug. 1985. Public discussion with Jessie Kesson, chaired by Isobel Murray, held at the Edinburgh Book Festival, 20 August 1985.

188 '"Nine to Four" Classroom Vanished Long Ago' In *Sctn*, 20 Aug. 1985. Article about teaching; see also correspondence later in the same week.

189 'The Gael Prefers to Write in English' In *Evening Express*, 14 Nov. 1985. Interview with Andrew Knight.

190 'An Hour with Iain Crichton Smith' In *Gaudie*, 27 Nov. 1985. Interview with Steve Fraser.

191 'A Hymn to the Great Songs' In *Sctn*, 21 Dec. 1985. Review of Sorley MacLean's *Ris a' Bhruthaich* (Stornoway: Acair, 1985).

192 'Books of the Year' In *Sctn*, 21 Dec. 1985. Iain Crichton Smith selects his favourites from the year.

193 Untitled review in *Gairm*, 1984/85, p. 383, of *Casan Ruisgte* by Donnchadh MacLeoid (Glasgow University, Roinn nan Canan Ceilteach, 1985).

194 'A Note on Gaelic Criticism' *Towards the Human*.

195 'Real People in a Real Place' *Towards the Human*.

196 'Sea Talk by George Bruce' *Towards the Human*.

197 'The Feeling Intelligence' *Towards the Human*.

198 'The Power of Craftsmanship: The Poetry of Robert Garioch' Also appeared in *Towards the Human*.

199 'A Lust for the Particular: Norman MacCaig's Poetry' In *Chmn*, 45 (vol. 9, no, 1 [1986]), 20-24.

200 'A Poet's Response to Sorley MacLean' In *Sorley MacLean: Critical Essays* edited by Raymond J. Ross and Joy Hendry (Edinburgh: Scottish Academic Press, 1986).

201 'Gaelic Poetry in Translation' In *Teaching English*, 19, no. 2 (Spr. 1986), 15-22.

202 'Derick Thomson: Concern with Gaelic Culture' In *Radical Scotland*, 23 (Oct/Nov 1986), 38. Discussion of two poems, 'Coffins' and 'The Herring Girls'.

203 'War Poetry, the Corruption of Language, and Internationalism'
In *West Highland Free Press*, 31 Oct. 1986. Reply to a letter
published 24 October 1986, replying to his of 17 October.

204 Untitled review in *Gairm*, 1986/87, pp. 188-90. An *Seachnadh agus
dain eile* [The Avoiding and other poems] by Aonghas
MacNeacail (Macdonald, 1986).

205 Untitled review in *Gairm*, 1986/87, pp. 381-84. *Bailtean* by
Maoilios M. Caimbeuil (Gairm, 1987).

206 'The Whole Being of a Man' introducing *Poems 1932/82* by Sorley
MacLean (Philadelphia: Iona Foundation, 1987).

207 'Introduction' to *Scottish Short Stories* (London: Collins, 1987).

208 'Scottish Twentieth-Century Poetry' In *Wen Yuan*, 1 (1987), 65-85.

209 'Three Generations of Poetry' In *Chmn*, 52 (10, no. 3, Spr. 1988),
85-87. Review of *Perspectives: Poems 1970/86* by George Bruce
(AUP); *In the Kibble Palace* by Stewart Conn (Bloodaxe Books);
and *The Way We Live* by Kathleen Jamie (Bloodaxe Books).

210 In *GH*, 11 July 1988. Interview with Lorn MacIntyre (date 30 May
1988).

211 Untitled review in *Region and Nation Newsletter*, 1, no. 2 (Spr.
1988), 27-28. Review of *Bruges-la-Morte* by Georges Rodenbach,
translated by Philip Mosley (Paisley: Wilfion Books, 1987).

212 'Intensity of Poetic Writing at its Best' In *Scotland on Sunday*, 7
Aug. 1988. Review of *Best Short Stories from Stand Magazine*
(1987).

213 'Duthaich air ghoil le eachdraidh' In *Sctn*, 21 May 1988. Iain
Crichton Smith reports on his visit to Israel.

214 'Urram do Sgriobhadair' In *Sctn*, 23 Jan. 1988. Interview with
Ronnie Black.

215 Letter in *Sctn*, 31 May 1988, protesting at suspension of
Reverend Alexander Murray of the Free Church for asking Mgr
Thomas Wynne to deliver a prayer at a meeting of Highland
Regional Council's working party on religious affairs.

216 'Deified Ideals' In *TESS*, 1988. Review of *In the Kibble Palace: New and Selected Poems* by Stewart Conn (Bloodaxe).

217 Review of *Eliot in His Time: Essays on the occasion of the fiftieth anniversary of The Wasteland* edited by A.W. Litz; and *T.S. Eliot: Between Two Worlds* by David Ward.

218 'Lapidary Master' Review of *A Universal History of Infamy* by Jorge Luis Borges.

2 Plus 2 (Lausanne)

Aberdeen University Review   *AUR*

Abstracts of English Studies

Agenda

Akros

Alba Mater (Aberdeen University)

Alma Mater (Aberdeen University)

Ambit

Annual Bibliography of English Language and Literature

Antaeus

Antioch Review

Aquarius

Argo (Oxford)

Aristophanes' Middle Finger (Dundee)   *AMF*

Artful Reporter (Manchester)

Bad Seed Review (Newcastle upon Tyne)

Bananas (London)

Bibliothek

Blind Serpent (Dundee)

Book Review Digest

Book Review Index

Booklist   *Blst*

Books in Scotland   *BiS*

Box of Rain (Leeds)

British Book News   *BBN*

Cairn

Calgacus (Kyle of Lochalsh)

Catalyst (1320 Club)

Cencrastus   *Cenc.*

Centre 17

Chapman   *Chmn*

Chirico

Clanjamfrie (Dundee)

Cleft (Edinburgh College of Art)

Cracked Looking Glass (Maida Vale, London)

Crann (Aberdeen University Celtic Society)

Critical Quarterly   *CQ*

Critical Quarterly Poetry Supplements

Daily Telegraph   *DTel*

Dream (Aberdeen)

Echo Room, The (Newcastle upon Tyne)

Edinburgh Review   *ER*

Eilean an Fhraoich Annual (Stornoway)

Ellery Queen's Mystery Magazine

Encounter Enc.

English

Equivalencias (Madrid)

Facar air an Fhacal

Feedback (Edinburgh)

Financial Times FT

Form (Argyll)

Gaidheal, An

Gairm

Gallimaufry (Dundee)

Gambit (Edinburgh University)

Gaudie (Aberdeen University)

Glasgow Herald GH

Glasgow Magazine

Glasgow Review Glasgow Rev.

Guardian Gdn

Helix (Ivanhoe, Australia)

Honest Ulsterman (Belfast)

Horsefeathers (Cambridge)

Index of American Periodical Verse

Innti (Raghnallach, Eire)

International Poetry Review

Jabberwock (Edinburgh University)

Kenyon Review

Leabhraichean Ghaidhligh

Lines Review	*Lines*
Listener	*Lsnr*
Literary Review	*Lit. Rev.*
Littack	
Logos	
London Magazine	
Lot 49 (Edinburgh)	
Malahat Review (British Columbia)	
Masque	
Meridian (Merseyside)	
MLA International Bibliography	
Modern Reading (London)	
Modern Scottish Short Stories	
New Departures (Stroud)	
New Gambit (Edinburgh)	
New Measure	
New Poetry	
New Review	
New Saltire	
New Statesman	*New Stn*
North 7 (Highlands and Islands Development Board)	
North-East Review (Aberdeen)	
Northern Light (Aberdeen)	
Oasis (London)	
Observer	*Obs.*
Orbis	

Ossian (Glasgow University Celtic Society)

Outposts

Palantir (Preston, Lancs)

PEN Broadsheet

Phoenix (Glasgow)

Pick (South Croydon)

Planet (Dyfed, Wales)

PN Review (formerly Poetry Nation)

Poesie Vivante (Geneva)

Poet (Glasgow)

Poet (Madras)

Poetry and Audience (University of Leeds)

Poetry Australia

Poetry Book Society Bulletin and Supplements

Poetry Dimension Annual

Poetry Glasgow

Poetry Information (London, then Newcastle upon Tyne)

Poetry Ireland Review

Poetry Nation

Poetry Now

Poetry Quarterly

Poetry Review   *P. Rev.*

Press and Journal (Aberdeen)   *P&J*

Proem (Edinburgh)

Prospice

Radical Scotland

Reality Studios (London)

Resurgence (Dyfed, Wales)

Review (Oxford)

Review of International English Literature, A   *Ariel*

Rubble (Strathclyde University)

Saltire Review   *Saltire Rev.*

Saltire Society Newsletter

Scotia

Scotia Review   *Scotia Rev.*

Scotland's Magazine

Scots Independent

Scots Review (Edinburgh)

Scotsman   *Sctn*

Scottish Educational Journal

Scottish Field

Scottish Gaelic Studies   *SGS*

Scottish International   *Sc. Int.*

Scottish Literary Journal (and supplements)   *SLJ*

Scottish Literary News   *SLN*

Scottish Poetry One et seq.

Scottish Review   *Sc. Rev.*

Screever (Stoke on Trent)

Scrivener

Short Story Index

Sian (Hebridean Writers' Cooperative)

Sidewalk (University of Edinburgh)

Spectator	*Spec.*
Spirit	
Sruth	
S.S.T.A. Magazine	
Stand (newcastle upon Tyne)	
Stornoway Gazette	*St. Gaz.*
Strata	
Studies in Scottish Literature	*SSL*
Sunday Times	*ST*
Tablet	
Teaching English	
Times, The	
Times Education Supplement	*TES*
Times Higher Education Supplement	
Times Literary Supplement	*TLS*
Tomorrow (Oxford)	
Tracks (co. Meath, Eire)	
Transactions of the Gaelic Society of Inverness	*TGSI*
Transatlantic Review	
Verse	
Voice of Scotland	
Wen Yuan (Peking)	
West Highland Free Press	*WHFP*
Windfall (Edinburgh University Poetry Society)	
Words (Markinch, Fife)	
World Literature Today	*WLT*

Yearbook of English Studies

Year's Work in English Studies

Zebra (Bristol)

ZLR (Nottingham)

Zygote (Ayr)

Aitken, W. R. *Scottish Literature in English and Scots: a guide to information sources* (Detroit: Gale Research, 1982)

Anon 'A Checklist of Modern Scottish Literary Manuscripts in the National Library of Scotland' *Bibliothek*, 9 (1979), 81-152

Contemporary Novelists (St James's Press, 1986)

Kidd, J. and R. H. Cairnie *Annual Bibliography of Scottish Literature*

MacLeod, D. J. *Twentieth Century Publications in Scottish Gaelic* (1980)

Messerli, Douglas and Howard N. Fox *Index to Periodical Fiction in English, 1965—1969*

Sader, Mari (ed.) *Comprehensive Index to English-Language Little Magazines 1890-1970* (1976)

Smith, William James (ed.) *Granger's Index to Poetry*, sixth, seventh and eighth edns

—— *Granger's Index to Poetry: 1970-1977* (Columbia U. P., 1978)